D1474139

FUTURE PHILANTHROPY

FUTURE PHILANTHROPY

The Tech, Trends & Talent
Defining New Civic Leadership

RYAN GINARD

ISBN 13: 978-1-63489-478-4

Library of Congress Catalog Number has been applied for.
Printed in the United States of America
First Printing: 2022

26 25 24 23 22   5 4 3 2 1

Cover design by Josh Durham
Interior design by Patrick Maloney

Wise Ink Creative Publishing
807 Broadway St NE
Suite 46
Minneapolis, MN, 55413

To Diane, Roman, and Ruby.
You inspire a future worth fighting for.

CONTENTS

Acknowledgments

Writing this book has had many similarities to that image of an iceberg that periodically pops up on LinkedIn showing that no new idea or project appears overnight (you know, the ones with the "buzzy" hustle-porn anecdotes shown lurking beneath the surface). And while stopping short of being my own cliché, *Future Philanthropy* has been built up over the years across many conversations, conferences, and pushing the limitations of my cloud storage in terms of articles, podcasts, and audiobooks that have helped inform and shape my thinking.

People always say to surround yourself with smart people, and I have been truly blessed in this regard, throwing my hands up in praise to those I'm lucky enough to have worked with, I have ideated with, and who I can call my friends. That's why I want to give a special shout-out to my coffee and craft beer caucus who have listened, challenged, and contextualized many of the assumptions and predictions contained within these pages, and done so with such a genuine level of candor and mutual respect, understanding that our approaches to progress are just as much complementary as they are shared.

Thanks to (in no particular order) James Halliday, Hampton Dohr-man, Jessica Kort, Pearl Hoeglund, Trevor Blair, Sean Elo-Rivera, David Lopez, Brittany Bailey, Robert Foster, Matt Gorham, Dike Anyiwo, Tim Wheatcroft, Sam Tsoi, Karim Bouris, Lee Barken, Jared Aaker, Ben Katz, Jacob James, and Megan Thomas. I value your ideas, your passion, and your drive—and appreciate your willingness and reluctance to hear my ideas on the future of philanthropy, civic engagement, and a better discourse. I look forward to reconvening soon!

To those who saw something in me and my potential contributions both to the field at large, and within their own organizations—when my resume screams "most likely to leave after two years"—thank you. Your faith in me and your ability to keep me focused on my day-to-day goals, yet embrace my ideas no matter how much it challenged the organization's comfort zone, was what kept me hungry for our shared success.

Karen Begin, Nancy Jamison, Renato Paiva, and Blair Sadler, I appreciate all you do and all you are.

I'm also thrilled about my fledgling career at the University of Texas at Austin. While Brent Winkelman and Zak Richards will probably frown at me saying it's cool to be able to raise money for robots (when our scope is much more than that), there is a certain type of magic in working at a higher education institution where you are helping donors create a legacy that transcends traditional giving and creates one that forges a new path toward a future we can't yet comprehend.

I want to thank the folks and organizations that make up the Philanthropy California alliance and those of the United Philanthropy Forum. I appreciate all you do to educate donors and foundations on effective philanthropy, knowing that effectiveness cannot be achieved without justice. Props to Dave Biemesderfer for building a bigger, more inclusive tent; this was a true gamechanger for the field.

The San Diego Leadership Alliance (SDLA), including the "Breakfast Club" of Liliane Lendvai, Juan Vargas, Paola Illescas, and Nikki Weil; Emerging Practitioners in Philanthropy (EPIP); and the Fieldstone Leadership Network have also had a lasting impact on how I approach my work, effect change, and mobilize coalitions for good. SDLA and EPIP felt like family, something that has become more and more important to me as I navigate being a husband, a father, and an active citizen.

The biggest amount of love and appreciation, though, falls squarely at the feet of my wife, who has been my best advocate, supporter, and COVID-era office colleague. She lets me engage with both my creative and political sides, understanding my motivations for doing so and supporting my nontraditional (read: non-American) approaches. I think she knows it keeps me sane, and I guess her hope is that I eventually run out of ideas. The fact is, though, she and the kids inspire me to be more and to do more—so, sorry, babe, I can't see that happening any time soon.

To my extended family and friends back "home" in Australia, thank you for providing me with some welcome respite from the usual day-to-day pressures through your advice, support, dry wit, and humor. The fact that the time zones don't affect my workday is also perfect, needing ample time to digest your insatiable thirst for sharing Australian political memes that no one would understand stateside. Y'all keep me grounded, and I hope one day I'll be back to fight the good fight with you.

Finally, the actual book. Thanks to the Wise Ink team for agreeing to work with me and guiding me through the process in a way that helped me keep and amplify my voice. I was supremely lucky to find a values-driven publisher like yours and was blown away by your passion for the subject matter and for excelling in herding the cats, as it were. Five-star review coming to you on Yelp!

To those who backed this project on Kickstarter, thank you for believing in this project. It not only helped build momentum for its release but from a personal standpoint it was extremely humbling that you would step up and endorse this work. Whether you supported me personally or you just had a natural curiosity in the subject matter, it really meant a great deal. Thank you to Stephen Chin, Bernie Ripoll, Andrew Smith, David Sligar, John Gillon, Raff Ciccone, Sean Elo-Rivera, Becky Phillpott, Sheena Watt, Laura Fraser Hardy, Trina Engler, Jordan Ginard, Namit Trivedi, Ryan Schaller, Nhu Tran, Matt Fettig, Matt D'Arrigo, Ken Rahmes, Dimity Paul, David Shaw, Lexus Turnell, James Turnell, Constant Wilson, Scott Page, Sharon Payne, Nate Fairman, Dennis Brewster, Anthony Cianflone, Linda Le Tran, Brad Pagano, Justin Nunez, Sam Orr, Brett Collett, Sam Ryan, Alison Macintyre, Alex Ryan, Matt Burke, Rob Mills, Phil Keleman, John Rahmes, Cameron Reid, Michael Bauer, Tim Page, Daniel Blake, Stacey Ginard, Ashley Miranda, Karl Maftoum, Kristin McBain-Rigg, and Nadia Clancy.

Thank you to all those who agreed to be featured in this book as an emerging leader. It's important to show what can be achieved in the field by those who are actively doing so. Far too often, we put the big foundation leaders on a pedestal when it's the people in the engine room who are really getting things done and pushing us to new levels of greatness. Y'all are inspiring, and I hope we get to partner again on other projects or things that, you know, end up changing the world. Adriana, Alison, Efrem, Erin, Krystian, Laila, Laura, Meggie, Michael, Ruby, Sara, Sarah, Seyron, and Zahirah, I look forward to seeing your stars continue to rise!

Thank you to Beth Kanter, who wrote the book's afterword—an important piece on seeking balance in our work as we seek to understand and navigate a two-speed approach to change: on one hand, the immense emotional weight the country still holds as we move toward healing and social, racial, and environmental justice; on the other, the unforeseen consequences of rapid technological change and how it impacts our current being and surrounds. Social justice work is hard, and can be trying on both the mind and body, so let's not forget that. Let's be kind to ourselves, and be aware of the real prospects of burnout and what that means to our mental health. We must continue to check in with one another to ensure we remain connected to and supported by what matters most.

I hope folks are clued in to the work and influence of Beth Kanter on the social sector. A pioneer for tech trends and a champion of workplace vitality, it was her book *Measuring the Networked Nonprofit*, which I received for free at a Council on Foundations conference, that helped me understand that data was essential for putting together the case for change.

And last but by no means least, thanks to Trista Harris, who has truly pioneered philanthropic futurism over the past five years and shown folks like me that there is a space for them in organized philanthropy and nonprofits through championing the ideas of tomorrow (and in unison with the social sector) to tackle the defining issues of our time.

I had the pleasure of interviewing her at an EPIP event the evening before the San Diego Grantmakers conference in 2018. It was the prep for this event that really turned my head toward future-focused thinking around tech, trends, and talent—and that the intersection between this kind of thinking, together with a healthy dose of courageous leadership, can advance a real conversation about what our communities could look like five, ten, even fifty years into the future.

Trista's recent book *FutureGood* was also a big north star for me, and I recommend it to anyone looking at creating their next strategic plan. It's a primer, a roadmap, and an actionable guide for any organization looking forward, rather than being reactionary and mired in the status quo. I would also check out her backstory and how her tenacity and smarts got her into Richard Branson's inner philanthropic advisory circle. For someone who has read all of Branson's books (that's the English part of me), it was cool to feel one degree closer to someone who has also created unique approaches to those entrenched problems that defined a time gone by.

So, thanks to Trista, because there is no doubt this book would never have come into being if she had not blazed a trail for futurism.

In the end this book is a nod to all those doing great work in the field, especially those emerging leaders who inspire me daily. I also don't want to forget those who are leading foundations who are willing to try new approaches because they are compelled by their mission and personal values to find the best answers and approaches to aid their work, not just to please their board.

Thank God for Twitter in this instance: I can just add a hashtag and then discover what is going on, the innovative ways that folks are tackling current and historic issues, and better yet, read the replies of other folks praising their work. If you bypass the algorithm and search for good, you can see the unbridled positive potential of social media.

To all those reading this, let one thing be known: I appreciate all you do, because social change is sometimes a lonely and thankless act, and I want to reassure you that you are on the right path. Don't forget there are many folks like you working in solidarity and concurrently chipping away at a better tomorrow, and if we can inspire more people to join us in our work, the future of philanthropy will be bright.

It's time to get shit done.

Introduction

Philanthropy has a rich and storied history, yet in a constantly evolving society it can seem somewhat slow and reactionary to the issues critical to our work. There are plenty of folks out there talking about current trends that are informative, interesting, and thought provoking. But it can be argued that they are also adding yet another layer in this reactionary chain. The real question is: How do we move from talking about the future in incremental time frames and look toward one where we are truly anticipating future trends and laying the groundwork for their successful implementation?

This book seeks to address this question and more in the following ways:

- Asserting a belief that philanthropy is ripe for disruption.

- Acknowledging that certain elements of philanthropy need to evolve for the sector to remain impactful and, in some instances, to remain relevant.

- Acknowledging that society has become disproportionately structured in a way where there is no longer an opportunity for all.

- Addressing the need to conceptualize what the future might hold for philanthropy to help stimulate discussion and forge a more dynamic sector.

- Inspiring leaders and entrepreneurs in the field to be more creative in their approaches to raising funds for our community.

- Articulating thoughts in a "101 style" through low-tech jargon, amplifying ideas over process, and seeking social outcomes rather than technical inputs.

I'm of the theory that philanthropic futurism is best served by a generalist approach and understanding of technology and society that can

1

enable them to see, inhibited, its future applications through the lens of the social sector—knowing enough to be dangerous, as I like to say.

Yet for thirty years I was more of a dreamer than a futurist. Someone who believed they would leave their mark on the world, not because of any deep fire inside that propelled me to challenge the status quo, but one of deep-seated privilege that was reinforced by society telling me it was there if only I wanted it. Please pass go and thanks for the $200.

I was more entitled than enigmatic during my youth, and this was ultimately patterned onto my psyche by my parents and society at the time. I was born on the outskirts of London to a working-class family during the Thatcher years, with my parents embodying a very materialistic form of aspiration, one fueled by capitalism, consumerism, and the relentless need to look successful in the face of all who knew them.

My father's thirst for that outward-facing achievement became a dangerous facade that tore at the seams of our larger family fabric, and one that built a foundation of entitlement, amplified in part because of modern-day populism and the fact that he never struck it rich. It was far easier to blame others than take responsibility, and predictably, that attitude ended up driving a wedge between us that was irreparable in the end, but one that could have been easily solved if he had the courage to admit his faults and duly accept mine.

This isn't to say my parents were bad parents. They loved each other very much, and this bond helped keep a roof over our heads and our family together where many others went their separate ways during that time because they weren't able to balance the life pressures that coincided with the recession of the early 1980s. I saw this contrast frequently, and I vividly remember being at a friend's house, hanging out upstairs, and then hearing a terrifying scream. We ran downstairs and toward the sight of his mother covered in blood from where his stepdad had battered her with a phone, when phones were big, heavy plastic units. This memory still shakes me to this day and has me wired a different way when it comes to talking about issues of equality and feminism.

But for all the togetherness, that was mainly reserved for just my mom and dad. They had an unbreakable bond to which I never belonged and was never invited to be a part of. This made the early stages of my childhood an extremely lonely experience, and I got into unnecessary trouble at school on a consistent basis just because acting out was my opportunity to be seen.

Yet you wouldn't have guessed it if you visited our home. Countless trophies we won took pride of place on the mantelpiece. Mentions of me and my siblings filled a big scrapbook, photos capturing our milestones adorned the walls, and the constant loop of family videos played during the holidays. But when you peeled back the curtain you would see they were just symbols of my father's "success" as a parent and that every big moment was never captured through the lens of his camera. Because they were never there. I can't for the life of me remember my parents together at an event that had any meaning to me.

This background is what drew me to public service. In the absence of my parents, I had to seek my own community, seek other mentors, and seek meaning, and I have felt the need to pay it back ever since.

I am far from ungrateful, though, and as a parent myself, I understand that I was probably not aware of, or privy to, many of their own sacrifices. My parents did one thing, however, that changed my whole life trajectory, for which I am truly thankful. In 1997, they made the decision to move our young family to Australia, and while I had only one year left of high school, it was a no-brainer moving, especially with an opportunity to start my life again to avoid a potentially darker path from the one I now walk.

This move halfway around the world afforded me the opportunity to take a good hard look at my future and challenge myself to be better. To do better, be a better person, and be a better citizen. I knuckled down at school, and while my grades weren't fantastic, they were much higher than they were in the UK and allowed me to become the first in my family to go to college.

After a year or so at James Cook University, a regional university in Townsville, North Queensland, where I took classes in law and physics before understanding that business was the only curriculum I could understand and apply, I moved to Brisbane and the Queensland University of Technology (QUT). One of my close friends there invited me to join the Student Guild as the sports and recreation coordinator for the

Carseldine Campus in the city's northern suburbs. I thought it would be cool to organize events and meet new people. Within a year, I was leading the finances, operations, and policy for an organization with forty thousand members, over one hundred employees, and a million-dollar budget.

In this role, I also sat as a student representative on the University Council, Student Academic Affairs Board, and the Student Appeals Board, standing up for students' rights and leading major campus-wide campaigns to save essential student services in the face of voluntary student unionism and to address ongoing sexism in sports. In addition, I worked nationally with some of the most inspiring (and aspiring) student politicians in the country, many of whom are now senators or federal or state representatives, driving some truly progressive policies that are envied the world over.

And this was all in my early twenties. What a steep learning curve! And what a rapid maturing process! Another chapter of my life was written, one that made me grow up, see beyond my selfish tendencies, understand my flaws, and check my privilege.

After graduating from QUT with a business degree in management and advertising, I made the transition to political staffer, running marginal seat campaigns both statewide and federally. The campaigns I led leveraged more than AUD $2.5 billion in civic infrastructure for our region during the five years I worked in the federal electorate of Oxley. This was particularly important given that it was one of the more diverse and economically challenged electorates in the country, with large indigenous, Vietnamese, and Samoan communities. It also helped give me real insight into the issues of marginalized communities, their customs, and most importantly how their communities rally around each other—collectively lifting up their faiths, their businesses, and the success of their families as first-generation Australians—much of which I held an affinity for or could directly relate to. It was a pleasure to serve them and advocate for their interests daily.

At this time, I also ran for the Brisbane City Council, the largest city government in the southern hemisphere. I lost to the then opposition leader in what was technically an unwinnable seat, but one in which my campaign bucked the swing, even outperforming our mayoral candidate on a majority of the booths. I ran on an active transport platform, pushing back against the uninformed plans for a spate of roadworks, advocating for better public transport options, and defending green space. It was a fun experience and helped me become a better staffer and civic leader. Understanding how a candidate feels, interacts with the public, and articulates a vision for change is a truly unique perspective that campaign staff can never truly capture.

Then, in 2010, a once-in-a-generation flood struck our region, with the worst hit being the one in which we lived, the Western Corridor between Brisbane and Ipswich. The floods peaked at 14.6 feet, with more than 200,000 residents affected and property damage amounting to AUD $2.4 billion. There is a surreal photo of two kayakers paddling over the area where the federal electorate office resided, which only served to highlight the devastation on our local community. So we got one of our three-by-three-meter pop-up tents, put it up in the suburb of Goodna, a central location in the district, and began the cleanup, because we needed to do something—anything, really—to help our community recover as quickly as possible.

This natural disaster caused a state of conflicting emotions. On one hand, it restored my faith in humanity. Folks came together to help one another. People from as far away as Sydney took leave from their jobs to put on gloves and work all day for free. On the other hand, it showed how fragile life can be. It proved that having a roof over your head and food on the table is nothing to take for granted.

The electorate office's number was rerouted to my cell. Every night I took calls from residents who didn't know what to do or where to turn. They cried uncontrollable tears, pouring out their troubles to a complete stranger and, occasionally, sharing suicidal thoughts. It was a rough time for the community, and it would take a lot of healing and rebuilding to get it back on track.

This episode changed me. While it reaffirmed that I was in the right line of work, it also prompted me to take a step back and think about what the next steps might be. I was burnt out, but fearful that if I moved on I would be letting people down. Working in service of your

5

community always bears a unique pressure that is hard to explain. It also lends itself in search of a balance that is often unachievable.

So I did what most people do when they are searching for answers and have a high disposable income: I booked a trip to Europe to go find myself.

Little did I realize this would be the trip where I would meet my future wife. We met in Rome, and in a truly serendipitous way. She was from San Diego, so I had some choices to make for us to be together. Within eight months, I resigned from my job, left my countless books of political memoirs in a box at my family's house, and set out for California. In hindsight, it was a crazy decision and could've gone in a number of different directions, but we are now happily married and the parents of two great kids, a maladjusted rescue dog, and a donor-advised fund (DAF).

I dabbled in a few things after I moved to the United States. I helped launch a government relations and public policy department at the US Green Chamber of Commerce, freelanced as a journalist for the *San Diego Uptown News* (successfully delivering front-page stories regardless of my penchant for vowels and an *s* instead of *z*), running the community engagement efforts of the semi-pro soccer team the San Diego Flash, and then—like a moth to a flame—back into politics as a field organizer for the California Democratic Party on a red-to-blue targeted campaign. I loved the adrenaline, the urgency, the conversations with swing voters, and the team camaraderie of that work. Through every campaign I have ever been on, I have developed lifelong friendships and met folks who have challenged or enhanced my political views. But the hours were long and extremely demanding—hardly complementary to raising a young family. So when the campaign was over (eking out a close win), I chose to be more intentional with my next career move.

That's when the world of philanthropy came calling.

A role at the San Diego Foundation with its charitable giving team opened up. In essence, the role was fundraising, yet it had a lot of potential to be so much more. On paper I didn't sync up with all of the job responsibilities, but I was lucky enough to have an amazing person in my corner to help me get my foot in the door for an interview. Brittany Bailey, who I had met on the Scott Peters for Congress campaign, wrote an email to the hiring manager that was so good that I actually blushed when I read it. (Brittany is awesome, and in a complete role reversal, is now a political staffer herself for the progressive mayor of San Diego.) After navigating four interviews, I was the new manager for charitable giving and the Civic Leadership Fund, the foundation's annual fund that raised resources for the newly formed San Diego Foundation Center for Civic Engagement, which I would later run myself.

Philanthropy became a great fit for me. It was still like working for the community, but instead of asking for their vote, I was actively finding them funding opportunities to lead their own neighborhood change. The Civic Leadership Fund, which I ended up leading, became a truly dynamic vehicle for the foundation, shifting their membership to a younger and more diverse group of leaders, raising up their voices through a new steering community (which was the first ever majority people of color committee in the foundation's history), with the goal of helping inspire larger donors through a range of unique events that sought to bring in nonprofits and community leaders rather than keep them at arm's length.

I touch on my experiences at the San Diego Foundation throughout the book to highlight examples of how community foundations are missing out on a range of opportunities to be at the forefront of civic engagement and catalyze shared solutions that can create a real vibrancy and sense of purpose in our communities. *They can, and should, be more than just charitable banks.* But as you'll find out later, my approaches were sometimes at odds with leadership. The fact that I was gently reprimanded in the nicest of ways for openly calling out the need to move beyond "old white money" should have been ample warning that traditional philanthropy was not ready for the type of change I was selling.

From there, the next step was a grassroots nonprofit. As with my political candidacy, I aspired to understand all facets of the sector I work in. So shifting from a funding institution to one that actively cultivated the support of their fund holders was a no-brainer. That landing spot was Access Youth Academy, a truly unique education program whose mission, programming, students, and leadership were the perfect mix of grit, inspiration, and vision. This urban squash program helps low-income youth become the first of their families to graduate from college, since many colleges with squash programs (especially on the East Coast) were struggling to fill and diversify their scholarship spots at the time. (One of those students' stories was captured on the episode "The Jaguar," part of Apple TV+'s *Little America* series, and is well worth a look.) The program is similar in structure to the cradle-to-career approach of the Harlem Children's Zone in that it realizes a student's struggles weren't over when they were accepted to college. This is why Access implemented a twelve-year program that supported these kids through high school and college and even two years after college graduation, where a donors' networks became much more valuable than their dollars.

Everything that Access did was strategic. They found a stellar school partner in the country's number-one transformative school, the Preuss School at UCSD. They targeted students who weren't necessarily good at sports or didn't have straight As, but had an unquestionable resolve. They interviewed the families about the commitment they would make to their child for both accountability and buy-in, and they recruited some of the biggest influencers in the city to join their board (at a $10,000 give), helping them scale this success and amplify their impact. Access will be moving to a state-of-the-art squash and education center in the coming years, coincidentally located in one of the nation's twenty-two Promise Zones, an Obama Administration initiative (coincidentally) inspired by the work by Geoffrey Canada and his Harlem Promise Zone model. This process of how promise and opportunity zones are helping leverage new funding opportunities for nonprofits and reimagining the math of traditional capital campaigns will be discussed in more depth later in the book.

After receiving confirmation from the City of San Diego that the funding mechanisms were in place for $12.5 million in New Markets Tax Credits, I felt that this was the perfect time for a new challenge, and the perfect time for Access to bring in new blood and a new energy as they moved to a new phase of fundraising. I was approached about a job opportunity by a board member of San Diego Grantmakers (SDG), a membership organization made up of 120 local foundations and corporate and government funders. This newly created position was charged with building new resources to sustain and then grow the organization on the back of a $1 million capacity-building grant. It was the perfect progression for me, and with San Diego having such a small philanthropic footprint compared to other metro areas underpinned by big corporate funders, statewide foundations, and large family foundations whose namesake products you have definitely bought at one point, it was honestly one of my last opportunities to get back into the sector.

I was drawn to SDG due to my admiration of their then-CEO, Nancy Jamison, and respect for their staff. At one point before my time at the San Diego Foundation ended, I was heading to one of their events and thought, *Damn, there is an actual energy and willingness to discuss the difficult issues and get shit done here.* It was refreshing. Later, my interview with Nancy lasted an hour or so. She was a kind, engaging, and highly intelligent leader who was happy to share the spotlight, guide you through both internal and external "hiccups," and also challenge you to be more. We talked about the current state of philanthropy, the opportunities for the sector, and the desire to enhance the current organizational culture. I swear I could have sat there the entire day and not run out of things to say or learn.

When I joined SDG, one of the first things we worked on was finalizing a new strategic plan for the organization. We added the term *future focused* to our values. We wove equity, social justice, and opportunity for all throughout the document, not just adding it in a byline but calling it out. We highlighted the need to lift up new forms of funding such as giving circles and impact investing. We effectively had engineered a new DNA that compelled us to rewrite our entire mission and vision. Change is possible if you're willing to show a bit of courageous leadership, take time to intentionally recruit the right people to your staff and board, and "lift the hood" of the organization and do what is necessary to make a real impact, not just keep yourself in a job.

It was also at SDG where I found more meaning in my work. I have often found myself in awe of others in my field as they have demonstrated a real connection with what they do—an unrivaled passion that spurs them to act—whereas sometimes I have found myself questioning my direction, given the lack of fire or emotional attachment to a cause. I'm empathetic, I know it's the right thing to do, yet I wouldn't effectively give up everything for something or someone else. It could have also been a symptom of impostor syndrome too, something emerging leaders tend to deal with daily.

Then something clicked. As part of a concerted effort to walk the walk of equity, Philanthropy California (a coalition of Northern California, Southern California, and San Diego Grantmakers) hired a consultant to educate us on the history of race, challenge our assumptions, and discuss everything from allyship to white supremacy and whiteness.

Racial training opened my eyes. Coming to the US with no real historical education of the country allowed me to approach the work with an open mind and to view this country's past with a critical lens and curiosity, asking why the US "is like it is." Slavery, equal rights, and the ongoing scourge of police brutality are stains on the American story, and we should be doing more. We should be fighting for justice and change and holding our elected officials and those who are sworn to protect us accountable so they can become better, fairer, and more just—and, in many cases, so they can stop compounding the reasons why certain sections of our community continue to live in fear.

It was at this time I also had a child and decided to become a US citizen. The bare minimum I could do to ensure our communities felt respected, protected, and connected was to vote.

I still continue to learn as much as I can about the systems that have been built to protect the current status quo so I can identify ways I can use my privilege to help this movement for change and to lift up others. I can get my foot in the door—and damn right I'm not walking straight in, but rather holding it ajar so I can bring others with me and ensure they get their seat at the table. We can deal with this table in a number of ways, which you'll see as I introduce each major pillar of this book. I'll also speak about a number of operational strategies that can help with diversity, help marginalized groups get into philanthropy, and ensure pay gaps and other inequalities are eradicated, as well as how technology, while having the potential to lift up those disadvantaged by our society's constructs, can just as easily harm that progress due to implicit biases moving from consciousness to coding and any unintended consequences of artificial intelligence (AI).

However, it's possible that you may read this book and think that it doesn't go far enough or that I could have used this platform more effectively. My response is that there are better spokespeople out there who better understand these issues because they ultimately live them. The best role I can currently play is to support and amplify their work at every opportunity. I have included a list of those doing great work in this space as a reference in this book. Please check it out and don't shy away from difficult conversations about what you can do and how you can help.

There are many things I look back on from my time at SDG with a real sense of accomplishment: the formulation of the Equity and Innovation Fund, doubling the organization's operating budget to $4 million annually, and creating a new public policy committee and three-year policy agenda, to name a few. When Nancy retired from her position as CEO, I knew it was time to move on. I had joined the organization to learn more from her, to grow not only professionally, but also personally. And I did.

Within those two years, I decided to not be just a connector, but also try and see myself as a potential leader in the field. I had always promoted others ahead of myself as I continued to grapple with what could be my own future. In the back of my mind, I had always thought I could return to Australia and help drive reforms in their philanthropic sector, perhaps even run for office again. My wife and I also discussed the potential of moving to another city so we could realize our own dream of home ownership and build a foundation for our kids, since we couldn't afford to buy a house in San Diego. It was as if every year I had to go through the painstaking process of having to recommit to my current life, career, and city.

So, instead of being crushed by my continued indecision, I decided to take any opportunities that might help grow and further develop my own skills instead of letting them slide by.

That year I became a fellow of the San Diego Leadership Alliance (SDLA) and was accepted into the Emerging Nonprofit Leaders cohort for Fieldstone Leadership and became chair of the San Diego chapter of Emerging Practitioners in Philanthropy (EPIP). The latter needed a bit of TLC, a new north star, and the recruitment of a new leadership group—something to stop the constant membership turnover in a city where eligible members were few and far between. The north star ended up being the chance to showcase our city to the nation by securing host-city rights for the EPIP national conference, which unfortunately was postponed for 2020 due to the COVID-19 pandemic.

So while Nancy challenged me to be more, my extracurricular experiences and learnings with the aforementioned groups gave me the confidence to proactively search for that next challenge, which came in the form of a chief of staff role at National University and its ambitious $185 million philanthropic project funded by founder of First Premier Bank, T. Denny Sanford. I speak extensively about this experience later in the book as a possible shift in how uber-philanthropists approach and tackle issues at scale without needing the scaffolding of a large foundation.

I know what you may be thinking: *OK, OK, I get it, you have shown that you have an understanding of philanthropy, but where does technology layer into this conversation? How are you an authority on the subject?*

First, I'm far from being an authority. However, I do have an interesting background when it comes to tech, and the more I look at it, the more I see my father did have a positive influence on my career after all.

My dad's jobs ran the gamut of what was available. At different points, he worked in printing and aged care and ran an antiques store that later morphed into a sports shop. Eventually, he ended his day-to-day working life as a cleaner. He would rather be remembered, however, as an inventor—and to his credit, there was merit in that claim. He was very creative and secured a number of international patents. Sadly, he lacked the trust, patience, and follow-through to make it past a home-made prototype. He always tried to rope me into the marketing, especially when I moved to the US. (He was particularly enamored of the TV show *Shark Tank*.) His ideas were simple innovations, but he had hundreds of them, and therein lies the lesson: There are many ways of making things better, and tech can help us explore these options and help accelerate those that show promise.

I have long ideated ways to improve civil discourse, increase civic engagement, and get out the vote through tech. Some have been successful, though none have been scaled. But they all have impacted my understanding of technology's capabilities and possible applications. I have learned how to use code to make enhancements to white-label offerings and show that these ideas work, not just in principle but also through successful prototyping. My main question, however, was always this: How do you move from moments to movements and navigate the barriers of civic, government, and nonprofit tech adoption?

After speaking with a number of founders in this space, I identified that it was too expensive, too cyclical, and not fully accessible. It's as if the tech world has been warped into a view that commercialization is the only pathway for user adoption and that success is either an "exit" or an IPO.

I shudder at the thought of all the amazing ideas, technology, and people who have fallen by the wayside because they fell short of these key indicators. Imagine if folks who were snapped up by Google, Facebook, or Amazon had pivoted their work to be more civically focused. They could create something that would increase voting by 30 percent in midterm election years, reduce chronic homelessness in cities by 90 percent, or even bring in millions of dollars and increased representation to a local community by helping secure a full count in the most recent census. A civic ideas bank could even be created to capture all of the flashes of inspiration by our community, no matter how outlandish those ideas may be. It would be very much like an online museum of an individual's ingenuity, a way for people to share their work and learnings regardless of their success and to sift through potential solutions that could unlock the potential of a similar idea they are working on.

I am now at the University of Texas at Austin and one of the few directors of development placed within a single department, working to identify individual donors with an interest in making major gifts to Texas Computer Science and meeting with our national network of alumni and donors to keep them up to date on departmental initiatives and faculty research. My current role is the perfect intersection of my passion and my skill set. Texas Computer Science is a top-ten ranked program in the country, and the city of Austin is fast becoming one of the biggest tech hubs outside of Silicon Valley, with Apple and Tesla recently announcing new campuses to be built in the best place to live in the US, according to the *US News & World Report*.

I have been enamored of Austin ever since I visited it for the first time in 2016, when I spoke at South by Southwest (SXSW) on the topic of "Civic Leaders Need New Civic Technologies," and while the highlight was meeting Grumpy Cat and not actually speaking, the city jumped to the top of our list should we ever move from the Cali-Baja region. Although our move was hampered by the COVID-19 pandemic, meaning that we haven't even explored our new city due to being isolated for more than eight months and counting as of this writing, I have sincerely enjoyed working with some truly brilliant minds in the tech space and am buoyed by what the future might hold for both UT and me, having been exposed to the work that underpinned a successful $20 million National Science Foundation grant in AI and the establishment of a new Machine Learning Laboratory, of whose work and research inspires much of the final pillar of this book.

I am a proud student of the future. I believe that our society, when working in unison, can move mountains. I believe that our communities, when working together, can part the seas of discontent. And I wholeheartedly believe that when folks are connected to opportunity and their eyes are opened to their full potential, we can set this world free. The fact is that we are not even talking about the future beyond hyperbole and aspirational rhetoric. And you wonder why even the most optimistic of folks don't believe? The best they can do is merely hope.

If anything, *Future Philanthropy* is my attempt to help folks believe in our sector again. This is the real change we need right now, because someone is more compelled to act when they believe in a better world, and not just hope for one. But is hope a luxury in today's society? Do people have the time or the energy to go that extra mile for what they believe in when the systems they seek to change are mining their time, talent, and resources for all they're worth, all the while leaving them exhausted at the end of the working day? Hope for many is having food on the table, a roof over their head, and job security, not engaging in the most complex and defining issues of our time.

SOME NOTES ABOUT THIS BOOK

First, let's spell out what this book is not. This isn't a woo-woo diatribe about the concept of hope, the need for a once-in-a-generation leader to unite a fractured and polarized society, or a book about the invisible force of personal purpose. This is about understanding what our futures might hold and how a combination of both talent identification and retention, coupled with providing those talented people with the tools and systems to go from good to great, can develop solutions that, if successful and adopted into law, can help folks get back to even.

The ideas contained within these chapters are rooted in intentional shifts that, if applied in some fashion over the coming decade, will begin to compound in a way which will reweave the very fabric of our society, from one where battle lines are drawn depending on your politics to one where we link arms out of a mutual respect for each other and wanting nothing but the best for our family, friends, and neighbors. "A rising tide lifts all boats" is a great slogan on which to pin our hopes, but not at the expense of those drowning below.

This book also shies away from providing recommendations for change based on how other countries have tackled some of the themes discussed in this book. While it highlights some of the differences in a featured piece on the state of philanthropy of both Australia and Saudi Arabia, I have long found the narrative of "Well, it works there," to be a lazy strategy that doesn't appreciate that our histories, systems, and cultures are different. I do profess to using the "Innovation doesn't need to be new, just new to you," approach in some of my work, but policies do not come turnkey, and even the family-friendly ones embraced by most Scandinavian countries aren't easily constructed the way IKEA would have you believe. If people think that change is easy, then they don't truly understand anything about civic participation and the battle for ideas.

So you now know what it won't be. Let's talk about the fun stuff.

The book is structured across three main pillars: trends at the tipping point; talent, operations, and human resources (HR); and the "flagship" pillar of future technologies that have the potential to revolutionize our sector. Topics are introduced and addressed in long form with ideas, insight, and potential applications laid out for you to adopt and ultimately advance. It tackles everything from impact investing to giving circles, diversity, equity, and inclusion (DEI) to the jobs of tomorrow, and also what the sector might look like in 2030 and beyond—including what AI, machine learning, and even quantum computing mean and can do for charities the world over. There's also a bonus section that looks at a number of institutions that could be revamped with a philanthropic focus, including the postal service, professional sports teams, and even GivingTuesday.

My favorite part, though, is highlighting fourteen emerging leaders in philanthropy and tech. These folks truly get shit done, and I have had the pleasure of working with them in a variety of different capacities over the years. These Future Features are as much thought provoking as they are inspiring, and they are a good way to see change in action, realizing that these leaders' determination is indeed palpable and ultimately infectious! There is no doubt in my mind that they will be leading foundations, sitting in Congress as elected representatives, and ideating the solutions that will improve the lives of millions of citizens.

Future Philanthropy has been a two-year labor of love that began with an interaction with a virtual reality (VR) display at the Clinton Global Initiative in New York, which sparked a fascination about what the future of philanthropy might look like, from tech to trends and through to innovative new thinking that seeks to tackle society's most pressing needs. This book hasn't just been a simple pen-to-paper exercise. It has been an immersive experience across all facets of philanthropy, both from a professional and personal standpoint including:

- **ideation and experimentation**—building prototypes for civic engagement tools that were focused on democratizing donor-advised funds (DAFs), getting out the vote, and rebuilding civil discourse.

- **learning and listening**—participating in a yearlong diversity training to understand and question the root causes of racism and inequity, engaging with my community in more unique ways and participating in a number of innovative leadership cohorts.

- **traveling and speaking out**—discussing civic technology at SXSW and VR/AR donor engagement at the Public Relations Society of America's International Conference (PRSA ICON), and traveling to DC annually for Foundations on the Hill.

- **convening and writing**—hosting book clubs, immersive events, a live podcast, and ultimately creating a blog that underpin many of the ideas you will find in this book.

It hasn't been smooth sailing, either. The conversations, opportunities, and efficiencies I have raised with my organizations in the past have been met with a befuddled look and a "maybe next year" kind of response. I feel like a little puppy getting a pat on the head most of the time.

Make no mistake: Talking about the future demands attention and respect because the costs of inaction sometimes far outweigh those of action. What I'm proposing is not groundbreaking. The tech is already out there and has been proven to work. It just needs to be reimagined for a new use. Once I pushed for a simple VR station at a Grantmakers conference. It fit the theme, since we had renowned futurist Trista Harris as a key speaker. But there was a real disconnect between leadership on how it worked, what value it would bring, and what participants would take home from it. Futurism is just as much opening people's eyes as it is advancing society. So instead of people being wowed by an immersive experience and moved by a story of impact and walking away with the idea of what could be, they received a pair of cheap sunglasses featuring our logo instead. Gotta love a missed opportunity.

There really needs to be a future-focused social sector conference. Many organizations have tried, but none have truly succeeded. In fact, nothing I have seen has come close to the Clinton Global Initiative Conference. This event wasn't about the star power. Nor was it about getting attitude from Daymond John after asking for his ID, watching Dikembe Mutombo making Chelsea Clinton jump way off the ground to give him a high five, or missing out on meeting Bill Clinton because I had to leave for a Chvrches concert at Central Park. Rather, it was a life-changing experience, and not just for me. It brought together people and companies with real resources to make a difference and curate their participation in ways that fostered collaboration around key conference themes. After each keynote, members would break out into rooms and thrash out ideas and bind partnerships or discuss ways to make some demonstrable change in our world over the next year. This event tackled disease, conservation issues, educational access, and attainment—you name it. Once collaborators agreed to a plan of action, a buzzer would sound, and they would announce their agreement on stage, then report back the following year.

Wow. What I would do to recapture this approach and help facilitate real bipartisan, cross-sectoral commitments to change and then keep them all honest in a transparent and accountable way. This conference impacted millions of people and contributed to a legacy that will be illuminated over the course of time, not picked apart in today's egregious cancel culture.

Let's just say that my initial contribution to a new movement is this book. *Future Philanthropy* is a blueprint for bold change and a call to arms for anyone who feels they are being held back. Now is not the time for sitting on the bench waiting to be called up to the big dance.

Now is the time to stand up and be counted, taking a big bet on yourself, and rallying around the next generation with the attitude that these new leaders can be the ones who repair a fractured society and restore the aspirations that come with living in the United States of America—the future successes you envision for your children when they are born, the excitement of starting your dream job, or the promise of a brighter future for those who fled persecution and risked it all for freedom and a safe haven for their family.

I truly hope you find this book thought provoking and will keep it within arm's reach wherever you make your mark. This isn't a how-to guide, it's a "how could we" guide. So blaze your own path and effect the change you want to see in this world, as if your future depends on it.

PART ONE

THE TALENT OF TOMORROW

CHAPTER ONE

Inviting New People to the Table

If I had a dollar for every time I was in a conversation about the need to bring more folks, new voices, or new ideas to the table, I would have the capacity to buy a lot of tables. And not just those IKEA ones—I'm talking fancy tables with smart screens built into them.

Of course, they are right on the money (excuse the pun), but are we on the right track or just tracking the right conversation?

We talk a lot about systems change, understanding that if built, rebuilt, or—in more passionate circles—dismantled, then that can allow people to thrive, and our society to thrive with it.

Systems are key, that's true. But the "system" as it were still needs people to review it, ideate it, and, of course, implement it. I think we definitely have the energy for change, but do we necessarily have the right people in place to change it?

Given what transpired across 2020, I don't think we do.

That's why it's important to underpin this book by taking a proactive look at social-sector talent and how we can start building a better foundation for change; looking at those new voices, approaches, and partners; and putting them in a position to be successful.

We need to help folks get back to even based on the disadvantages they inherited at birth, and then we have to support them in their professional development to ensure they reach their full potential, all the while looking at opportunities to step into leadership roles and become those powerful voices, complete with lived experience, that our sector is crying out for.

It should be a fluid process rather than a forced outcome—an intentional, strategic step forward rather than a byproduct of fortune. We need to take control of our futures, not just take a reactive approach to change that is determined by outside forces. Black Lives Matter is a movement, it wasn't a moment. All the companies and organizations that diversified their staff, diversified their boards, and changed their narrative must be motivated by a shared vision of the future and not the fear of being left behind or overtaken.

Diversity is not just a box to be ticked; it is a commitment to change for the better, a change in which fairness is key and justice is at its core.

Change is driven by people, not processes, and as part of our commitment to getting back to even, we should lead with talent rather than tech. Tech is what accelerates and enhances change, it isn't what drives it.

With that in mind, it's time to accept that your employees mean everything to your organization and that the current levels of pay, investment in professional development, and retention efforts are way below par.

This first pillar highlights what is required to attract, keep, and elevate nonprofit talent. It explains how to challenge current narratives of what our workforce looks like, how it acts, and the environment it operates in. It charts a path to what steps we can take now and over the next decade to ensure that our sector is the most dynamic and impactful it can be—a place where workers' identity can have both legacy and currency, rather than being made to choose by the pressures of an outdated view of success.

This section also introduces the first Future Features on emerging leaders who ultimately chose to be the difference rather than simply play a role. You'll find more in-depth insights on how they see the future of philanthropy weaved through each of the four pillars of this book, with the first three being . . .

MICHAEL WARD JR.

Michael Ward Jr. is a social entrepreneur focused on increasing the upward mobility and social capital of underserved communities, specifically people of color. Michael currently lives in Austin, Texas, and is the president of the Austin Urban Technology Movement (AUTM). AUTM is a nonprofit that bridges the gap between the technology industry and the Black, Brown, and Latinx communities through job placement, career development, and networking opportunities. Michael is also the cohost of *Culture Crawl ATX*, a podcast that invites random guests to engage in conversations about controversial topics.

Originally from Miami, Florida, Michael earned a bachelor's degree in political science and global studies from the University of North Carolina (UNC) at Chapel Hill. While at UNC, he spent some time studying in France and worked for the International Communications Volunteers (ICV) in Geneva, Switzerland.

After graduating from UNC, Michael started his career at Oracle selling both front-end and back-end enterprise software for cloud and on-premises technology. During his time at Oracle, he also led their Black employee resource group, Alliance of Black Leaders for Excellence (ABLE), across the United States, Canada, and Brazil.

After Oracle, Michael transitioned to ADP as a professional employer organization (PEO) district manager where he learned the impact human capital management (HCM) has on a company's sustainability, culture, and bottom line. He also spent some time in the Austin start-up community, working as the vice president of operations at Primal 7, a fitness and physical rehab company.

MEGGIE PALMER

What if women—and men—never had any doubts about their worth? What if the anxiety associated with negotiating could be overcome? What if building confidence created new opportunities and value for employees, their colleagues, and their company? This is the world entrepreneur and former foreign correspondent Meggie Palmer envisions, and she's using technology to make it reality.

Described by many as a confidence creator, Meggie—who lectures at Columbia University and Barnard College and writes about gender and diversity for *Vogue*, *Marie Claire*, Women's Agenda, and News Corp—founded the consulting firm PepTalkHer in 2016. The start-up's mission is to close the gender pay gap by empowering professional, aspirational women and their allies to know and negotiate their value. Meggie and her team lead practical, fun, engaging corporate consulting and training programs for global businesses, including JPMorgan Chase, HSBC, and Revlon, that enable leaders to develop—and retain—their best staff.

In the US, legislation is underway that will mandate fair and transparent compensation. Meggie is already helping several large companies, such as Salesforce, Contently, and Protiviti, get ahead of the change, using technology to facilitate the transformation. Reevaluating and rebalancing the pay scales can be a sensitive subject for many CEOs and HR leaders, but it's an increasingly significant issue as consumers move buying power toward businesses with representative teams and inclusive values.

PepTalkHer has grown to a community of more than twenty-five thousand members, frequently partnering with brands such as Anheuser-Busch, Erno Laszlo, and Salesforce, which want to engage with the PepTalkHer community and attract talent. In conjunction with experts, PepTalkHer also developed a proprietary curriculum to help organizations retain, engage, and reward millennials and high-potential talent. In 2019, Meggie launched the PepTalkHer app in collaboration with *Vogue*. Using the nudge theory of psychology, the app aids users by sending weekly prompts to help them reflect on their weekly wins at work. It aims to make performance reviews less painful and helps to shift users to a growth mindset. Tracking data and images, it allows users to export and print their "brag book" to better advocate and negotiate at performance review time.

Meggie is a changemaker, and her optimism and passion for the future translate to the boardroom and the stage. She's regularly quoted in the press and interviewed by the likes of NBC and *Glamour*. A passionate and inspiring speaker and coach, she was a keynote speaker at Salesforce's annual conference, Dreamforce, and she recently headlined a conference for *Vogue*. She's emceed and hosted dozens of events globally, including for the European Union at its International Women's Day event at SXSW. Meggie was also invited by Nico Rosberg to speak at his Greentech Festival in Berlin.

During her days as an award-winning foreign correspondent, Meggie filed stories for global broadcasters, including Animal Planet,

BBC World News, Channel 7, CNBC, Discovery Channel, and SBS Dateline. Her journalism honors include a New York Festivals TV & Film Award, UN Media Award, a Walkley Award, and being named Queensland Young Journalist of the Year.

In addition to PepTalkHer, Meggie is also founder and CEO of Sliding Door Media. Drawing on her fifteen-year media career, she uses analytics and anecdotes to train high-level executives of disruptive, game-changing businesses to communicate their message across platforms and audiences using the power of storytelling.

A volunteer lifesaver and proud member of The Wing, Meggie currently sits on several not-for-profit boards, including Burn Bright, an organization teaching values-based leadership to schoolchildren throughout Australasia. She also serves on the US board for ELEVA-CAO, an NGO for women in tech.

ADRIANA LOSON-CEBALLOS

Adriana has successfully fundraised for local, national, and international nonprofits working in the fields of human rights, social services, social justice, and arts and culture in Mexico City, New York City, San Diego, and Washington, DC. She has almost a decade of experience writing proposals for city, county, state, and federal grants that have resulted in significant annual portions of the organizations' budgets. She has also obtained foundation funding from family, community, institutional, and foreign foundations, with grants up to $1 million.

Adriana's experience in foundation fundraising has resulted in strong donor prospecting and cultivation skills, as well as a successful creation of evidence-driven strategies based on the organization's customer relationship management (CRM) data. She has developed a corporate membership program for a social service organization in NYC and worked with corporations to obtain organizational support in the form of sponsorships, grants, and partnership opportunities supporting the corporation's corporate social responsibility (CSR) goals. Contributing to the strategy around individual and annual fund appeals, and working fundraising events, she has developed fruitful relationships with donors and boards at various organizations.

Adriana has an MA in human rights studies from Columbia University and is currently completing a PhD program in leadership studies with a concentration in nonprofit and philanthropic management at the University of San Diego.

———————————

Throughout this book you will see new leadership in action—and I hope you see yourself in them, their work, and their backgrounds. Lifting up those getting the work done is something that needs to be part of our collective role in championing change and inspiring those new folks we continually speak about bringing to the table. Let's just make sure we have enough chairs from now on, and let's be patient in filling them. This is a generational journey we are embarking on and one that will no doubt be full of trials and tribulations.

CHAPTER TWO

Investing in the Engine Room

OUR LEADERSHIP PIPELINES ARE LEAKING
A GENERATION OF CIVIC TALENT

Anyone who has met me knows that it's pretty much a given that I'm going to talk about what I call the "professional cliff face" within our first two meetings. It's not just for the sake of being a rabble-rouser, or that I have found myself in a state of perennial flux during this decade and that I am simply venting. It's that by disregarding emerging leaders and not setting them on a pathway to leadership that they can see, contribute to, and in a small way control, we risk losing them as true civic assets to our communities in the future. And by civic asset I mean someone who is actively participating in the progress of their community in a multitude of ways, helping move money for good, leading on boards and committees, volunteering and leveraging all of their skills and influence to make their region an even better place to live and work.

The cliff face in this instance is that we are constantly built up earlier in our career, fast-tracked to middle management by our late twenties, and very active in our local community, mainly because of fewer responsibilities and a larger disposable income. There is a vast array of emerging leadership programs available to help build up and sharpen our talents, knowledge, and networks.

Then come our thirties. Life happens, we get into more serious relationships, we get married, we have kids, yet more importantly we find ourselves still in middle management. Those who sit above us in senior leadership roles have been there for what seems like an eternity, waiting for their own chances to lead. (They were effectively in the same position as us a decade or so ago.)

So we drift. We find more connection and purpose in family life. We get a mortgage, we care for our elderly family members, we coach our kid's soccer team. We continue to work hard and try to block out other distractions to ensure we get that promotion, because that will make our lives easier, or so the story goes.

The reality of the matter is that once you fall into a different routine, it is more difficult to reengage with your community in the ways that most excite you. Justifying knocking on doors for a few hours on a Saturday morning for a ballot measure rather than attending your kid's dance recital is a difficult task. And when you add the compounding effects of stress, fatigue, and frustration, it's much easier to reach for a glass of wine and the remote in the evening than it is to hop in your car to drive to city hall and speak about why a dog park in your neighborhood is a positive thing.

I hear about it way too often and, excruciatingly more so, see it way too often. People who, in my eyes, have all the traits and tenacity to lead our community to greatness slip through our grasp because of the log jam of leadership. They move to a bigger city with more opportunity, they move out of the social sector to the corporate world saying they will be back, more enthusiastic than ever to help make that change we always discussed—and they never do. Because life happens and we default to newer talent who have more time to support campaigns in a variety of ways and are ready for populist fights in real time, not taking a few hours to get back to you as they renegotiate who is cooking dinner that evening.

It's a vicious cycle. And you know what? When that person above you or that long-serving CEO leaves, they rarely hire from within, citing the need to change gears and bring in new ideas and experience. Most of the time this comes in the form of someone from another city or state entirely. Sometimes you just can't win.

I'll be blunt: Philanthropy is the worst at pipeline management. Community foundations even more so.

While I admit to some scar tissue from a previous role in an organization that moved from long-term stability and staff tenure to a toxic atmosphere of gaslighting and being managed out of the organization, the practice that stuck with me the most was overlooking talent from within. (Those who missed out on promotions all went on to much bigger and better roles—go figure.) So, what strategies could exist to help keep our best and brightest on that upward trajectory with momentum and the support of their organizations?

Contract Limits. Much like term limits in politics, four- or five-year contracts for leaders that can only be renewed once might help yield a number of benefits for public entities, including a more focused commitment to results, more transparency and accountability to the community, and an opportunity for periodic change and the ability to manage the organization's evolution and transition. However, we would be naive as a sector to have a periodic drain of institutional knowledge. A nationally supported "golden gurus" program—which was initially pioneered in Australia—for philanthropy in which a CEO, during the last one to three years of their term, would be available for mentoring and/or consultant work with other foundations would be invaluable.

Cross-Training. Future leadership talent should be identified early and supported by the organization. This could be developed internally in a number of ways, but it makes sense to expose those employees to different functions of the organization and lifting up their skills in areas in which they are lacking. For example, a program director could be trained in nonprofit finance, or a development director could be asked to lead a new place-making project.

Professional Training. It can be awkward to ask for financial support to take professional training. Yet I find it strange that the main opportunity to ask about it comes during the budgeting process or an annual review. It's like open enrollment for benefits where only a major qualifying event can drive any flexibility in the budget.

Likewise, it's much easier asking for $1,500 to travel to San Francisco for a conference than it is paying for your Certified Fund Raising Executive (CFRE) accreditation or joining your local leadership cohort.

Why is that? Is it because they feel you are personally benefiting and may leave shortly thereafter? If so, that's shortsightedness and insecurity from management who can't see the inherent benefits. Conferences are low-level learning opportunities; they're great for networking and sparking ideas, but hardly add to your skills and expertise in the field.

Most employees don't want to ask for things for fear of rocking the boat against the strong current of power dynamics. Leaders should actively look to plug their shining stars into opportunity and reap the benefits of skilling their team up, keeping them engaged, and ultimately keeping them focused on the mission and loyal and energetic to the cause.

SABBATICALS

There are two applications of a sabbatical that would tremendously benefit organizational leadership, future leaders, and the community at large, all of which could go a long way in addressing the problems outlined within the scope of the "cliff."

Leadership Sabbatical. There has been an emerging trend of this first type of sabbatical in the philanthropy sector. Funders are seeing the benefits of funding a mechanism to increase retention, encourage new thinking and leadership, and provide stability for organizations on the tipping point of change.

The Durfee Foundation, a family foundation that rewards individual initiative and leadership, has driven this approach over the past twenty years, providing stipends for leaders to take time away from the organization to reflect, refresh, and recharge, and provide their organizations with a consultant whose role is to support the interim leadership team as they prepare and manage the period of transition. One founding executive director in particular benefited from the experience, coming back with a renewed vigor and energy for the role while having their operations director take more responsibility ahead of a move to a larger facility and doubling the number of people the organization could serve.

The program that supported this process was a joint effort based in

San Diego between the Clare Rose Foundation and Fieldstone Leadership Network. This program, known as the Clare Rose Sabbatical Program, provides an annual award to four nonprofits in the following ways:

- Individual stipends and expenses of up to $40,000 to cover salary, benefits, and travel to reflect or otherwise renew themselves in whatever manner they propose.

- Additional support of up to $5,000 is made available to successful candidates' employing organizations that are willing to establish a permanent, revolving fund for professional staff development.

- A fund of $2,500 to appropriately compensate or reward the leader or team that filled the role of the executive director during the sabbatical.

- Up to twelve consulting hours to aid in the preparation for, be on-call during, and assist in the reentry from the sabbatical.

And these numbers aren't plucked out of thin air. The whole approach is underpinned by a strong logic model created in collaboration with the Caster Family Center for Nonprofit and Philanthropic Research at the University of San Diego and enhanced through a five-year systematic evaluation of the program. The data derived from the program's participants demonstrated that the program strengthened nonprofit leaders, built organizational capacity, and contributed to a vibrant nonprofit sector.

At the end of this program, some leaders decided it was time for a new beginning. And guess what—the person who replaced them was the individual who filled the role in an interim capacity. Thus, programs like this help showcase a leader's talents and let the board see those talents in a new light. This is an important hurdle to overcome for many leadership aspirants, and a reason why many are overlooked when it comes to their opportunity to step into the CEO role.

Job Sabbatical. Foundations can also consider letting talented staff they would like to keep long-term go on an extended period of absence to explore other interests. For example, they could allow staff to take leave without pay for a year to work in a government department or support the work of a national affinity group. Those employees would benefit from the exposure to new ways of applying their knowledge and learning both soft and hard skills, while the home organization would reap the benefits upon the employee's return. This could also be in the form of a "job swap," in which two organizations agree to have their employees effectively swap places. Those organizations don't have to essentially be the same. One could be a foundation and the other a chamber of commerce, for example.

Today's job market is extremely fluid, with some individuals jumping between jobs regularly and others staying at organizations for more than ten years. (The latter is becoming more of an outlier than the career norm.) Regardless of what folks say, this isn't just a Gen Y thing. In the end, people like stability and the opportunity to grow into their roles, be supported, and reach their potential. So with a bit of creativity, some focus (and some foresight) around staff retention, we could build a new bridge rather than create a new cliff face. And for that our sector and our communities will stand to benefit.

NONPROFIT MONEYBALL:
DISCOVERING NEW TALENT TO HIT YOUR FUNDRAISING GOALS

The Moneyball thesis is simple. By using statistical analysis, small-market baseball teams can challenge for success by accruing assets that are undervalued or overlooked by other teams (and selling ones that are overvalued). Through a nonprofit fundraising lens, this thesis could be compared to a small organization regularly securing large donations that have traditionally been captured by larger national entities and institutions such as the Red Cross, American Cancer Society, or large universities.

In today's society, where nonprofit-sector information is more accessible and transparent than ever before, it's not just the mission of the more established charities that yields larger donations. There are considerable disparities at play, and one of them is the ability to secure the very best in fundraising talent.

Fundraising for smaller organizations is tough. You are more often than not wearing many hats. You are also inversely disadvantaged through your own success—through higher expectations, the need to raise more funds to keep up with service demand, and the like. And when there are lean spells, you are the first to feel the pressure from those previously singing your praises.

If you're raising money for a small nonprofit organization, what's compounding the issue is that your donor base and prospect pipelines are much shallower than larger organizations in your space. The majority of nonprofits traditionally have only enough liquidity to last three months if the funding dries up. Salaries from these nonprofits are also modest at best in a time when costs of living are far outpacing wage growth and regular Consumer Price Index (CPI) increases.

In short, if you're fundraising for an entity with an annual budget below $1 million, you face the constant threat of job insecurity and are (probably) underpaid.

In addition, your chances of exceeding your fundraising expectations are stacked against you as you are competing against large development teams. And that doesn't even include the marketing, event, and research support these teams have the luxury of tapping into organization-wide.

Moneyball is definitely a defining story line for the professionalization of sports. Statistical analysis has become a key driver for progress in professional major league franchises, with organizations looking for any edge they can get as they chase sport's immortality. This also rings true in other sectors. For example, a financial analyst can use stats to help them find undervalued stocks and bonds. So why is philanthropy so slow to use additional data points to assist with talent identification in fundraising?

Creating an innovative nonprofit is difficult, especially without the right talent. Hiring the right employees for the right roles at the right time is critical, and this requires good resource management. That's why we need to lean more on HR data and, in the future, look to new approaches and tools that can help with our decision making. Let's break down some simple approaches that nonprofits can use now to identify new talent and compete for a greater slice of that fundraising pie.

Look Beyond the Traditional Markers. With a deeper bench of skills, organizations can tackle the most complex social problems. But where does HR find this new generation of nonprofit game changers? And how does it attract those individuals? The great news is you don't have to look that far. Literally hundreds of those game changers are working in your communities on a seasonal basis. But who are they? Community organizers and political field staff are well versed in the importance of metrics, with a strong sense of what the end goal is. These emerging leaders also work tirelessly around the clock on cause-based issues, exist in large numbers, and are readily available (especially post-campaign). They are well connected, hardworking, and jacks of all trades. Many of them also specialize in fundraising, with all of them understanding the importance of the "ask." Their challenge, however, is that they probably don't hit all the job prerequisites, and that's where the problem lies. How do we help nonprofit organizations identify these transferable skills via the application process and ultimately look outside the box to de-risk their candidacy?

Empower Your HR Team. Nonprofit benchmark reports have shown that nearly half of the human resource executive staff who were surveyed identified an increase in their overall organizational influence—predominantly through more recognition by top-level executives that HR plays an integral role in executing an organization's mission. This represents a big opportunity for nonprofits and both public and private foundations to increase their capacity, be more impactful, and achieve their goals through the identification and development of talented staff. As social justice moves away from transferring wealth and toward building social infrastructure to help all members of society reach their potential, the sector is also seeing a parallel shift from purely program-based philanthropy to a campaign-like approach where engaging and building nontraditional constituencies and developing cross-sector partnerships are key to delivering tangible outcomes to those they seek to serve. The study, which was undertaken by XpertHR, reveals a renewed acknowledgment of HR's role in achieving organizational success and, on further reflection, its ability to equip organizations with new talent that will adapt to the rapidly changing philanthropic sector.

Encourage Inclusive Recruiting. The rigidity of minimum qualifications is slowly shifting as the modern workforce evolves, with credentialing fast replacing the prestige of the college you attended and the specialization of your degree. However, plenty of research still shows bias in how job descriptions are drafted and reviewed. This has to be a focus of ongoing change to ensure equality of opportunity in the job market. Many folks read job descriptions and opt out of applying as they don't "see themselves" in that role or they discredit their chances before they even apply. This is a major factor in the continuation of unequal pay for women and people of color. The immediate medicine for this systematic issue is to review the language of the role and ensure things such as educational requirements reflect the bare minimum for the relevant career experience.

Look Beyond Your Network. In addition to making job descriptions more inclusive, expanding your reach when advertising your job is paramount. Along with all of your local recruitment sites and specialized nonprofit job boards, start sharing your opportunities with Hispanic Chambers of Commerce, Black business society chapters, and workforce partnerships and alliances that provide job search and career development resources to all job seekers, regardless of income or background and at no cost to the candidates. These networks are not only dynamic in helping amplify talent, but their members are also the ones at the forefront of societal change. Your organization would be all the richer for their participation, whether applying to your roles or serving on your boards. So reach out authentically and build enduring partnerships that can help advance each other's missions.

Stop Salary Cloaking. While legislation has been passed in several states making it illegal for employers to ask for an employee's salary history, a subtle change to job advertisements could lead to savings in time and resources and play an important role in retainment levels and issues around pay parity. Salary cloaking is the practice of not posting a salary range for that role, arguably in the hope of attracting strong candidates without having them opt out of the opportunity at first glance. This is problematic in the nonprofit space as wages are notoriously low to begin with. Over the course of the recruiting process, it wastes people's time with searching, applying, screening candidates, and interviewing, just for a candidate to say, "No thanks, I have a family to support." I cannot stress this part enough: When an employee takes a lower salary, it perpetuates wage gaps and affects the employee's lifetime earnings and—to be frank—their sustained satisfaction in the position. The *Chronicle of Philanthropy* reported on the fact that most fundraisers only last sixteen months in their role and then move on for better pay. There is always a high cost of turnover, and this can be addressed on the front end by adding the simple detail of what you are willing to pay. I'll discuss salary cloaking in the nonprofit sector (and why it should end) in chapter 3.

Be Creative with Job Titles. I rarely refer to myself as a fundraiser, articulating that I am a philanthropic advisor when asked. A title at the end of the day is just a way of identifying a point person in what should be a strong "fundraising culture" of an organization. There is so much that goes into an ask, and I have found that donations come predominantly as a byproduct of strong donor research, cultivation, and stewardship—along with a killer case for support. Continuing with the Moneyball hypothesis, the individual managing a certain prospect can be likened to that of an American football quarterback studying the playbook, devising strategy with the head coach (CEO), and on game day executing the drive up the field and either scoring a touchdown themselves or passing to a receiver or giving it to a running back to make the score. At the end of the day, you select the best person to make an ask, whether it be a board member, the CEO, or an administrator sending out a membership renewal email.

Business cards in the fundraising space traditionally show fundraising, development, or advancement in the job title. However, research on the effectiveness of fundraiser job titles shows that *director of advancement* polls the lowest. Fundraising roles may garner more attention from out-of-sector talent if we devise new titles such as philanthropic advisor, charity analyst, or NGO resource strategist, to name just a few. Be creative about which job titles make the most sense to help facilitate more immediate understanding of who is engaging with the donor and why. Tricking donors into conversation by not being honest about why you are reaching out is a recipe for disaster.

Upgrade Your Systems and Adopt Automation. So you are excited about the diverse talent pool you have sourced for your next open position. That's great! The last thing you want is for your internal systems to let this potential finalist fall through the cracks or be snapped up by another organization because you took your time. (If they applied for your job opening, there is a high probability they are applying elsewhere too.) By analyzing and reassessing your organization's hiring process, you can ensure everyone who interviews with you has a great experience (thus improving your brand and standing in the sector) and that candidates feel supported through the onboarding process, ultimately setting them up for success.

Today's hiring process should have elements of standardization for consistency, tools that capture all of the information gathered on candidates, and automated components to ensure that the time taken from posting the role to that hire's eventual orientation hits established benchmarks. A great tool for this is Smartsheet, a platform that can be tailor-made for your internal needs and has the capacity to generate action items when candidates move along to additional stages of the process. Coupled with weekly reports to managers to ensure transparency and identify bottlenecks, tools like this can give your organization best-in-class processes at a fraction of the time and cost of a large acquisition team.

Expect to see big strides over the coming years for numerous HR offerings and applications. Google has been redefining the sector with their early research into data-driven HR focused on the optimal length of the hiring process, leading to Google's "Rule of Four" for interviews. Data collected from Google's 2016 interviews indicated that 95 percent of the time, panels of just four interviewers made the same hiring decision as panels of more than four interviewers, a decision that saved both time and money. So be rigorous and patient in your hiring process, as the return on investment for getting the right fundraiser on your team can be a true game changer for building capacity toward your organizational goals.

Use Assessment Tools. What do you do when you can't decide between two finalists for a role? Let's say that one of those candidates comes from a traditional fundraising background, and is credentialed as a Certified Fund Raising Executive (CFRE), and the other has limited experience but has been more successful in raising funds over a smaller period of time. More often than not, organizations take the safer option, which is the one with more years of experience and the professional qualification. Yet what if there was one more data set that could help make a more informed decision?

Cultural fit is just as important as an employee's skills and experience. By using behavioral assessments at the front end of the interviewing process, leaders can measure future indicators around performance and motivation, with the end goal of designing and building high-performing teams. Tools like the Predictive Index (PI) allow you to run your job description through its platform, develop a desired range for an employee's behavioral and cognitive fit, and gather further input from team members who will regularly interact with that individual to refine the key indicators of success and help develop particular interview questions based on the candidate's profile. Talent optimization strategies will be covered in more depth later in this chapter.

This, however, might be reserved for larger organizations, given that the average candidate would not like to have their resume (or cognitive skills for that matter) screened by an algorithm. A study conducted by the Pew Research Center found 76 percent of US workers would not want to apply for a job that screened their resume in this way, with most who were surveyed thinking the algorithm would do a worse job than a human.

But the path to innovation is seldom a smooth one. The good news, though, is that innovation doesn't have to be new. It just needs to be new to you—and why wouldn't you explore the hiring practices and rationale of larger organizations and their HR practices? Data-driven HR also helps to remove a certain level of human bias from recruitment efforts and opens the door to undervalued talent just as long as nuance is applied to ensure particular groups aren't being overlooked at the beginning of the process.

Consider taking calculated risks in your recruitment processes because, at the end of the day, it's a simple equation. There is a lot of talent out there with relevant and transferable skills. People who can motivate others to vote and donate in support of critical community issues can replicate this process (with a little fine-tuning) to turn supporters into donors and community volunteers into civic leaders. So whether you're swinging for the fences or just trying to get your operations to first base, it's definitely worth looking at.

While Moneyball didn't win the Oakland A's a World Series championship, the methodology was successfully applied at the Boston Red Sox organization through Theo Epstein. It eventually helped them end an 86-year drought to win the World Series. And then when he went on to the Chicago Cubs, it helped them end their own 108-year curse.

What fundraising campaign will be your World Series? And what team are you going to assemble to achieve your most audacious goals?

PHILANTHROPY'S NEXT WAVE OF JOBS AND HOW TO GET THEM

A career in organized philanthropy vis-à-vis a nonprofit seems pretty good from an outside perspective. And it wouldn't be wrong. Salaries in organized philanthropy are some of the highest in the nonprofit sector, growing on the strength of investment performance and additions to endowments. This also leads to more job security—and, as a result, lower turnover and a generationally segmented workforce. But the sector is changing rapidly, and this is going to disrupt a long-held status quo.

Traditional grantmaking approaches are changing. The vehicles through which funds are being invested are changing. Philanthropy is transitioning from funding as a charitable transaction to one with a social justice lens at its core. To adapt to this paradigm shift, the sector is going to need new voices, experiences, education, training, and expertise when it comes to executing these dynamic new takes on how we support programs and projects looking to deliver real impact for those they serve.

And it's not just the type of staff that will need to change. It's also the jobs that support the work.

What are the new jobs we can expect to see over the coming years? And how can people crack into this field with purpose rather than "accidentally" find their way there?

Jobs of the Future. Futurism is all about understanding the current trends and seeing how they can be applied in the future. But to do this you need to have a thorough grasp of the sector's current position and be able to identify where gaps still exist.

From a jobs perspective, Philanthropy New York created a good snapshot of current jobs in the sector and their core functions, with everything from accounting clerk right through to program officer and beyond. These positions will still exist to a certain degree. Yet if they are to deliver the scale and impact we envision (and need) over the next decade, they will either evolve or be replaced by positions that reflect the community dynamic or that are more tech focused with digital solutions and delivery at their core.

The Future Roles[1] of a Modernized Philanthropy. As we move into a new decade and see new generations coming of age in the workplace, these are

---

1 Given the specialized nature of these jobs, it's important to highlight ongoing issues around equity, especially when it comes to positions in financial investing and tech development, which see far lower employment numbers of women and people of color than other sector-wide roles mainly due to access of senior level experience in newer sectors. Philanthropy should continue to expand its efforts to diversify its staff and better reflect the communities it serves. This begins through its recruitment efforts—job descriptions, requirements, and where open positions are advertised.

the new positions that (in no particular order) will be common fixtures in philanthropic organizations the world over:

- **Investor Relations and Business Analysts:** These roles will support the traditional chief investment officer (CIO) position and help inform/diversify portfolios beyond the traditional markets and into impact investing and socially responsible investments (SRIs).

- **Product Managers and Coders:** Over the next decade, big philanthropy will shift away from establishing large private foundations and link with more nimble alternatives such as nonprofit universities, associations, affinity groups, and other niche funder tables to begin building platforms, tools, and even physical products, providing them at no cost to drive market adoption. This approach will look very much like a social enterprise or start-up with deliverables required over a set period of time, where the project will either sunset or be absorbed by the sponsoring entity or, ideally, adopted by the government.

- **Fundraisers:** Fundraisers aren't as regular a fixture in large private foundations as one might expect. They have never had to fundraise, given that their operating funds are derived from fund management and investment returns on their corpus. However, with a need for foundations to expand their unrestricted funds to fuel trends toward new programs and rapid response efforts, development staff will be needed to develop and execute new fundraising plans and partnerships beyond traditional revenues.

- **Legal Officers:** As philanthropic organizations commit to tackling systemic issues such as immigration, homelessness, and human trafficking that persist and affect some of the most vulnerable in our communities, an on-staff lawyer will be able to help advise on the constitutional, legal, and legislative aspects of advocacy and contracts that will go beyond a traditional Memorandum of Understanding (MOU) and funding agreements. Contract law expertise will also be needed for those seeking to drive action on impact investing and supporting the legal aspects and mediation for potential mergers of local nonprofits.

- **Organizers:** As foundations increase their footprint and impact in the community through traditional grassroots engagement, they will begin to take the nontraditional route of hiring organizers rather than just funding them. At first this will be more partnership based, but the need to have a more dynamic staff that can help work in (and with) the community to drive real change that supports their advocacy will become apparent. This shift could occur as a result of the evaluation process of philanthropy's work on the census, especially if it leads to large undercounts in urban areas.

- **Journalists:** Journalism, as we know it, is under attack. Whether it be dangerous rhetoric around its motives from DC or a dramatic shift in the traditional revenue models, we are seeing major layoffs in staff, the consolidation of local publications, and moves from for-profit entities to a nonprofit model (for those not currently a viable venture capital acquisition option). Philanthropy is acutely aware of the need to keep quality, independent media outlets operating at the hyperlocal, municipal, and state levels and has a long history of also fueling new innovation, as the sector is uprooted by the changes in how folks get and digest their news. (The Knight Foundation is a great pioneering example of this.) Philanthropic institutions have plenty of possibilities to evolve from traditional marketing and communications (marcom) approaches as they lend their voices to critical issues in their communities, with their own virtual newsrooms setting the table for critical civic discussions.

So How Do We Get These Jobs? I receive many questions on how to get a job in philanthropy, and I'm aware that much of the advice you can find on the web is to focus on "following your passions" and working on your soft skills. What I'm here to tell you is that there are far more practical approaches that will get you closer to your dream job and help you thrive when you get there.

Use Power Mapping. This is a visual tool and process that is often used by social justice organizers to identify people of influence in order to build a comprehensive lobbying strategy and effect change through groups and individuals. This methodology can be readily applied by those seeking to break into the philanthropic sector. Just list all of the leaders who are driving change and innovation and align with your values or where you want to be career-wise and then create a sub-tier listing of emerging leaders with whom you want to connect. Follow and connect with them on social media, learn which groups they align with, and then begin tracing back the dots. These lines will then lead to those top-tier leaders (given the common two degrees of separation we see through the sector), and you will have a warm lead who can connect you.

Network. Many opportunities exist within the philanthropy sector that are geared solely toward engaging new and diverse voices in the field. Keep an eye out for conference scholarships that give you full program access, including the pre-conference networking events, and link up with the professional groups that can help expand your knowledge and understanding of the sector's nuances within your region. Your local chapters of the Association of Fundraising Professionals (AFP), Emerging Practitioners in Philanthropy (EPIP), and the Young Non-profit Professionals Network (YNPN) are great organizations to connect with. Join a committee and then progress to the board. It's a great experience, and you learn quickly about programming, fundraising, and governance with the focus on your own professional development.

Build Your Own Informal Groups. Create an informal group of your peers (which can be organized through a simple Facebook group) and meet regularly to discuss opportunities and sector trends and to work through ideas and pain points to advance your respective careers. This approach has been applied in a number of ways: roundtables where prominent community leaders are invited to speak, book clubs and happy hours that layer in local viewpoints, and the more intentional and intellectually enriching 8-3-1 events championed by fellow futurist Trista Harris in her book *FutureGood.* The overall premise for that type of event is to gather eight individuals for three hours to discuss one major issue affecting their community.

Become a Funder. What better way to learn more about organized philanthropy, grantmaking, and your community than by joining or starting a giving circle? Many giving circles let members give at a level that is meaningful to them, and there are plenty of platforms (such as Amplifier and Growfund) that help you receive and distribute funds to make the process as simple as possible so you can focus on the giving part. Other options include opening a donor-advised fund (DAF), which is very much like a charitable bank account. It is more expensive to open this kind of account, with the lower end establishment fees needing an initial contribution of between $2,500 and $5,000. However, DAFs may become exponentially more affordable in the near future, which will be discussed later in this book.

You can also consider pitching to your parents or extended family the benefits of establishing a family fund as a way to give back to your community, espouse your values, and invest in your professional development. It will bring your family closer together while bringing you closer to a possible career move.

Pursue Your Credentials. While degrees and master's programs are questionably still prerequisites for senior level and executive positions, the institution from which you receive it is becoming far less important in the greater scheme of things. The core lessons from an MBA and MPA (master's in public administration) are what is of the most value. Many private nonprofit universities now have monthlong courses, meaning you can graduate in little over a year. Together with the availability of additional professional accreditations such as the Certified Fund Raising Executive (CFRE) and Certified Nonprofit Professional (CNP), there are plenty of options to build out your resume while building up your own experiences. Don't let a year go by waiting for the right time or trying to be flexible for the right position. Get back to school, get credentialed, and you will get ahead in the long term. It's a lot more affordable than you think.

Join Learning Groups. There is an abundance of new niche leadership organizations—progressive, identity-focused, city- and sector-specific cohorts—spreading out all across the country, providing participants with core skills across organizing, strategy, and PR. The best part of these groups are the strong bonds you make with sector-wide peers and the alumni network to which you now belong, one where numerous job and other unique opportunities are made available.

Take a Leadership Role on a Nonprofit's Board or Committee. Join the board of a nonprofit to learn about governance and the real needs of a social-sector organization. Understanding the difficulties of fundraising, sustainability, and capacity will give you a greater appreciation of those that are the main beneficiaries of philanthropic funds and give you a unique lens when it comes to enhancing the process and impact of a funder's investment. This is also where you will be at the same table as funders—with many major donors of those organizations (both corporate and individual) traditionally playing leadership roles. One pitfall to be aware of is that people who are at the beginning of their career feel they have to be asked to join a board or shy away from service due to "give and get" requirements. This is not necessarily the case. Seek out organizations where mission and values align, volunteer or serve on a committee to get a feel for that organization, and then state your case to join that board and manage their expectations. You will be surprised at how accommodating organizations will be for the right skills, ideas, and energy.

Don't Mistake Skills for Experience. I firmly believe that generalists— those who have applied their talents to a multitude of different roles and sectors over their career—have strong transferable skills and know enough to hit the ground running (and in a number of cases have a higher ceiling in terms of their potential). The earlier example of non-profit Moneyball on page 32 showed how nontraditional candidates with a diverse yet complementary set of experiences can be the ace up an organization's sleeve. Don't be deterred from applying for that dream job due to those elusive "preferred experiences and qualifications." You never know what the hiring manager is looking for or which candidates have built out that particular talent pool. Remember, you have to be in it to win it!

Apply for a Fellowship. This is technically a one-year paid internship and a position you will still need to apply and interview for, but one that more often than not results in becoming a full-time employee. The added benefit here is twofold—the position is often endowed or named by the donor who has made this capacity-building position possible, which provides that extra bit of prestige, and the role is normally created to help drive a particular issue or emerging trend in the sector. This is a great opportunity to make yourself indispensable to the organization.

Brand Yourself. Highlight your skills in a way that complements your resume and enhances your personal brand. A personal website allows you to build out a portfolio of your work and refine your personal narrative, values, and goals in ways resumes just can't. Immediately after you finish this chapter, go to a domain marketplace and buy your name or a close derivative. Set up your personal email and link it to all of your networking bios and cover letters—it looks super professional and gives you more control of your content.

Blog to Your Heart's Content. Think of it as a way to develop your voice and a complement to your professional growth. Over time, it could also lead to speaking and consulting gigs if leveraged correctly. Refining your voice on social media is all well and good, but according to Maria Peagler, the founder of the now-defunct socialmediaonlineclasses.com and now her own digital marketing consultancy, resonance and relevance are earned only for minutes, hours, or days on social media channels, while blog post content lasts around two years. Play the long game by building quality over quantity in terms of content, regardless of what fly-by-night influencers say. Trust me, they don't know our sector if they are trying to make a quick buck.

Work with a Mentor. Plenty of articles out there discuss the benefits of identifying a mentor. Given that the philanthropy sector is quite niche and narrow, receiving wise counsel and feedback on how to navigate a career in the sector is extremely important. There are also other benefits such as being taken to major events as their guest, leveraging their networks to recommend you for potential roles, and acting as a reference. In truth, many of these connections have helped me open doors I didn't even know existed at the time. This can happen to you too!

Engage Online. There has never been a more accessible way to connect with leaders in the field. Build lists of leaders whose work and values you admire or aspire to and interact with their posts. Develop your own voice and cultivate your own audience by using hashtags such as #Causes, #Philanthropy, #DoGood, #Charity, #SocialGood, and #Change. Another great use of time is to periodically host a Twitter chat, which lets you moderate a conversation and connect with individuals in an intentional way. Promote the chat ahead of time, and ask my favorite question: "Who is doing great work in X?" Then write up a summary and tag all those who participated to continue the conversation and continue building rapport with likeminded individuals.

Volunteer. Can't afford that $1,000 ticket to SXSW EDU? Heck, most professional half-day summits are $100 or more these days too. However, there is a way in if you miss out on conference scholarships, and that's by volunteering. Reach out to organizations hosting interesting conferences in the field and volunteer to help out at registration or to be a note taker in breakout sessions. This will probably result in a shift from two to five hours (with the bonus of meeting and greeting guests and VIPs who you probably power mapped by now), and then you'll have the opportunity to check out the rest of the conference for that day. Hot tip: Get involved with the conferences of regional associations of grantmakers and the big National Philanthropy Day functions. National associations that will need local support may also come to your city. And here's the kicker: you'll likely get a complimentary lunch too, and executives these days aren't just eating the rubber chicken.

If you want a job in philanthropy it's important that you understand that identifying and acquiring the skills, experience, and leadership required to deliver real impact through an evolving philanthropic landscape is paramount. And with a number of recent changes and emerging trends in the sector—and the possibility of many more over the next decade—more opportunities and entry points now exist for you to approach this career shift or promotion in an intentional way.

THE UNTAPPED POWER OF FUNDRAISER COLLABORATION

Let me share a tale of nonprofit secrecy via text messages that's fictional but based on reality:

> Fundraiser A: "Want to go for a drink after work? It's been a rough day"
>
> Fundraiser B: "Sorry, I can't catch up tonight. I have a big grant application to write that's due tomorrow"
>
> Fundraiser A: "Oh, which foundation?" (Note that this question is emanating from a point of intrigue, given that the fundraisers don't actually have the same deadline approaching.)
>
> Fundraiser B: "Oh, it's just for our core programming." (Note the vague and deflecting response here.)
>
> (Fundraiser A's phone shows little typing dots for Fundraiser B on and off for about five minutes.)
>
> Fundraiser A: "OK, good luck! When you are free we should catch up and share what we are both working on" (Note that this is Fundraiser A's way of saying, "What other grants are you hiding from me?")

Sound familiar? Why is it that discussing funding organizations and their upcoming grant cycles is somewhat secretive?

Funding for nonprofits is not a scarce resource. When I first started in fundraising, I found it perplexing that discussing which foundation's funding opportunities I was applying for was sort of a taboo subject. It was like I was directly affecting someone's fundraising income forecasts with my basic probing or uncovering the lost city of Atlantis to which they had the only map—both of which were equally dramatic, might I add.

I made up my mind early on in my philanthropy career that I would be collaborative wherever and whenever the opportunity arose. A "rising tide lifts all boats" mentality was—and still is—a strong north star in my goal to improve my community. And while certain regions are not awash with oceans of cash in the organized philanthropy space, our sector is best served by working strategically together.

That's when I developed a networking group to shine a light on grant opportunities and information on the tactics and gatekeepers that would improve our chances of all being funded. Once a month, I would convene with six development staff—three folks I had invited, the other three chosen by a peer I had asked to be my cohost for that month—to discuss current funding opportunities, the strategy to secure those potential grants, and any other development-related issues. This helped to diversify the attendees, expanding each other's networks and focusing the conversation on outcomes rather than catching up on a purely social level. Friendships obviously spawned out of this process, but we couldn't forget the purpose and the promises we made to our participants. My monthly cohost and I would also ensure that everyone represented different sectors to help break the skepticism, stigma, and hesitations around discussing work with perceived "direct competitors" who, in many cases, they had never met.

These meetings were some of the most honest and authentic conversations about the sector I have had in my career. Sharing backstories, tactics, and contacts and then discussing our own current roadblocks in getting to an ask with that of an engaged yet objective peer group was priceless in our mutual goals of making budget and maximizing our respective successes. If they win, we win, or so the saying goes. Each session was also held in the strictest confidence; individual donor names were not shared, just important context to information that can be readily found on an organization's Form 990, Return of Organization Exempt from Income Tax (even if they are sometimes hard to locate if you don't have that map of Atlantis).

I was also a board member for two prominent local nonprofits when I hosted these meetings, so this information was also great to share with those organizations' respective executive directors and development staff. Public knowledge should be disseminated publicly; it's a good habit and one that is truly appreciated by those you share it with. It also feeds into the broader landscape with folks quick to say, "You should connect with X, he/she is dialed in and might be able to help." There is nothing better than civic referrals to help build name recognition!

The networking element here should not be underestimated. It helped me gain insight into different approaches, tactics, and experiences from other fundraisers that have been priceless to my own development. It also helped me identify more dynamic local fundraisers who I would have no hesitation in referring for new job opportunities in the future, ones where they would benefit from new talent, rather than the usual group of fundraisers who bounce around local nonprofits every two years or so. The fact that my trusted peers select them to join us provides such a strong legitimacy to who they are. It helps us connect on a personal and professional level more quickly than perhaps bumping into them at a conference.

These sessions are easily replicable. Consider actively seeking to build a solid network of fellow travelers to help advance emerging trends, practices, and narratives as a way of challenging what and who is funded.

Michael Ward Jr.

The Curator of Digital Talent, Change, and Opportunity

When the internet was created, it was envisioned to give people unparalleled access to information and opportunity. But access always comes at a cost, and opportunity has never been equal. Therefore, the jobs of tomorrow and future opportunities to build wealth in a new digitized economy were again taken advantage of by those who had the means to do so. Predictably, the economic disparities faced by Black and Hispanic communities began to manifest themselves in new ways, with the stark contrasts in digital access leading to a racial tech gap that now threatens their future career paths and ability to break historical cycles of inequity.

Michael Ward Jr. and his organization, Austin Urban Technology Movement (AUTM), combat these issues by building opportunity pipelines that target the talent gaps in an industry by addressing the challenges around recruiting, retention, and employee engagement. And while talent is the bridge to social mobility for the communities he serves, it is transformation that he seeks.

Michael may be working to build a new tech future for underrepresented groups, but he is squarely focused on the bigger issues at play. This means tackling the very systems that philanthropy inadvertently props up.

"Philanthropy needs to stop giving to the same organizations that have not solved the problem yet," he says. "We need to stop giving money to predominantly white or white-led organizations that are serving our Black and Hispanic communities; they cannot relate to or fully understand their life experience and challenges. The current model is just a checkbox for companies and individuals to feel good about themselves, without actually focusing on the outcomes or benefit of the communities they serve." In other words, it's a collaborative effort, with part of that effort needing to come from philanthropy in terms of listening, meeting those doing the work where they are, and being receptive to trust-based principles of partnering for change.

Collaboration with other nonprofits and businesses is also needed. Michael and AUTM are under no illusions of the need for an intersectoral approach to fostering digital equity or a more integrated workforce development program with our education system. Reaching out to people and organizations with shared goals ensures there is the collective consistency needed when pushing for reform and that you can amplify each other's work and successes.

Working in the tech space also provides Michael with the ability to be future focused in identifying where gains can be made for his organization and the communities he serves. Leaning into new trends, Michael ensures those he serves are prepared for the jobs of tomorrow. But he notes one piece of legislative change that would be a game changer for his community.

"Free education. Let's ensure everyone is educated for today's workforce, understands technology, and is given the opportunity to acquire the skills needed to thrive in a rapidly digitizing, automated US economy," Michael says. "The American system is designed to do what it was set up to do. Segregate, divide, and protect the status quo. It has permeated our economic, political, and social decisions for hundreds of years, and it's time for justice, equity, and opportunity for all."

While Michael understands what's at stake and has charted his own path to achieving change, he feels philanthropy can play a role and help accelerate achievable solutions, such as:

1. Providing internet access for low-income, underserved, and underrepresented communities.

2. Connecting low-income, underserved, and underrepresented communities with technology devices (mobile hotspots and computers).

3. Upskilling and reskilling low-income, underserved, and underrepresented communities to get into the tech industry.

"Philanthropy should be the capital-like investment needed for nonprofits to be successful and accomplish their mission," he says, "and I hope they are willing to hear our call."

Tech gives everyone an opportunity to be optimistic for their future as well as the future of generations to follow, many of whom will benefit in perpetuity from their hard work, courage, and sacrifice. That sacrifice isn't the burden of any one person either, with our community needing to be bolder and better than ever before. Yet we need individual people to step up and mobilize our communities—and there is no better advocate than Michael and AUTM.

CHAPTER THREE

Challenging the "Systems Quo"

SHOW THEM THE MONEY:
HOW SALARY CLOAKING IN THE NONPROFIT SECTOR MUST END

When you buy a new house, you'll likely go to a real estate aggregator like Zillow or Redfin, enter your search parameters (which will be primarily determined by your budget), and then identify which homes you might want to tour. The price for the home is listed, which helps you decide whether you want the house or can afford it at that price, and sellers in most states are mandated to make a disclosure statement should anything be wrong with the home. This is a transparent process, front loaded to avoid wasting everyone's time or seeing deals fall through. It would be odd to enter into escrow without having an understanding as to the cost of the house or a figure agreed to in principle.

So why is the process different for individuals searching for jobs?

Job hunting and hiring have changed dramatically over the past twenty years. Jobs sites can now find the right person via sophisticated algorithms, and we have the ability to share opportunities with our peers in real time across direct messaging and social media apps. (Imagine back in the day having to clip out a newspaper ad and mail it to someone!) These advancements, and the ensuing transparency in the marketplace, are also seeing the advantages that employers had long held in recruitment and contract negotiation being eroded at a scale at which unions could never have dreamed.

The power is now beginning to shift toward a new workforce demanding flexible working schedules, positive corporate social responsibility, and the ability to receive unique insights into workplace culture via websites such as Glassdoor. Couple this with the facts that workers change jobs several times in their careers rather than remaining with one company, and now organizations are doing a lot more to attract and retain talent while prioritizing internal reflection and action on their own issues and limitations.

Right now, we are in a unique period of history where all the pieces are in place to turn the table upside down and set out on the path to true pay equity and wage fairness. That's the corporate angle, of course, but it's one in which the social sector can draw up a similar blueprint.

So how do nonprofits begin to take the lead and tackle this challenge, especially when wages are traditionally low in the first place? Well, it's complicated, and structural, but within immediate reach if there is a genuine long-term commitment to addressing it.

The first step is to do the internal work and review your own structures.

Policies and Procedures

I previously worked in a role where six of the eight employees were director level or above, and the only people of color were the two folks who weren't. This wasn't by design; the organization was fiercely committed to social justice and equitable philanthropic practices. However, the organization grew quickly, and there were difficulties in identifying people for what were very much emerging, niche roles. Policies were put in place to make hiring practices more inclusive—words used in position descriptions, equivalent experience vis-à-vis educational requirements, and actively identifying and expanding networks through which to share the opportunity, including Black and Hispanic chambers of commerce and urban leadership groups.

Have your organization's structures, policies, and procedures evolved or become dated over time? Because as you know, diversity is not just a faucet you turn on and off with each new hire. I encourage you to review your policies, update them as needed, and introduce new ones where there are perceived gaps. Test them in real time with your next hire or vendor selection, review them at the end, and make additional changes where needed. Have a periodic review be part of your commitment to building an award-winning culture.

Job Descriptions

This also relates to the organizational chart. Are there too many levels of management? Do employees know their pathways for career growth within the team? Many staff are not set up for long-term success at nonprofits due to a lack of planning by leadership who often hire folks at the top of their bands or create titles that enable little growth or the ability to develop essential management skills beyond the scope of their day-to-day duties—including managing staff. This should be articulated before new staff are hired, in order to set an employee's expectations in how they can progress in the organization.

Job standardization, realignment, and potential reorganization (with a commitment to no layoffs if necessary) should occur at this point if positions have similar duties or are skewed because of tenure or scale. This includes eliminating irrelevant requirements such as lifting twenty-five pounds, having a driver's license for office roles, and—for all that is good in this world—the vague statement "other duties as assigned."

Compensation

Once positions have been finalized, a thorough review of remuneration should occur, with appropriate salary ranges established and linked to CPI increases and associated budgeting taking baseline merit increases into account. This should be shared with each staff member in a way that they understand where they are, where they can go, and, most importantly, how they can get there. New staff should be placed on the first rung on the salary structure and only placed at the midpoint if it can be justified by management. If there isn't room for promotions in the short- to mid-term, then these employees should at least be afforded yearly pay increases rather than be trapped at the top of a rigid salary scale.

Pay Audits

Once the structures are in place to ensure people are remunerated adequately and fairly, with their growth a key focal point of the organization's values and staff investment strategy, then it's time to address your organization's current pay gaps and equity in the following steps:

1. Ensure salary ratios between your highest and lowest earners are within acceptable industry standards.

2. Review current salaries, identify where gaps may exist between people doing the same job, and correct those gaps. Bring all pay up to the highest level; don't bring people down to the median.

3. Ensure labor laws are not being violated with contract, per diem, and part-time workers and that interns are remunerated. Wage theft is a common practice for low-wage and undocumented immigrant workers and has no place in the social sector.

4. Repeat this process annually. No one should ever fall through the cracks.

Also remember that pay gaps and pay equity are different in this regard, and your board would be well served by understanding the nuance. If you are the staff member leading this charge, ensure that the narrative is that this review is to tackle organizational disparities across gender and race in line with the mission and values of the organization.

Once your own house is in order, it's then time to go out and find that perfect candidate—and you will, if you jettison some of the practices that have long plagued the sector and that have diminished the earning capacity of generations of workers over their lifetimes. That's not even including the larger effects that broader social and economic factors have had in reducing the earnings of women and people of color over the same time period.

So what are those important next steps?

Again, Stop Salary Cloaking

This is the simple first step in making fair and equal pay a reality for the philanthropy sector. As discussed on page 36, salary cloaking is the process of posting a job without the salary range and one that brings with it a plethora of other problems and compounding effects:

- **It perpetuates the wage gap.** This has already been covered, but it's important to note that salaries in the nonprofit sector are already low.

- **It discriminates.** Women and people of color are more likely to opt out of applying for roles, as they don't think they meet the requirements.

- **It's deceitful.** It's important to build trust with a prospective employee instead of allowing them to get emotionally attached to the role and then have them consider a situation they would not have entered if they knew of the salary range in the first place. A great remedy to this, and to ensure this situation doesn't happen vice versa, is to reaffirm the salary and benefits package prior to them moving forward in each stage of the hiring process. There's a reason it's called "cloaking"—the very definition means to hide, cover, or disguise. And while it might not be intentional, it certainly can't be justified as a budgetary constraint.

- **It's a waste of time.** Why spend time reviewing resumes, organizing and participating in interviews, and running background references just to reach an easily avoidable impasse in salary expectations?

- **It's expensive.** Remember, time is also money.

Avoid Asking About Salary History

Currently, asking for someone's salary history has now been banned in nineteen states and a number of large metropolitan cities, and for good reason. It can result in pay discrimination, shifting the negotiating power into the employer's hands. *This must be expanded nationally.*

Past income shouldn't matter, and these new state laws effectively stop the practices of tying salary offers to past earnings. As we mentioned before, having set salary ranges for each position and sharing it in job ads will effectively mean people are paid for their experience and qualifications. It allows upward mobility and higher lifetime earning potential, meaning a happier and more motivated workforce—critical components for nonprofit retention.

What Actions Can You Take?

Firstly, just do it. Add the salary to your job descriptions and advertisements. It's free. If you feel that your salary is too low for the role you are seeking, then either don't post it or realign the skills accordingly. Maybe even take a chance on someone who doesn't quite meet the requirements but has a high ceiling and would benefit from your organization's investment in them.

Find Your Champions. Everyone in the philanthropy sector—individuals as well as nonprofits, membership organizations, and representative bodies—should reach out to elected officials and unions to schedule a meeting to discuss these aforementioned issues and potential solutions. Find your legislative champion and help catalyze legislative change by rallying the sector behind your cause.

Establish Industry Watchdogs. Nonprofit associations, universities that focus on nonprofit research, or other publicly funded entities would be good stewards of this discussion. They could act as knowledge brokers for advocacy efforts and play watchdog for a new era of salary transparency. Current sector-wide salary reports are not nuanced enough to tell the real story, with larger entities skewing salary range estimates for certain positions. Instead, these watchdogs should aggregate and annually report on advertised salaries and create a bot that routinely responds via social media should a job be advertised with no salary included.

Ensure Job Boards Play Their Role. Make the salary a required field for those wishing to advertise their role. You're providing a service to them, but don't forget you are providing a service to your community too.

Ensure Grantmakers Also Share in This Onus. Organized philanthropy could do a number of things to support this practice. They can advocate against salary cloaking and prohibit the disclosure of salary history in all workplace negotiations. If grants are project based and the hiring of new staff is part of budget projections, then this should be reviewed to ensure that the salary is fair and reasonable for the work outlined, with the caveat that any advertising of this role includes the salary.

As Albus Dumbledore from the Harry Potter franchise once said, "I don't need a cloak to become invisible." This is indicative of how many people continue to feel invisible and that their experiences and skills are not marketable. This is a false assumption. Parts of our society have been historically exploited in small ways to maximize profits and stretch budgets, which has ultimately lost hundreds of thousands of dollars in earnings for millions of workers. Closing the pay gap and unraveling the compounding issues of pay inequities (remember, there is a difference!) are all within reach if we have the energy to make smart, pragmatic changes. It's a generational commitment that can be identified from a person's first day of work, so let's support their upward trajectory and the economic benefits to our society that come with it.

TALENT BEYOND BORDERS

Every candidate who lived in a different city than where our offices were and made it through the initial screening process was put forward to me as the hiring manager with caveats I had not asked for, nor was thinking about.

- "What are their motivations for the move?"

- "Why would they want to move from [insert name of current employer/city] to come here for this salary?"

- "There is no doubt that they are just trying to get to [insert city] and we will be used as a stopgap until they find something better."

This line of thinking needs to stop. Who are we to make assumptions about someone's motivations to apply for a position?

The nonprofit sector should be actively courting talent to move into our sector. If business is actively recruiting folks regardless of location and also providing them with relocation packages, then we need to get with the times and realize this as a viable strategy.

It's just another nonprofit stigma that needs to be overcome. If we are looking for a stellar candidate, one who we see as a key to improving our impact, culture, and bottom line, and we find that person in another state, then why is it so hard to justify a further $2,500 to subsidize their move, especially when you can add contractual clauses that will protect your investment and ultimately de-risk looking at someone from outside your network and the city you operate in?

Remember that talent is just as important as tech and that the right people can help you achieve your future goals. If we have learned anything from 2020, it's that location is just a place you log on to your computer and that working in a remote capacity can increase options for us to attract the best talent to our organizations.

Nonprofits should also be open to remote employees and those who wish to relocate out of the local area. During the COVID-19 pandemic, I had a number of random conversations with folks (mainly people we were buying furniture for our new house from) who shared that they were letting their leases run out or selling up and either traveling the country, moving to a more affordable city, or moving back to their hometown while still remaining employed with their current company.

Workplace flexibility will become more of a deciding factor than ever when it comes to who people work for. If your organization isn't solely place based, you seek to benefit from this as talent becomes more accessible and more mobile than ever before. And, surprisingly, philanthropy is actually leading (and granting) this change.

Tulsa Remote, a program founded by the George Kaiser Family Foundation, offered 250 people the opportunity to relocate to Tulsa, Oklahoma, by providing people with a grant spread out over the course of the year. This grant helped with moving expenses, provided a monthly stipend to help them navigate (and be supported financially in) the early stages of their transition, and presented the remainder as a welcome gift at the end of their first twelve months in their new city. Recipients of these grants were also given space at a coworking facility, which helped new residents to plug in quickly to a new collaborative community. The George Kaiser Family Foundation was motivated to underwrite this program as a way to enhance the current local workforce by attracting a diverse new talent to a forward-focused municipal administration. The program has now had multiple cycles and has added an upfront payment option for new residents buying a home. G. T. Bynum, the mayor of Tulsa, spoke at the first Upswell conference in Los Angeles, which I also attended. He discussed the Tulsa Remote program at length and how it was woven into his strategy of data-driven economic mobility. A large part of that strategy was also leveraging some of the biggest foundations in the local government space, including Bloomberg Philanthropies, the Bill & Melinda Gates Foundation, and the Ballmer Group. Bynum's bet was that by using data, he could identify the local skills shortages and then target young folks who were not currently working or going to school to get the credentials to fill that need. It's also an approach that could be replicated for a range of other local indicators and outcomes.

Hawaii also launched a Movers & Shakas program in late 2020, where they would pay for your airfare and provide lodging or workplace benefits if you stayed at least thirty consecutive days in Oahu. The idea behind the initiative was to recruit and nurture talented professionals to help build more resiliency into the economy, which has been heavily reliant on tourism and devastated by a severe drop in visitors because of the COVID-19 pandemic. The goal was to build a network of remote workers who work alongside and volunteer at local nonprofits, including the Chamber of Commerce Hawaii, Girl Scouts of Hawaii, and Hawaii Literacy.

Workforce development is a big focus for the social sector right now. Organized philanthropy is beginning to see how initiatives that drive up the local economy are a great return on investment and also ease its burden as a reactive social safety net. Helping create more, and better-paying, nonprofit jobs in the communities where philanthropies are located is a smart economic growth strategy, especially when you realize that the sector is the third largest employer out of eighteen major sectors of US workers and directly works to protect and lift up the vitality of our cities and towns.

With many folks being priced out of their cities for a variety of reasons, it would be great to see place-based foundations (predominantly those that built their wealth in the regions they serve) be the driving force in generating the jobs of tomorrow and attracting new talent. This would help rejuvenate their cities, which were ironically affected due to talent leaving over the past few decades to seek new pastures.

THE NEED FOR STRUCTURAL (NOT JUST STRATEGIC) SHIFTS IN TECH ADOPTION

Digital infrastructure, capacity, and capability are going to be important components of driving tech adoption in what is a rapidly evolving digital economy. In other words, start getting in place those team members who can facilitate and accelerate the change you envision.

There is a big disconnect between what's needed and when it's needed. The 2020 State of Philanthropy Tech, which is researched by the Technology Association of Grantmakers and provides insight into tech adoption by the sector, identified that seventeen to one continues to be the average ratio of staff to information technology (IT) staff. It also identified that 40 percent of IT departments do not have any DEI programs, and only 12 percent have programs to develop a pipeline of diverse leaders—all things that intersect the major pillars of this book, and all things that show that we are not equipped to embrace and leverage the full benefits of current and emergent tech options. Only 51 percent of respondents expected to see their IT budget increase in 2021 too, and that's with COVID-19 exposing the limited effectiveness of our service delivery models.

The Salesforce Nonprofit Trends Report also shows crucial stats on this topic. (And on a personal note, I really enjoy Salesforce's global scale, the quantity of its statistics, and the fact that it provides its CRM for free to nonprofits. That's good CSR in action right there.) It has only produced two reports thus far, so it will become more impactful and telling in the future. But it has already shaken out as an important snapshot of the sector's current adoption, strategies, and staffing for all technology, software, and IT needs. Its scope is already up from 450 respondents in 2018 to 725 nonprofit leaders across North America (305) and Europe (420) for 2019. Given that more than 30,000 nonprofits use Salesforce, this is a pretty strong sample size with a margin of error of 5 percent and a 95 percent confidence level.

There are three key takeaways from the 2020 Salesforce Nonprofit Trends Report that are of particular interest:

1. 93 percent of respondents state a lack of IT or technical staff is a challenge to their organization's adaptation of new technologies. This is important, given that a deeper dive into this report shows that 55 percent of the use of technology is actually championed by IT.

2. 85 percent of nonprofits surveyed said technology is the key to the success of their organization. This ultimately reflects an understanding that fully aligned strategies, underpinned by data, are more likely to succeed.

3. 75 percent of respondents say that how to measure and report data is a challenge. Synthesizing, evaluating, and informing decisions through data are key to any organization's long-term success. This high percentage is particularly a cause for concern.

Much of the commentary that I have witnessed online following the release of this report has been criticism around perceived flaws in the strategies being employed by nonprofits, rather than trying to highlight the foundational elements required to realize the transformative opportunities of leveraging available tech options—you know, the little issue of organizational capacity. In short, vast swaths of the sector that are embracing tech solutions (going beyond simply logging onto a CRM or employing a social media tool) are still light-years behind the for-profit sector in regard to achieving a fully realized return on this kind of investment, one that the business sector is so accustomed to.

A great article from *Yale Insights* (from the Yale School of Management) provides some real nuance to the hypothesis that nonprofits just don't get it yet. It features a robust Q&A with members from Compass (a group that inspires business professionals to engage with their local communities) that discusses the transformative value of technology and what the future might look like with a more strategic direction. The article is framed by a typical out-of-touch question: *Do nonprofits take the digital world seriously?* This is troubling for many reasons, and the reality is that this will forever be the disconnect if nonprofits are viewed as a business model in dire need of support (or saving) from the business community.

To combat this misconception about how nonprofits do their work, we need to focus on reeducating business and philanthropy on not only the day-to-day needs of our sector but also how they can lift up our work to drive new efficiencies and outcomes from technological advances. Here's how we can achieve this.

Create a Seat for Tech at the Table. If you are going to do one thing this year to advance your approach to tech, it is to get someone from the industry on your board. They can provide a strong and trusted voice on the topic for your governing body, champion the need for having tech at the core of all you do as a modern and dynamic nonprofit, and lead any visioning activities or proposals the organization is advancing for the future.

Inform Funders of the Need to Increase Funding or Support. It's time to be honest and forthcoming with funders about the need and opportunities in funding nonprofit tech. It should no longer be bundled up with operations and viewed as an essential capacity-building endeavor. A deeper understanding and realization that tech infrastructure helps leverage impact—indirectly helping serve more clients by identifying data trends that make programming more efficient, and automating processes to enable staff to tackle bigger vision projects—should make funding tech a no-brainer.

Share IT Staff and Resources. As previously stated, much of these issues revolve around capacity. But for some nonprofits, an IT manager or equivalent is indeed a luxury and, in some cases, a role where there might not even be the work for a full-time equivalent worker. However, sharing an IT person through an intermediary or having a shared resource in a locale that houses a number of nonprofits might be a constructive way of tackling the possibility.

Invest in "Tech Raisers." TechSoup is an organization geared toward providing nonprofits affordable solutions on hardware, software, and tech training. Many of these offerings are free or at greatly discounted prices, so they are the perfect vehicle for potentially building out requests that can help expand their tech capacity and can help connect all the dots between nonprofits, donors, and the products they are seeking to acquire. TechSoup could also consider building a crowdfunding platform—a "tech raiser," if you will—to help facilitate the raising of funds and the dissemination of discounted technology more fluidly. This would be a potential win-win and help TechSoup expand its understanding of sector needs and fulfill its own mission.

For funders looking to take the initiative here, check out the Technology Association of Grantmakers guide to investing in digital infrastructure, which eloquently states that grantmakers are increasingly recognizing that social change in the digital era requires an investment in technology. "This investment is more than tools alone; rather, it's a commitment to building digital skills, capacity, and new platforms to unlock the knowledge, passion, and collective strength of civil society over time as the relationship between technology and society continues to evolve." The guide that is referenced at the end of the book also provides a roadmap on how you can build both your own digital capacity and that of the sector at large.

Data Philanthropy. Creativity is what spurs innovation. It is also what challenges the status quo and should not be confined to a budget line. For those smaller, scrappier nonprofits that simply cannot afford to adopt any of the aforementioned strategies, they can think outside the box and seek partnerships with local tech groups, collaboratives, and individual people, sharing their data and providing hackathons with the fuel they need to help deliver new, informed solutions.

Request Government Support. Internet access has become a vital tool in development and social progress since the start of the twenty-first century. Broadband internet penetration rates are now treated as key economic indicators, with the United States struggling to remain in the top twenty in terms of its rate of broadband penetration and the speed of its infrastructure.

Broadband investment, where fiber is delivered to not-for-profit offices, libraries, and universities, is another opportunity to accelerate the accessibility and impact of world-class download speeds in the sector. While this would largely be a federal government endeavor, it could also be a complementary part of a progressive municipal approach to spur economic activity. Note: The Federal Communications Commission (FCC) was directed to create a plan to include a detailed strategy for achieving affordability and maximizing use of broadband to advance, among other things, civic participation, education, and community development as part of the American Recovery and Reinvestment Act of 2009.

All of the above suggestions are ways for organizations to become better able to creatively shift to—or at least be encouraged to move forward with—new approaches in regard to their future tech adoption. Let's also remember that we need to increase capacity if we are to embrace appropriate strategies. Salesforce sums it up best in its Nonprofit Trends Report:

> Technology is the great equalizer and can unlock the power of data while providing personalized experiences. It allows nonprofits to reach new audiences, serve more communities, respond to new challenges, or optimize opportunities. Innovative technologies create many new scenarios to operate smarter and increase efficiency. To do this, nonprofits must embrace new tools to become the social change platform their constituents are demanding. When digital transformation is set aside, a nonprofit is more susceptible to disruption from other nonprofits that modernize. The consequences of nonprofit erosion are even worse, because nothing replaces their impact on society. This leaves a rip in our social fabric.

MEGGIE PALMER

Confidence Creator in Chief

Getting paid what you're worth, what you deserve, and what your experience demands through self-advocacy is, in our eyes, an act of social justice. You are lifting up not only your own value but also that of millions more who have been underpaid as a result of their gender, color, beliefs, or ability. Equal pay for equal work must be the goal if we are committed to true fairness in the workplace. But before we can achieve this, we need to immediately address the pay gaps that exist in organizations, our industries, and broader economies.

One person mobilizing this change is Meggie Palmer, founder of PepTalkHer, who has set out to translate women's professional contributions into successful negotiation strategies and use the data derived from the PepTalkHer platform to inform changes in business practices, hiring, and workplace culture.

"We're on a mission to close the gender pay gap because as it stands," she says, "the gender pay gap will take more than one hundred years to close. That's way too long for our liking. So, we investigated how we could help.

"We saw women's confidence being eroded away by toxic workplaces. We watched women be offered—and then accept—salaries lower than their worth, and we heard women tell us they struggled to believe in themselves. These stories were even worse for women of color, pregnant women, and women who dared take maternity leave. The discrimination is mind-blowing. It was heartbreaking just as much as it was a dangerous marker for the notion and narrative of an individual's upward mobility. So we built something that could be your cheerleader, effectively serving as a career coach in your pocket."

The PepTalkHer app helps you track your career successes. It uses AI to coach confidence and negotiation and to give you a pep talk when you need it most—and who better to have in your corner than Meggie?

"PepTalkHer is essentially an online brag book," she says. "It prompts you to collect your wins at work, giving you data to back up your pay raise and promotion conversations."

Your true value isn't defined by company-wide key performance indicators (KPIs). In fact, a broader national narrative needs to occur right now around the dignity of work, not the meritocracy of it. Contributions need to be recognized, appreciated, and rewarded. That's the reason Meggie's company is essential in helping folks count the things that are often not counted, keeping track of all their achievements and benchmarking their salary. This will become even more important when automation potentially redirects workers from management, administrative, and manufacturing roles to core service areas such as education, healthcare, and the social sector.

In a nonprofit setting, the "ask" has become synonymous with the final step in donor cultivation, yet we might be missing the most important context of it entirely. Employees have to speak up for themselves and ask to be remunerated for their worth. If they don't, they're potentially leaving hundreds of thousands of dollars in lost career earnings and benefits on the table.

"PepTalkHer is a free app," Meggie explains, "but we do not operate as a nonprofit. It would fundamentally be going against our values if we were, but we are acutely aware of the deep, deep inequities that persist in that sector. We are big fans of not-for-profits also doing work in this space, like the American Association of University Women (AAUW) and Time's Up. We are supporters of organizations including the Women's Prison Association and the National Domestic Workers Alliance."

Though more women are becoming nonprofit CEOs, the 2020 Nonprofit Compensation Report from Candid showed that their salary packages still lagged way behind those of their male peers, and for organizations with budgets of $25 million or greater, that gap averaged out to around 18.5 percent. "One woman was promoted to CEO of a major company," Meggie says, "and she didn't ask for a raise. 'I'm lucky!' she said. I said, 'No way!'"

Women in the US who are employed full time earn eighty-two cents for every dollar earned by men, according to the Institute for

Women's Policy Research. At the current pace of change, it'll be 2059 before women reach pay parity—unless you're a woman of color. Black women will be waiting until 2130, while Latinx women won't achieve this milestone until 2224.

Yet with Meggie leading this important crusade for economic and social justice in our workplaces, and with millions of underrepresented and underpaid workers standing tall, a new future may be heralded in much sooner than we think. Because in the end, data is there to inform actions, not be a prisoner of them, and PepTalkHer could be your ticket to career and financial freedom.

CHAPTER FOUR

The Evolution of Need

Dissecting the Next Decade of
Where We Work and Who We Work With

TALENT OPTIMIZATION: FINDING, ALIGNING, AND
HARMONIZING AN ALL-STAR CAST OF CHANGEMAKERS

People are your most important asset. There is no dispute around that. Yet how can we identify those values-aligned people, who will help drive your organization to new heights, and who will remain happy and productive in both the good times and the bad? And how will technology ensure these folks are identified and elevated to your attention in the most competitive job markets?

Consider what's best for your organization. Is it having someone come in for two years and help your organization level up and then move on? Or having someone who will stay for at least five years to methodically build and grow a program over time?

Here are two other questions that may be keeping hiring managers up at night:

1. How do we know what we are getting—or, most importantly, who?

2. How do we use tech to help ensure our candidate pools are as diverse as they are dynamic?

Recruitment has historically been a minefield of inconsistency. It is full of biases that have spawned jaw-dropping research around the percentage of interview callbacks for white- or Black-sounding candidates. It sees folks benefit from either directly or indirectly knowing someone at an organization who has managed to get them noticed or—for the sake of interpersonal politics—screened by HR. And you have hiring managers skimming hundreds of emails and making decisions based on a hunch and not by any sort of science except thinking "he/she looks like they are worth talking to."

The end goal for recruitment is always to fill the job vacancy. It's the process's most binary function. But it's time we went beyond that to find the best fit, both for the position and for the culture of the organization.

In my past hiring roles, whether overseeing the process or as the hiring manager, I have approached it seriously and with growth in mind—for myself, the employee, and the organization as a whole. I would take the time to think about the candidates rather than rush through my immediate feedback, pondering what weaknesses of ours this person can cover, what the ceiling could be for our team with this missing piece in place, and how the candidate might challenge us to be better. I wanted to present my case both qualitatively and quantitatively, and for a while I became fascinated with finding useful ranges of data sets to help me make more informed choices. I created a reporting structure and policies that would elevate these additional insights so they also informed others who were asked to participate in panel interviews. This also gave employees the tools and training to enhance the process for both themselves and the candidate.

This standard is what is commonly referred to as talent optimization, something I am a big proponent of. It is a way to layer in more scientific methods when building candidate pools and lowering the risk of a bad or underwhelming hire, which can be a very expensive mistake, especially for a nonprofit organization.

We must continually seek better ways to evaluate candidates. My bet is that in a few years, tech that screens behavioral traits and cognitive abilities will become the norm, not just a tool used by large tech firms.

I should also mention that I'm a certified Predictive Index (PI) practitioner. PI is an award-winning talent optimization platform that aligns business strategy with people strategy for optimal business results. It helps groups design great teams and culture, make objective hiring decisions, and foster effective employee engagement.

More than 8,000 clients and 350 partners use PI—Nissan, Docu-Sign, and Subway, to name just a few—across more than 140 countries.

It was the platform I felt could best help me succeed in my hiring hypothesis. It not only helped me review my position descriptions (both current and future) but also took into account the expectations of this role from other members of staff, providing me with a 360-degree viewpoint of who might best succeed in a particular job.

After these initial internal surveys, a job target was generated, which would then be used to highlight those that aligned best with the skills, capacity for critical thinking, and defining behaviors. Candidates at different stages of the hiring process would then take both cognitive and behavioral tests, with those whose results fit within the identified ranges being elevated to the top of the list.

The main stumbling block for the scaling of talent optimization software is the fact that there is a disconnect in what the testing means and how it is used. This isn't a pass or fail scenario; it's just another data point. It shouldn't be a way to disqualify candidates early in the process and is probably best used to screen your finalists if you are struggling to choose between them. Note: If they are like-for-like candidates, always go with the diverse hire.

Talent optimization isn't just about the hiring process, either. I am still finding new ways to help empower managers to build high-performing teams, analyze employee engagement and take customized action, uncover and grow leadership potential, increase productivity, and ensure a great job fit for employees and candidates despite all the day-to-day challenges thrown our way.

As an aside, my wife is an exceptional technical recruiter, and we have discussed this as an opportunity for the social sector for a good year or so. When she became a captive audience member of my enthusiasm during the COVID-19 pandemic, our conversations advanced into her creating her own company, which I assist on occasions when she has a "tech for good" client. While she is pretty much going to win employee of the year each year, I have appreciated the chance to learn more about the ins and outs of hiring and build upon what I have gleaned from the Predictive Index approach, enhancing it through a nonprofit lens.

Creating a boutique consultancy, Beacon Search Partners, made sense, especially given our shared twenty-five–plus years of nonprofit management, development, and corporate talent acquisition experience, ranging from small start-ups to nine-figure nonprofits, community foundations, and private universities, right through to high-volume and fast-paced technical recruitment at Fortune 500 companies. We are both passionate about hiring the right people because we understand what's at stake for those our clients serve. That's why we are now continually looking for talent to ensure our applicant pool is the most dynamic yet robust one available to our clients when a hiring need arises.

We also have a deep commitment to diversity—shaped by our personal and professional experiences and training—and felt we could support many of the things mentioned in this section. We understand the challenges and opportunities of equitable hiring practices and want to help guide our clients through this process in a positive way. This includes inclusivity screenings of the organization's job descriptions, their hiring policies, and their interview questions to ensure people feel comfortable sharing their whole selves throughout.

Adopting a modern "recruiting for good" persona, we began partnering with dynamic nonprofits and tech companies looking to hire exceptional talent to help lift up their communities. The great thing was that we could hold true to our values when deciding who to work with. Here are those values:

- **Collaboration**—partnering in an open, authentic, and meaningful way to ensure the best outcomes for our clients and the best experience for our candidates, further strengthening the work, impact, and reputation of the nonprofit sector as a whole.

- **Equity**—believing the social sector needs to hire talent that reflects those they seek to represent and that their contributions can create the systems and opportunities that can lead to equity for all.

- **Future Focused**—anticipating, identifying, and implementing future trends in hiring practices to ensure our clients are receiving the very best service and applicant pool possible.

- **Impact**—approaching our partnerships not to simply fill a position but to ensure our clients are hiring candidates who will make a measurable and long-term impact to their organization and the broader sector.

- **Courage**—demonstrating conviction for our values by challenging our partners to look beyond traditional networks and approaches in the search for the best talent available.

The thing that really had me giddy with excitement when we created this search firm was a new nonprofit assessment I created for the company that has now become known as our Beacon FIT (Future Indicators Test). This assessment reviews candidates prior to presenting them to the client by measuring direct and indirect work experience, values alignment, and communication (for example, do they have a consistent voice both personally and professionally on social media).

In supporting mission-driven companies and moving beyond the basic acquisition of staff to one of talent optimization, we are leveraging new trends and cutting-edge tools. And while my wife does the lion's share of the work, I am happy to play a small part in catalyzing social change when the kids go down for the night.

And you know what? We are already seeing it. After securing $100 million in Series C funding and an FDA emergency-use authorization for its rapid, portable, molecular point-of-care COVID-19 test, Cue Health partnered with Beacon Search Partners to rapidly scale its workforce. We are proud to have supported this innovative company in helping identify and recruit the talent needed to tackle a global crisis.

We also partnered with ResultsLab, a social impact firm in Denver that transforms the impact of social good organizations through building their capacity to engage in data-informed decision making, and San Francisco–based UpMetrics, which was looking to build out its new impact investing vertical, which was a terrific addition to its core work of empowering organizations, funders, and investors to be more data driven and maximize their impact.

Companies like UpMetrics and ResultsLab will grow exponentially over the next decade as they use data in new and innovative ways to influence their decision-making and help identify the key inputs and results of their work. (This field, as well as the opportunities for non-profits to benefit from its adoption, will be covered in more detail later in the book.) My wife and I were happy to identify a dynamic and diverse pool of candidates for these organizations' new leadership roles—and yes, there was a little bit of nonprofit Moneyball applied there too.

Talent optimization, if used to strengthen a talent pool rather than try to engineer the perfect candidate, will help make amazing things happen, just like what Cue Health has been able to achieve. With AI sure to accelerate and scale these capabilities over the coming years, the ability to identify and recruit the very best talent for nonprofit organizations will eventually be just a few clicks away.

ARE WE HEADING FOR A NEW VIRTUAL REALITY FOR NONPROFITS?

For many people during the COVID-19 pandemic, the immediate question was, *When should we expect to go back to work?* The question they should have been asking was, *Do we really need to go back to work?* We aren't talking about the actual work. That will continue in earnest. And no, we are not here to expound on the wonders of Zoom or flexible working arrangements (which we already know are great and much needed, thanks for asking). We are actually talking about the bricks-and-mortar component of work, which is under a little more scrutiny—and which might not make sense for nonprofits anymore.

Nonprofit budgets are no doubt being reviewed amid the current reality, and the continuing concerns of lower revenues will bring into focus the larger fiscal outlays, of which rent is often the second largest expense after personnel. Organizations are now realizing that some services can be delivered virtually, including in the areas of education, training, and healthcare. While essential services are arguably best still delivered in person, improvements in delivery methods through technological advancements like computational health, AI, chatbots, online communications, and education platforms are accelerating the quality and accessibility of viable alternatives.

What effect are these potentially profound realizations having on executives whose current office for the past year was more likely their kitchen table than an overpriced electric standing desk? The answer must surely be these questions: What is in the organization's best interests moving forward? Is there an ability to modernize and deliver comparative or better services all while reducing expenditures and delivering on the core mission?

That answer should be a resounding yes. If anything, the COVID-19 pandemic pushed us to use technology that, in hindsight, our sector probably should have already adopted. It's high time that boards and organizational leadership had a real discussion about what is critical moving forward, because folks are quick to cut staff and freeze travel and other expenditures that slow down cash flow issues without confronting them head on.

Why don't we seriously look at how much we pay in rent and ask what the alternatives are?

Why is it that a physical space has become a symbol of success or a necessity for a business?

What is the point of a boardroom if it's only used once a month anyway?

The reality is this problem has been bubbling under the surface for a long time because of a one-dimensional viewpoint of how nonprofits do business. Real estate has been forcing the hand of nonprofits for the past decade, with escalating rents pricing organizations out of the very areas they serve. Gentrification is a very real issue for communities, and while it's more acute at the individual and family level, the impact isn't lost on nonprofits.

This issue hasn't been lost on funders, either, with examples such as the *Status of Bay Area Nonprofit Space and Facilities* report, commissioned by Northern California Grantmakers and the San Francisco Foundation, which were concerned that the cost of office space in the region had increased every quarter since mid-2010 and five years later sat at 122 percent higher than when those increases began. This report showed the vast majority (82 percent) of the 497 nonprofits that responded to the report's initial survey were concerned about the negative impact of the real estate market on their long-term sustainability. Sixty-eight percent of respondents also thought they would have to make a decision about moving in the next five years. Furthermore, 38 percent had moved at least once in the last half decade.

With many metropolitan areas suffering from similar pressures, nonprofits should be using this critical insight as the impetus for some real conversations when formulating new strategic plans. It's not like there isn't a wide variety of options to consider, either, including the following:

- **Roles and Responsibilities:** Is it absolutely essential that all staff be on-site? Could development and marketing staff predominantly work from home? Could project management platforms such as Monday, Wrike, or Asana be used as a way to drive workflow and accountability? Can meetings be held by Zoom?

- **Service Delivery:** Do all "workshops" need to be in person? Can savings be made by moving classes online or by shifting to a hybrid model that captures a significant amount of detail from clients before meeting in person (or ascertaining whether the need to meet in person is even needed)?

- **Rent or Buy:** Is renting your best option for long-term stability? With options including New Markets Tax Credits, Community Development Block Grants, and other capital campaign approaches, organizations can seek to invest in their communities or look to partner with other organizations to create nonprofit hubs. Manchester Bidwell Corporation is a good template for what can be achieved with that approach, weaving itself into the very fabric of the community and addressing gentrification ahead of it taking hold.

- **Consolidation:** A number of nonprofits have grown exponentially over time because of demand, but nonprofits are not like consumer products. The greater the need, the higher the cost. There just isn't any economy of scale to be had here with tangible offerings and in-person services. Some organizations have expansive reach because they have a number of satellite offices. Could organizations consolidate into one larger headquarters and have regional staff work remotely? The National University System, which includes universities such as JFK University, National University, Northcentral University, and University of Seattle, has more than thirty campuses across the West Coast of the United States. With most of their courses becoming more flexible through online offerings, they are starting to consolidate to one major campus and keeping other prominent sites where feasible or out of geographic necessity. It's a smarter model and reflective of the evolving nature of a hyper-connected community.

- **Mergers and Acquisitions:** While this topic will be explored in greater depth later in the book, now is an apt time to mention it. With many nonprofits at risk of closing down their services for good (much like many for-profit businesses are forced to do), there may be opportunities for organizations to merge so they can financially strengthen each other and move to one shared address. Alternatively, boards may reach out to organizations that are rumored to be struggling to acquire or absorb some of their programming, assets, or staff to come out of this crisis with a new energy in tackling issues of commonality such as homelessness, education, or food access.

Funders should also come together to discuss this issue more broadly as a way to facilitate a difficult conversation about sustainability and the more prevailing question of how many nonprofits are too many in a given locale. Funding surveys or strategies much like those mentioned from the *Status of Bay Area Nonprofit Space and Facilities* report (which evolved into a broader campaign by the Northern California Grantmakers called the Nonprofit Displacement Project) could provide a benchmark of how to tackle this issue head on. The next steps would then be a blend of the following:

- **Policy and Legislation:** Rental caps, rezoning, and government support.

- **Communications:** Sharing results more broadly to highlight the impact of potential displacement.

- **Technical Assistance:** Providing funds to facilitate moves, space planning, negotiating leases, underwriting and guaranteeing loans, and other legal matters.

If anything, the coronavirus pandemic has shone a light on our most entrenched operational issues and provided space for the conversations we have long been dreading (or avoided due to the "busyness" of how we used to work in the past). We should welcome those conversations and work better to break out of this nonprofit deficit mentality.

You can do the math too.

First, forget about the office space being donated. That's just counterintuitive.

Next, multiply 250 square feet per staff member or those who regularly use your services on any given day, then multiply it by the per-square-foot rate for Class B office space. (Check out CBRE or an equivalent for real estate market reports in your region.) Once you have worked out that initial cost and added utilities and other associated costs, review it based on alternative scenarios, many of which have been highlighted above, and then see where savings can be made.

Finally, imagine where those savings might be applied. You can even decrease your projected revenues as a counterweight.

As for that fancy boardroom, it might be time to say goodbye to that rich mahogany table and those leather swivel chairs and embrace the conference rooms of board members' corporate offices or renting a coworking space for a couple of hours. Your volunteers probably won't mind, especially if it secures your organization's future and leads to more funding for frontline services and keeping talent.

PHILANTHROPY AS KNOWLEDGE BROKERS (OR, PUTTING KNOWLEDGE TO WORK)

I once described my previous role of leading the Civic Leadership Fund and the San Diego Center for Civic Engagement as just drinking coffee and connecting people. As you can imagine, this resulted in me receiving an understandably fair rebuke from my CEO due to it reeking of privilege. However, connecting individual people to opportunity was one of the highlights of my role, demonstrating the convening power of anchor institutions.

Take, for example, a screening of the documentary *Inequality for All* together with a Q&A with former Secretary of Labor and the movie's narrator and star, Robert Reich. This was a big coup for the Center for Civic Engagement and my last big event as staff lead. Whether I was motivated to go out with a bang or because I couldn't just sit back and watch a terrific opportunity be passed by for the sake of exclusivity and stewardship, I pushed back after hearing that the event would be in a private movie theater in La Jolla, one of the most illustrious cities in all of California, and that the screening would only be made available to selected donors and include a VIP reception with a meet and greet as part of the package.

If ever there was a disconnect between institutional philanthropy and the issue of income inequality, this was it.

I decided that burning all of my internal capital fighting for a broader audience was a risk worth taking, and leadership finally agreed to diversify the three-hundred-person-capacity theater into thirds, one for donors, one for students (as part of a partnership with UCSD), and the final one for community members. The latter highlighted the benefits of a strategic shift in how big philanthropy interacts with grassroots nonprofits. We had identified a number of civic leaders and organizations doing great work in some of San Diego's most underserved neighborhoods as part of a power mapping exercise a few months prior, and I felt they would benefit most from listening to and connecting with the facts, ideas, and action items emanating from a unique event such as this.

In the end, it was an amazing event. I still took flak due to the unfortunate heckling of the wife of the center's chairperson during the event (who abruptly left up the aisle with her husband in tow), but sometimes you have to take the rough with the smooth.

Little did I know then that this would be a great example of the need and potential for philanthropic knowledge brokers. And little did I expect that one of our board members at San Diego Grantmakers would share the story of this event five years later as of one of the best examples of civic engagement she had participated in. When I shared with her and others present at that meeting that it was an event I curated, and that it had been engineered that way as to highlight the benefits of expanding our tent, I couldn't help but give a wry smile.

Knowledge brokering is a role that acts as a connector and interpreter of new and emerging concepts, acting as a bridge for people seeking answers to questions on one side and those who have the answers on the other. The defining traits include translating technical info or hard numbers into something more accessible and understandable and providing links to knowledge, market insights, and research evidence while helping to convert that into practical tools, actions, and narratives. This role is becoming increasingly important because knowledge is a precious commodity these days, especially with the rapid advances in technology and the way we do, understand, and interact with things.

Leah Crockett, a knowledge translation coordinator and knowledge broker at the Center for Healthcare Innovation at the Children's Hospital Research Institute of Manitoba, outlined her role in layman's terms via a *KnowledgeNudge* article on Medium sharing that the role often involves acting as the "link" between people or groups, including the producers and users of research. This insight highlighted to me that knowledge brokers need the following skills to be effective in this type of role by:

1.   Relating to people with a broad range of background.

2.   Understanding different ways of thinking.

3.   Understanding the different contexts in which information can be used and share.

4.   Being able to critically analyze evidence.

These are the core skills I want to identify and lift up when hiring a program manager for a philanthropic project. The sector would benefit from some professional self-definition of these kinds of actors moving forward.

While think tanks are playing this role more broadly, affinity groups can also act as a bridge to actors across the ecosystem with their staff as educators, coaches, and catalysts to the adoption of new, emerging, and best practices. Groups like the Technology Association of Grantmakers and Philanthropy for Active Civic Engagement are prime examples of funders groups that could have a real role to play in the future. I mean, who is going to pick up the nuances of impact investing without a little hand holding in the early stages of adoption? My challenge to these affinity groups, however, would be to assume the role of flag bearers rather than service providers, proactively identifying organizations with which to partner and support rather than providing programming around new trends.

Philanthropy needs a mix of real expertise and the savvy to connect the dots with key people and organizations. These individuals don't need advanced degrees in the subject matter. Those who have an active interest in the field—and who can apply that knowledge strategically— can be just as, if not more, effective in the field. And what better stewards of civic knowledge are there than those entities that were set up in the same vein?

THE FIFTEEN RULES OF PHILANTHROPIC FUTURISM

Find your purpose.

Simon Sinek is synonymous with the Golden Circle, the concept of starting with *why* as the purpose, *how* as the process, and *what* as the result. And while I appreciate the foundational elements of this approach, my take on "purpose" as both a guiding force and north star has been hijacked over the past decade by my exposure to those who preach a conscious type of capitalism where the definition of success is to chase the waves before 8:00 a.m. in their sleepy, yet gentrified, beachside towns because that is the Zen image portrayed in their self-help book subscription boxes.

The future is what we make of it, and to say that we need to spend our entire careers chasing one, single most important pathway is a dangerous anecdote for success. Philanthropy is not someone's purpose.

I once was pulled into the conversations and design of a new "Chamber of Purpose," an intriguing coming together of businesses practicing and championing a triple-bottom-line approach to business. It made sense on paper, there were a number of people I respected as part of the process, and it seemed like they had the energy and the expertise to move it forward. But after a while you could see through the bullshit.

The word *purpose* should have given it away, but I'm a sucker for change.

After all the pleasantries and goodwill around this project had evaporated, and the people who got stuff done in their communities were burned or bad-mouthed for not rolling over to the demands from sections of leadership, we all saw the purpose movement for what it really is: business folks going through a midlife, failure-to-launch type of existential crisis. At the end of the day, all they wanted was either power (another CEO title) or clients for their consultancy side hustles.

Beware these kinds of actors in your philanthropy careers.

One of my first roles in the US was for an organization led by someone with these traits. I have never seen a nonprofit bring in so many unpaid interns month after month—hardly giving me a chance to learn their names, let alone what they actually did—which should have been a warning sign, but I just thought this must be how the country's workforce operated.

I shudder to think back on these experiences and hope that impact investing doesn't become their new "purpose" after their LinkedIn marketing or CBD-infused products tank.

So, no, I'm not a fan of the word *purpose*. In the end, just do what excites you and this will lead to career satisfaction. It's also how you will be successful in applying a futurism lens to your work.

You see, philanthropic futurism in its simplest definition is seeing and understanding future trends and technology and then understanding and articulating how they can be applied today to solve and support the finding of historical, current, and future societal problems. Being a career generalist is how you can garner that kind of insight. Predicting the future is just the fun part; it's really just a bet, yet one that can be better informed and calculated.

So why did I mention Simon Sinek when all I have done so far is to segue into a rant about a bunch of surfing frat boys? Well, I want to reaffirm I was not using his work as a Trojan horse to talk about my frustrations around a "Chamber of Purpose"; it's actually because he hits the nail on the head around rules and values.

It may just be semantics here, but the *why* should not be confused for purpose. I think that has gotten blurred in the wash. The why is your values; it explains the why of your behavior. The rules underpin the *what*.

I always mention the importance of values to folks who are grappling with the conflict of who they are at work and who they are outside of it. Working in the social sector should foster a freedom, or comfort, around intertwining both. You know, bringing your whole self to work, showing up, speaking up for what's right, and so on. At the end of the day, you must not shy away from who you are or you will be susceptible to being rolled over, and the purpose of this book is to inspire readers to espouse courageous leadership in all they do.

So start with your why, since, of course, Simon Sinek said so and has a really cool TED Talk on the subject. However, the why can be wired into your psyche by way of a values statement. And while I'll stop short of recommending a values retreat (even though that is indeed a trend that is occurring intergenerationally in philanthropy), I do encourage time for you to ground in, understand who you are, who you want to be, and how you will show up each and every day. These are the values that will guide your work both personally and professionally and will influence the decisions you make in uplifting your community.

My experience with values statements comes from a political background. If you want to run for office you must be able to withstand the ultimate question of motivation—Why are you running? You know when someone is running for higher office when they write a book that really gets to the crux of their being, what values fuel their public service, and how they are representative of the times. And trust me when I say that me writing a book that outlines my own values is completely coincidental.

My values are up on my personal website for all to see. I don't shy away from them, and neither should you with yours. Ultimately, it's who you are and, at a bare minimum, who you aspire to be.

The values I identified are future focused in nature and appeal to my sense of optimism and faith in our world to "get it right"—eventually. Because while there are amazing advances happening in our world and our sector (many of which are highlighted in this book), I ultimately wrote this book during a surreal moment in our time. We were captured by a global pandemic that provided plenty of time for reflection on the current state of our nation and how our lives can be turned upside-down in an instant. We realized that populism as our current guiding "vice" is fundamentally reactive and a danger to our economic and personal security. And while I won't get into the politics of it all, I will say that America needs to become a fairer, more just, and kinder country, and that it will take time to heal its current divides.

This is the lesson here: your values must persevere and will ultimately help you triumph. My values have aided my own development and help me grow beyond my deep flaws as a human. I, like everyone else, am a work in progress, and I'm happy to share my operators' manual:

- **Service:** The noblest motive is the public good, so I am best served committing to fairness, equality, and creating systems that lead to opportunities for all.

- **Courage:** I demonstrate conviction for my values by taking risks and being bold.

- **Future Focused:** I continually anticipate, identify, and implement future trends and solutions as my way of contributing to a more vibrant society.

Simple, right? In the end, you don't need twenty core values to rally around. That many won't fit on a sticky note that you can affix to your laptop. And when you list that many values, it means you don't actually stand for anything.

In my mind, values are a much stronger driving force in yielding the outcomes and behaviors you may want to espouse daily. However, you do need some rules to govern your actions and pathways and guide your decision-making. That's why I developed fifteen of them to help you approach your work in the social sector through a lens of futurism.

THE FIFTEEN RULES OF PHILANTHROPIC FUTURISM

1. **Understand that only government can change systems.** This is probably a surprising rule, let alone the fact that it's the first one listed. However, this was a sobering realization for me. For all of the funding, community standing, the ability to shape discourse, and the fact that many foundations will exist in perpetuity, the reality is that laws change systems and charity accounts for just over 2 percent of gross domestic product (GDP). So who is going to fund the revolution?

How does realizing this change your approach? Can it reframe your approach? Think of funding as a way to de-risk new community initiatives and provide government with both quantitative and qualitative data to invest more on proven programs. Think of community standing as a way to advocate for change and be a voice for those you seek to serve. Think of the ability to shape discourse as a reason to be a trusted convenor and strategic connector.

Also, think of perpetuity as somewhat of a civic Groundhog Day where you can ideate, tinker, and double down on solutions, knowing that mistakes can happen but that a strong evaluation framework can help you discover new ways to make a difference. The more philanthropy realizes its shortcomings in society, the more it can move away from picking up the tab for government cuts and begin leading new social innovation.

2. Innovation doesn't have to be new—it just has to be new to you. You don't have to reinvent the wheel. If an approach is shown to decrease chronic homelessness, look at why and then bring it back to your community, applying it in a way that makes sense and plugs in to current infrastructure. "Research, retool, and retrain" needs to be a nonprofit leader's new civic mantra.

3. The robots aren't going to take your jobs. Technology and automation are there to drive new efficiencies. Just remember that when routine tasks become obsolete in your workplace, and don't backfill that time with more mundane duties. Let that time be used for learning, exploration, and tackling new projects. Work under the assumption that tech will increase output and generate more jobs, not decrease them.

4. Stay the course. Change takes time; it certainly takes longer than a five-year strategic plan or that of a four-year presidential cycle. Set your goals and align expectations, contracts, and funding accordingly.

5. Sometimes you need to think not outside the box, but from a different box altogether. Radical innovation is substantially different from radical social change. Think about what tools or vehicles currently exist that might not be commonplace in nonprofits but could be gamechangers for your organization once applied. Don't adopt the old adage of "Why don't you run it like a for-profit entity?" Instead, remember that a 501(c)(3) is just a tax designation, not a business model.

6.   What does that even mean? Can you explain your ideas in a way a fifth-grader would understand? Does it pass the "so what" test? And for the love of all that is right in this world, please ditch the jargon, filler, and weasel words. Replace adjectives with data. Answer with yes, no, I don't know, or a number instead of giving a vague answer that sounds meaningful. I added a glossary of terms at the end of this book to help with this.

7.   Don't be everything to everyone. The social sector is way too nice. Trying to get everyone to understand your way of thinking is actually doing you and those you serve a disservice. The only reassurance your work needs is a simple thank you. You could donate a million dollars and someone will say you didn't give enough while another will say you gave it to the wrong organization. You can't win, and that's why you must lean on your values, make informed decisions, and trust your gut in doing what is right.

8.   Reclaim the word *philanthropy*. Ditch the Latin meaning of philanthropy from your lexicon. It's been used in the first paragraph of way too many blogs as a lazy on-ramp to promoting a GoFundMe campaign. The sad reality is that the word *philanthropy* does not elicit that powerful positive response it used to and is fast becoming seen as a construct of an evil capitalist society. Yes, it has flaws structurally. Yes, it has been used as a tool to decrease taxes and build unsavory individuals' reputations. And yes, it has been widely used as a charitable transaction over that of a charitable act. But we need to realize this is our sector's word, and we need to begin changing the stigma around it. Helping people understand that philanthropy *is* giving to your friend's 5K fun run, that philanthropy *is* volunteering at your local food bank, and that philanthropy *is* sharing legal advice with a nonprofit pro bono. It's time to not shy away from it and encourage others to lean into it as well.

9.   Convene, cultivate, and connect. Bring folks together, tap into subject matter experts, and build coalitions around change. Impact investing and public-private partnerships should be the outcomes of engaging different sectors in discussion about the most critical issues of our time. A shared understanding that all these issues are intersectional will help drive more informed decisions at the municipal, county, state, and federal levels. Oh, and be inclusive, not exclusive. We are all in this fight together.

10. Don't just shove your logo on it. Foundations have an uncanny ability to fund a project and take all the credit for it. They are quick to get out (and control the ensuing message) in that obligatory media release at the end of the funding cycle and use their large communications team to turn their results—whether planned or unplanned—into big marketing campaigns to yield even more donations. Instead of doing this, practice a new form of participatory place-based leadership. Know when to lead, when to stand side by side with community partners, and, most importantly, when to get the hell out of the way.

11. We are not all in the same boat. When I said that we are in a surreal moment of our time, I wasn't including the current civil rights protests. This is not a moment, it's the ongoing fight for racial justice, the ongoing movement against hate and prejudice that has been occurring over centuries. Philanthropic fragility is an issue right now. Many conversations are happening in the sector that focus on how to advance equity and equality in grantmaking. But are they leading to real changes to policy, staffing, and grantmaking practices? Or are they just fueling different content and speakers for their webinars? The call for action has been symbolized by all of us "being in the same boat," and that as allies we just keep rowing in the same direction. If we drop an oar, we pick it up and then keep rowing. I don't think we are in the same boat; I feel this saying, is another connotation of privilege. Instead, we are in the same storm, and there is still so much to be done before we even see land. Equity has to be front and center of the future direction of philanthropy. We all need to realize that when we make mistakes and our peers point out our flaws that we are not being called out, but are being called in.

12. Credential so you don't crater. I mentioned earlier that generalists are the best people to understand and conceptualize the future. They are also prone to become a jack/jill-of-all-trades and master of none, the career equivalent of being put in the friend zone. However, education is rapidly changing and, in what is no big surprise, is being rapidly disrupted mainly due to technology but also in part due to the effects of globalization and worker mobility.

I once met up with a fellow member of the San Diego Diplomacy Council who was adamant that I take my master's degree, stating that it was the passport to career success. Today, however, graduate studies are largely trending toward being simply a professional credential due to a range of capacity constraints, and getting these degrees from leading universities is more "paying into a professional network" than accelerating your career trajectory. So, getting your CFRE or a professional certificate in the social sector is beginning to support your career aspirations just as much as getting an advanced degree in nonprofit management or an MBA. And when it comes to futurism, you don't have to take formal training in computer science or engineering to understand machine learning or data analytics. Just hop on to LinkedIn learning and level up there in your own time.

Rounding out the fifteen are my three favorite fundamentals:

13. Ask. In other words, ask for more funding and support. Ask more questions about your approaches, goals, and vision. If you don't ask, you don't get.

14. Give. More specifically, give your time, talent, and money. Practice what you preach.

15. Get shit done. You can't talk outcomes into existence, and change isn't going to just happen by itself. The status quo loves talkers and procrastinators.

My favorite rule is number fifteen. I have built my reputation on it and am surprised no one has ever purchased me a novelty coffee mug with that slogan emblazoned upon it. If you can picture a Venn diagram with three circles—one that says "dream big," one that says "know how to have fun," and one that says "get shit done"—that intersection is the kind of people I want to work with and those I hope will get the most from reading this book.

When all is said and done, rules are fundamentally a failsafe for our values, norms, and—dare I say—morals. They are the balance of our lofty ideas and ideals, providing focus and a methodical approach to our work as change agents. So don't chase your purpose. Instead, chase a fulfilling life that complements what you care about, what excites you, and what in your heart of hearts can make a positive difference to this world. After all, that's the only thing we can control: our actions in making this world a better place than we found it. Because right now, for the first time in a long while, our younger generations risk being left in a worse position than those that preceded them.

ADRIANA LOSON-CEBALLOS

Optimistic. Courageous. Latina.

Adriana Loson-Ceballos manages to light up every room she enters; most likely because it's rare to see someone who knows themself, what has shaped them, and how they can bring that to their world. We first met when Adriana was the director of network resources for Emerging Practitioners in Philanthropy (EPIP). There I discovered how deeply spiritual and rooted in her culture and values Adriana was. She focuses her energy on reimagining philanthropy's flawed and undemocratic structures through her experience as a Latina in the United States, as a giving circle doctoral researcher, and as the founder of Colmena-Consulting to help us better understand how we come together to mobilize resources that create change, repair harm, and build power.

Adriana's dedication to showcasing philanthropy's power to create change is as revolutionary and inspiring as the lives of characters in Isabel Allende's and other Latin American Boom stories: "I consider myself to be a resource mobilizer and network weaver, cross-pollinating between movements and communities, endlessly working for a more just and equitable present and future," she says. "I guess all that is what I ultimately define as *filantropista*. I find purpose in the liberation and mobilization of resources—human, social, financial, and natural. The 'how' of this liberation and mobilization is what fascinates and drives me. I love studying how this is happening or how it has happened. More importantly, how might it happen while centering equity."

There is no greater understanding possible than that which comes from experience. Adriana's voice offers the sector an abundance mindset rooted in her lived experience growing up on the US–Mexico border. She offers her research and evaluation skills to collective giving groups, foundations, and academic centers—seeing the mobilization of the collective as a necessary source of study in liberation efforts. In the summer of 2021, Adriana launched Colmena-Consulting, where she studies movements, networks, fields, convenings, communities of practice, and collective giving models, such as in partnership with the Latino Community Foundation and Philanthropy Together. She also serves on two national philanthropy network boards, the Women's Funding Network and the United Philanthropy Forum, and is writing her dissertation on the Latino Giving Circle Network.

"We have a real opportunity, from funders to fundraisers, to intentionally let go of the remnants and relics of outdated systems that determine how and to where resources are moved," Adriana says. "It goes without saying that our connection to resources deeply affects how we experience everything. So for those of us working in philanthropy, we need to be looking at our proximity to resources and reevaluate the basic tasks of our job descriptions. We must reimagine what our jobs ask of us and how our organizations support this. It will take all of us to move philanthropy from contributions to attributions."

If Adriana's leadership is anything to go by, the future of philanthropy will center the power of the Latinx imagination, one which envisions a deeper, more courageous, and collective kind of charity for the future of humanity.

PART TWO

TRENDS AT THE TIPPING POINT

CHAPTER FIVE

Resetting the Table

I have always questioned the point to which vested interests keep the status quo in philanthropy, knowing deep down that the answer is more than likely about power and elements of fiscal conservatism. And I can't for the life of me see why folks would create endowments and keep funds in perpetuity just as a sustainability measure. That would be one element, of course, but not the sole reason for making an investment in an organization. It can't be.

To me, philanthropy is about legacy. The investments we talk about are really in the future vibrancy and vitality of the community at large, with the organization holding that corpus is the best vehicle to ensure that vision is realized.

Philanthropy is ever changing. We need to start taking steps toward a more innovative approach (and conversation) to how we do our work. That includes smarter investments in our portfolios, our people, and our partners. It's about flexibility, awareness, and an openness to make things right. It's about understanding that the whole role of nonprofits is effectively to put themselves out of business by solving the issues that drive its mission, not looking at ways to pump-prime the operations budget through aggressive tinkering in the stock market.

There are arguments to be made against the rapid professionalism of the sector, especially around the financial and administrative sides of the house. The bigger the organization gets, the more technocratic it becomes—and with it, the dilution of "what really matters." I'm talking here about the pioneering role of philanthropy, the ways that it convenes ideas, seeds solutions, and is nimble enough to take bets on our best and brightest individuals.

My real worry is that the sector is losing that spirit, that it's becoming more and more reactive in a populist world and shying away from being a key difference maker in favor of not rocking the boat (a.k.a. keeping the status quo).

But there are folks out there on the frontlines, working diligently, passionately, yet pragmatically. They are moving our sector toward one that is more accepting of change, and one that can see our future beyond the constraints of annual reports. They are fast-tracking the trends we are seeing in the sector and accelerating their implementation through leadership and influence and effectively resetting the table in a way that is inclusive, accessible, and, to be frank, more honest about the needs of the next few decades. I'm excited to feature three of them in the coming chapters.

SARA VAZ

Sara is community relations manager for the Nordson Corporation Foundation. In this role, she manages all of the corporate social responsibility activities for Nordson in the California and Colorado regions. Previously, Sara was the program manager for the Gary and Mary West Foundation, focusing her efforts on their youth employment and service animal portfolios. Sara has an MA in international relations from Alliant International University and has spent many years serving the refugee community in San Diego. She has served as vice-chair of the San Diego Refugee Forum and board chair of Somali Family Services. Sara now serves on the board of directors of Catalyst of San Diego and Imperial Counties, a regional association of grantmakers, and the Any Body Can Youth Foundation, an after-school program featuring a boxing gym built within the confines of a learning center/library in Southeast San Diego. She also served as the cochair for Women Give San Diego, a donor circle that funds nonprofit organizations in San Diego County that offer underserved women and girls the opportunity to enhance their participation in the regional economy and become fully engaged in the prosperity of their local communities. In addition to her work in the nonprofit community, Sara also owned and operated Link Staffing Services for a number of years.

SARAH MORAN

Sarah Moran is CEO and cofounder of Girl Geek Academy, a social enterprise on a mission to help inspire one million women into technology by 2025. She has been immersed in tech and STEM for most of her career. Learning how to code at the age of five and building websites and digital products throughout her teens, Sarah was confronted by the negative stereotypes around girls and tech within the teaching world. She has also worked across Australia and Silicon Valley, where she witnessed firsthand the challenges faced by women in the industry.

Sarah established Girl Geek Academy in 2014 alongside her four fellow cofounders as a place to learn, connect, and inspire change. The Girl Geek Academy programs are for girls from the age of five right through to ninety-five. Helping inspire a generational shift in the way political leaders, schools, young girls, and professional women think about and practice STEM, Girl Geek Academy has trained more than one thousand teachers in #MissMakesCode, the world's first hackathon for girls aged five to eight. That equates to a reach of more than ten thousand students in Australia now exposed to STEM education from the age of five.

Sarah's vision is to challenge the stereotypes and create positive and visible new role models—whether that's for women within the tech and games industries, making wearables, building start-ups, or executive leadership for women in large technology organizations. This also led to the publishing of a young adult fiction series with Penguin Books in 2019.

In 2018, Sarah was awarded the *Australian Women's Weekly* Woman of the Future Award and the QUT Young Innovation and Entrepreneurship Alumni Award. She was also a finalist for Cosmopolitan Woman of the Year.

An active community contributor, Sarah works with the Leonardo group and Science Gallery Melbourne; is a member of the Victorian Minister's Advisory Council for Gender Equality; is an ambassador for Brisbane City Council's youth program, Visible Ink; and is a member of the Future of Work Summit advisory board. She also sits on the VicHealth Youth Taskforce and is a VicHealth champion.

ZAHIRAH MANN

Zahirah joined the Ralph M. Parsons Foundation in 2017, having more than fifteen years of experience working with nonprofits in the Los Angeles region, including as a program officer at the Annenberg Foundation and program manager at United Way of Greater Los Angeles, leading a collaborative of private and public funders investing in solutions to end homelessness. Before entering philanthropy, Zahirah was a public interest attorney representing and advising nonprofits, coalitions, and governmental entities. She received her JD cum laude from Tulane Law School and her AB from Vassar College.

These three women are not just leading from the front. They are also opening doors for a new generation of voices, who gravitate to their work in building a united and intersectional approach to change. I hope that you too will follow their progress after reading their viewpoints on how philanthropy is shifting with new standards and expectations demanded by the communities they serve.

Sara, Sarah, and Zahirah are learners, listeners, and doers. And while the previous chapters have already spoken about the need for new talent, where we can find it, and how we can empower these talented employees to break through glass ceilings, the stories that these three women are about to share with you underpin it with real examples.

The next step is making sure the ecosystem is rebuilt in a dynamic way for leaders to thrive and that they have the tools, funding, networks, and support structures to enact real change. Otherwise, we will see that ceiling become the entire structure and one where we become afraid of using the stones we have fought so hard to acquire.

In the following chapters you'll learn about the new realities for organized philanthropy and the shifts it needs to make to remain relevant, together with the emergent tech and approaches putting the sector in a position to deliver momentous impact in the next decade. If we as a sector get it right, we'll see a new paradigm where success stories are just as important as the dollars invested, an important distinction in how funders see, understand, and develop a new standard of effective grantmaking.

CHAPTER SIX

The New Realities Shifting Our Philanthropic Landscape

THE RENAISSANCE OF REGIONAL ASSOCIATIONS OF GRANTMAKERS

This past decade has been a missed opportunity for our anchor institutions to forge a new civic compact with their communities. Less transactional, more trusted convener. Less prestige, more rolling up their sleeves and getting shit done. The community was calling for a more dynamic civic partnership in tackling some of the most critical issues of our time, and for a period of time, our community foundations were actively listening and beginning to build the internal infrastructure needed from a participatory community leader, diversifying their staff, public programming offerings, and grantmaking. They knew when to lead, when to link arms with key partners, and when to get the hell out of the way.

So whatever happened to community foundations being the focal point of a shift in organized region-wide civic engagement?

In the lead-up to 2014, with community foundations about to celebrate their hundredth year (Frederick Goff established the Cleveland Foundation in 1914), this truly felt like the sector was about to be redefined with a new public, philanthropic partnership forged as an important step in tackling the defining issues of our generation. Even President Obama was acutely aware of the opportunity and celebrated this centennial at the White House with one hundred leaders from the field. The White House later summarized the event in a statement, sharing that America led the world in developing a national culture of civic participation. "Together, we commemorated a century of achievement by community foundations and looked forward to the possibilities that lie ahead," the White House brief stated. The accompanying official White House blog post captured the essence of these possibilities by mentioning how community foundations were helping to tackle systemic challenges and were essential to achieving long-term success for the communities they serve.

So what has happened since then? (And no, it can't all be blamed on the forty-fifth president of the United States.) Well, authentic civic engagement slowly returned to its previous label, which was simply defined as *programs*.

Discretionary funds (many labeled as civic leadership funds that included memberships and tailored public programming) have been repurposed into simple annual funds to be used foundation-wide.

In addition, a number of brave new hires in organizations seeking to replace long-term retiring CEOs with leaders who came from a community, rather than from a fundraising or financial background, have recorrected their course.

Now these leaders are being replaced with the support of many long-term major fund holders, happily reintroducing themselves to the community as a charitable bank.

And you know what? That's OK.

Community foundations have thrived for one hundred years, and their business model will hold up for one hundred more, given that an estimated $59 trillion will be generationally transferred over the next fifty-plus years according to the book by Michael Moody and Sharna Goldseker—*Generation Impact: How Next Gen Donors are Revolutionizing Giving*. While many might see this as a missed opportunity for community foundations through a mission-based lens, it has actually opened the door for other players in the ecosystem, such as regional associations of grantmakers, to have somewhat of a renaissance in the philanthropic sector.

Regional associations are membership groups for organized philanthropy to learn, lead, and invest in their communities. They traditionally serve and represent local philanthropists, family foundations, corporate funders, and public charities by connecting funders to knowledge and resources and increasing awareness about philanthropy's role and potential for impact in its communities. These associations have been around for about fifty years and were slowly losing impact through the rise of national affinity groups that support more focused donor intent and collective impact around single issues. In addition, larger foundations didn't see themselves needing their services, and community foundations sought to shield their growing donor-advised fund (DAF) base from perceived competitors, which was a flawed perception. There was even a disconnect with their name and role within the community, with many associations calling themselves "[insert city/region here] Grantmakers," when in fact many of these organizations were not granting funds.

So what changed? And why are these groups growing when they arguably have a limited membership base to work with? To be frank, it was probably just that. For example, a regional association on the West Coast that had around 120 members researched the potential for growth based on all the region's foundations and found that if every single foundation joined as a member, based on current fees, they would only net approximately another $250,000 in revenues. Ultimately, if they wanted to reach the potential they saw in themselves, they would have to diversify their business model beyond dues.

This was not just a strong leader ensuring the future viability of just one organization. This was a story that formed part of a nationwide shift in the association model that has now resulted in these types of membership organizations becoming some of the most dynamic across all of the traditional actors in philanthropy. Many organizations that are members of the United Philanthropy Forum are redefining what is meant by organized philanthropy because:

- They are making big bets on new forms of philanthropy such as giving circles and impact investing by acting as fiscal sponsors in some instances and building up the ecosystem and running demonstration projects and deal flow where needed and appropriate.

- They are driving new conversations on equity, race, and real systems change, undeterred by the political leanings of some of their members and forging a new path. They believe that tackling these deep-rooted issues through the voice and resources of philanthropy is a way of improving the communities they serve through the work of their members.

103

• They are not only granting out their own dollars through collaborative funding mechanisms (development staff rejoice!), but they are also granting them out via the modern approaches they seek to educate their members on—full-cost, trust-based, and financial returns on their investments.

• They are collaborating on both a state and national scale to drive stronger outcomes. The peak body, the United Philanthropy Forum, only recently expanded its membership to include affinity groups, leading to a larger, more comprehensive network of funders that are learning from each other and understanding the intersectionality of our communities through a funder's lens. In California, the three associations serving the three biggest regions in the state—Los Angeles, San Diego, and San Francisco—formed an alliance named Philanthropy California to collaborate on joint programming, coordinate communications and policy, and fundraise for new projects.

• They are amplifying their voices through policy, advocating on behalf of their members not only for stronger legislation around charitable giving but also taking a stand on issues such as Deferred Action for Childhood Arrivals (DACA), the activity of hate groups such as those witnessed in Charlottesville in 2017, and the census. The latter is a sign of the maturation of the sector by tackling the issue from both a social and fiscal angle, submitting an amicus brief to the Supreme Court in relation to the citizenship question and ensuring a fair and accurate count to ensure the states they represent aren't adversely affected financially and are not disadvantaged politically from a potential change in representation due to a state undercount of its residents.

Sector observers would be wise in checking out the strides these regional associations have made in the past few years and how a strong north star can drive innovations while navigating the risks of being first movers in a sector notoriously slow in its engagement. The majority of these organizations are also changing their names with the times, with identifiable monikers such as Philanthropy Massachusetts (previously Associated Grantmakers) and the Maryland Philanthropy Network (formerly the Association of Baltimore Grantmakers) aligning with their new narratives and work.

Let's applaud the leadership and innovation of these groups while noting that they may also blaze a trail for a new relationship with their local community foundations. They both stand to benefit by working together. The associations get to deliver their programs to a larger audience, and in turn foundations benefit from more informed grantmaking and most likely more dollars being added by donors to their funds. And let's not forget about the communities they serve, communities that need their support now more than ever, and who will reap the rewards, support, and funding from a more intentional form of collaborative action.

PROGRESS OVER PERSONALITY: BUILDING A COMPELLING NARRATIVE AROUND NONPROFIT MERGERS

In part 3 of this book, which focuses on reimagining institutions, we'll talk about the Internal Revenue Service (IRS) and its potential role (and responsibility) in ensuring the nonprofit sector remains effective. But first we need to talk about one side of what I call a "book-ended" solution: tackling from both the front and the back end the yet-to-be-defined-if-it-is-even-a-critical-issue of whether there are indeed too many nonprofits. (Currently we have an average of forty per zip code and rising annually.)

The front-end fix is potentially reviewing the application of a nonprofit entity before it even forms through more rigorous scrutiny both in its taxonomy (classification) and its service area (geographical focus). The back-end fix is to encourage a national review, or at the very least having a more concerted national conversation on what is a healthy number of nonprofits, using a range of metrics and using a range of deeper learning data sets to inform any potential recommendations that may result from this exercise.

One of the solutions that might spin out from such a review would be the option (or active encouragement) of nonprofit mergers and acquisitions. But let's not kid ourselves here. That move would court a lot of controversy and pushback from the sector.

While mergers and acquisitions are largely celebrated in the corporate world or are a chance for founders of start-ups and their investors to "cash in" through an exit, the complete opposite view is held by large swaths of the social sector. Thomas McLaughlin, the author of *Nonprofit Mergers and Alliances*, highlighted this visceral reaction by observing that "to some in the nonprofit field, the idea of mergers is scandalous and distasteful." But why?

Maybe it's because in nonprofit land we always seek to keep a higher moral standard and respect for the communities we serve, sharing the values of collaboration as a way to deliver real collective impact. Maybe it's a pushback against the sometimes cutthroat nature of capitalism or something the sector simply cannot relate to, due to its rarity in our sector.

Then again, it might be time to keep an open mind, start with understanding how mergers work and what they actually entail, and dig deeper into the successes and failures of the event both qualitatively and quantitatively. Either way, philanthropy has a big role to play, regardless of any perceived conflicts of interest or the concerns of a gross overreach of their role in the social sector's ecosystem.

Before I do my own deeper dive, I want to address the narrative and stigma around nonprofit mergers and acquisitions, with the thought that we might need to drop the acquisition part of the equation.

The term *acquisition* is technically correct in some instances, such as when an entity ceases its services formally and its "assets" are acquired. It's also the more preferable operational move than just another nonprofit aggressively seeking to take over an organization.

That being said, I find it hard to fathom what a hostile takeover might look like for a volunteer board, and how you put a value on purchasing programs. It's not like you can just acquire a donor just as you would a mailing list. So let's get real and just call this process a nonprofit merger and simply spell out the benefits without losing the narrative due to muddied perceptions of a different application of the term.

Part of the issue is that there also isn't much research or information on past mergers available in easily digestible reports. The best one I have found comes from the *Stanford Social Innovation Review*, which has provided some key findings that point toward the potential of nonprofit mergers to become a potential tool in mission advancement and the scaling of program delivery. One report, from the Metropolitan Chicago Nonprofit Merger Research found that of the twenty-five nonprofit mergers that occurred in the Chicago region from 2004 to 2014, 88 percent of both those that were either acquired or were the ones acquiring another nonprofit reported that their organizations were better off after the merger. Other factors that polled highly were that the organizations that merged had a prior collaboration, they engaged in a third-party consultant or facilitator, or a board member was the one who advocated for it to occur in the first instance.

These are promising results, and while this may or may not be coincidental, shortly after the conclusion of this report, Forefront, a unique regional association of grantmakers that is effectively both the funders' and fundees' representative body, created a new program called the "Mission Sustainability Initiative (MSI)." According to its website, this program would "offer a full array of information and assistance that includes confidential counseling to nonprofits interested in strategic partnerships, information on the steps of such a process, educational programs, referrals to pro bono legal assistance, and experienced, paid consultants." Furthermore, "the MSI will also offer grants to selected nonprofits to cover some of the costs of exploring and implementing a strategic partnership." (Forefront defines *strategic partnerships* as nonprofit mergers, acquisitions, back-office collaborations, and permanent program partnerships.)

The one-time grants of up to $75,000 from the MSI effectively reimbursed all out-of-pocket expenses associated with any potential collaborations and saw around five hundred nonprofits attend its kickoff event. It is an early indication that this might be a thing the sector wants after all, especially if we strip back the personalities, politics, and perceptions around this potential mechanism for sustainability, financial stability, and organizational growth and impact. (I should note, though, that my thoughts on this are very much higher level and do not take into account the legal ramifications or the "in the weeds" issues of jobs, benefits, policies, donor and client privacy, and other concerns.)

There are a number of informative websites that provide more nuance on the subject as well as some handy checklists that can help your organization explore the conversation of the prospect of a merger. But if you are looking for something that really breaks down what this would entail, check out "Mergers, Alliances, Affiliations and Acquisitions for Nonprofit Organizations: Financial and Legal Issues," led by Venable LLP. It's a copy of one of their presentations on the subject and breaks it out in sections and handy bullet points to use as a bridge to the directions you may want to take.

I have had some experiences with facilitating such conversations. As part of my role at the San Diego Foundation I brought together two organizations that at the time seemed similar in many ways, including their mission, their programming, and their goals for increasing citizen diplomacy in San Diego and more broadly across the Cali Baja Mega-Region. A couple of meetings were held at the foundation (a more neutral venue), and while the conversations didn't go much further, it was clear to me that these conversations must always occur at a board level. Executive directors are too invested for a variety of reasons, and because of their pride and personalities, they occasionally can't see the benefits beyond their paycheck, regardless of the fact their organization may not exist in twelve months' time due to their downward trajectories. I also learned that nonprofit mergers do not happen overnight, nor do they operate in a vacuum. They need a neutral convenor to help them avoid the absolute minefield of issues that stands in the way of success.

This is where I believe philanthropy has a distinct role to play. The grant process rolled out by Forefront was one simple way of moving things forward, because the last thing you need in these negotiations is wondering who will pick up the tab.

Here are a range of other ways organized philanthropy might play a strong role in this trend:

- **Convenor:** Philanthropy can be a conduit for mergers by bringing nonprofit leaders together to learn more, sharing what the process entails and outlining the benefits and options available to them, should they want to advance such a move.

- **Connector:** By leveraging national networks such as the Council of Foundations, United Philanthropy Forum, and other service providers to identify tools, assets, and advisors that could provide pro bono support, funders can help finance local initiatives and also provide strong recommendations on process and professional support to advance conversations around mergers between interested parties.

- **Funder:** Philanthropy can always do what it was set up to do and disburse funds into the community to support initiatives and collaborations that forge stronger alliances, partnerships, and possible mergers. It doesn't have to be just covering legal or consultant fees. It can also fund essential infrastructure to help ensure the ongoing success of the new organization, including the support of staff, tech, and other tangible items.

- **Research:** If the sector believes that nonprofit mergers will be an essential part of creating a more sustainable, efficient, and impactful nonprofit ecosystem, then it should fund independent research that looks at the merits of such actions, outline every facet of the process, and also source and share the feedback from those who oversaw both successful and unsuccessful mergers.

Nonprofit mergers will no doubt become more prominent over the next decade as we learn more about and understand the need for them and (more than likely) after seeing some high-profile case studies that will probably become viral across board member listservs. And while they will predominantly remain a voluntary effort in establishment and execution, it doesn't mean that such mergers can't be legislated. Governments have consistently performed land reclamation for infrastructure projects and merged councils statewide when it has been deemed that change needs to occur for the betterment of the community.

If your organization is struggling financially or for direction or relevance, don't get caught in the cyclical trap of elevating a new board chair and hoping that their initial excitement and bravado is going to usher in a new period of growth. Maybe the more reasoned move is to have a discussion of what your fundamental mission is and whether that is better served by joining forces with a similar entity. The path of least resistance might be collaboratively through someone else's purview.

REDEFINING YOUR UNDERSTANDING OF ROI: MIXED REALITY AND THE RETURN ON IMMERSION

As previously mentioned, nonprofits should be weighing up as part of their future strategic planning whether they actually need a physical space for their organization, especially if their service delivery is not contingent on people physically coming to their location. Let's advance this a bit further and through the lens of newly available tech to envision what a virtual offering would look like and whether this kind of disruption will be realized in a positive or negative way.

Much of this clicked for me while I navigated the arduous task of house hunting in a new city during the COVID-19 pandemic. While the market has slowed a little due to a number of predictable factors, this has actually accelerated new tech to a level of expectation rather than that of a novelty, including 360-degree/3D virtual viewings and video chat tours. But the nonprofit sector isn't as nimble as other industries, so while some sectors pivot, advance, and identify or try new efficiencies through tech, the real risk for nonprofits is that they fall further behind in a rapidly evolving market, at a time when engagement and funding are down.

While there is much ingenuity out there and there is an opportunity for organizations to play a leading role in understanding and fast-tracking potential solutions that our society urgently needs, we will likely look back on this pandemic and see how it accelerated the urgency of adoption.

So how do you create a real virtual experience that can engage, inspire, and drive action from individuals and other potential partners? Simply shifting or mimicking traditional approaches and reapplying them via an online vehicle is not what we are talking about. Virtual fun runs will never take off or make any money and will dilute future gifts. So put that event binder of the novelty beer run from 2010 back on the shelf because the only thing that traveled 5K was your organization drifting from its mission. (Yes, I still have some scar tissue from the beer run.)

We must also seek (as a sector) to define a new ROI—not just a return on investment, but a return on immersion. This is largely a new term I am proposing, yet one that warrants broader discussion because understanding what statistics social sector organizations need to track to ensure they are capturing data and feedback in real time will ultimately assist in reviewing the broader effectiveness of these experiences.

Transition to Digital

So, what realistic options are available to nonprofits now or are on the cusp of being affordable in the coming years?

Firstly, acknowledge that this isn't as easy as flipping a switch. Such a transition would need to be rolled out over a period of time, with ample planning, software sourcing, trialing, migrating, training, and promoting the change needed to make your universe comfortable, understanding, and supportive of the proposed change. This would typically be over twelve months, and even then, that would be quite quick under normal capacity constraints.

By all indications, mixed reality (MR) is going to be the sweet spot for a shift to virtual options that could provide the best source on this new return on immersion. MR has gained strong traction recently and is outpacing the growth of the more established augmented reality (AR) options on the market. It's not just overlaying virtual objects in a real-world environment (think Pokémon GO) but anchoring them in ways that are interactive and have the ability to drive more commercial value and ultimately patronage and donations.

New Realities Across the Social Sector

The first steps to this new approach would be identifying goals and needs and then understanding your entry points. So what might these look like? Let's ideate this together.

Gala Events. When we talk about a new normal post-COVID-19, much of that conversation will center on the short- to mid-term reluctance of folks to participate in gatherings of one hundred or so people. This could spell the end of annual galas as we know them, and the revenues and impact of events of this size and scope will not be recouped by simply shifting to online alternatives such as virtual tickets, peer-to-peer fundraising, auctions, or paddle raises. The clues for a new trend might be seen in the popular All In Challenge, which sees unique experiences as the main vehicle for giving with the cause as a complementary component.

Imagine heading into a *Sims*-like world (the game that is), where you interact with others in the environment but when you engage in conversation a Zoom video plug-in kicks in. This could also help maximize attendance for those supporters out of state or for unique interactions with celebrities and key influencers. We are already seeing the emergence of these virtual worlds that activate a video chat function in real-time, including a 2D *Zelda*-like world in Gather.Town and this *Sims*-style approach from options such as Teooh and Virbela. It'll be really interesting what takes off and what the market looks like once matured.

Conferences. Conferences will also be hit hard as we recover from the pandemic fallout. There will be a natural consolidation of events, and those that do continue will be the ones that are unique and engaging and offer real learning opportunities. For the conferences that do remain, conference apps will probably see a major leveling up with 3D maps, interactive augmented-reality kiosks, real-time session engagement, and beacon alerts pinging your phone when you enter different areas. In this environment you won't miss a thing. Information sharing will be immediate and curated based on the information you provided at registration and refined as you move through the event. A number of boutique online half-day conferences and fireside chats will also fill the vacuum due to participants being more comfortable with large online meetings, travel restrictions, and budget crunches, for example.

Philanthropy. Organized philanthropy has the biggest opportunity here to set the table for new tech, make its grantmaking processes more inclusive, and—by showing a bit of courageous leadership—realize this is where the sector is trending. It could also provide a large portion of the funds to bring along the majority of the sector with it. Traditional processes like site visits can be all moved online with 360-degree virtual cameras being used to tour a facility and that footage being shared with the nonprofit afterward to help advance its work. Interviews can easily be conducted online, and with the addition of things like smart contracts (which will be discussed later in the book), new tech additions can help make the process more efficient and secure, building ongoing trust between funders and nonprofits.

Nonprofits. The key here for a virtual office is how to showcase services and capture the empathy needed to drive engagement and donations. Videos can move people but they still lack the authenticity and intimate nature of in-person experiences and asks.

A virtual office where individuals can still see your work in action and interact with virtual anchors including people, art, and other tangible solutions can help potential volunteers and donors understand the work at a deeper level and give them an opportunity to learn more and conceptualize how they can support your cause. The fact they can "drop by" at any time also makes your organization more accessible in ways that just weren't possible a few years ago.

Associations. There is no reason for national associations or those that represent large urban metros to have a fancy office in a downtown location. It is simply an inefficient use of membership dues (which make up significant portions of their revenues).

A virtual office, built around a dynamic and informative user experience, will help members find either the information or person they need quickly, help with member retention, and ensure the demand is for an outward-facing entity rather than an insular one. Associations operating in this format will also be able to hire the very best talent from the sector, not just those available in that city or willing to relocate to places with high rent and cost of living such as DC, New York, or San Francisco.

But what about VR? Wasn't that predicted to be the next big thing? Well, VR is still growing. But those cumbersome headsets are still making mass marketing difficult, and we are yet to see them become more affordable. It's also banking on gaming and not other practical applications of the tech to be the thing that helps it go mainstream. So we wait.

I still believe VR has the biggest potential for fundraising, but we should remember all of the conferences we have been to where the medium was underserved by poor software selections and leaning more about the tech itself than what it could do. This has led to a lack of connection and understanding of its potential in the nonprofit sector and to it being seen as a novelty rather than a possible necessity.

Nonprofit tech will be riding a pretty wild wave over the coming years with a new urgency from users and organizations alike as they seek to keep revenues flowing and folks engaged. After all, low ROI is a performance measure, and boards won't be satisfied with poor returns, especially with leadership being the key differentiator of how we are judging our organizations' responses to the pandemic.

SARA VAZ

Blazing a Path Toward a More Inclusive and Impactful Corporate Citizenship

If there is someone you should listen to regarding the future of corporate philanthropy, it's Sara Vaz, the community relations manager at Nordson Corporation, one of the most philanthropic companies you've probably never heard of.

Nordson, which engineers, manufactures, and markets differentiated products used for dispensing adhesives, coatings, sealants, biomaterials, and other materials, has charitable giving in its DNA (or bonded between molecules, in this particular case). The company is committed to philanthropy as per their articles of incorporation, which sees them contributing approximately 5 percent of US pre-tax profits to support charitable endeavors. That's not to be confused with the 5 percent minimum payout either, because along with a number of other incentives for staff, Nordson had shared approximately $100 million in grants during the past three decades to support charitable organizations across eleven countries worldwide.

Nordson's core product is pretty much symbolic of Sara's role in our communities too. She truly is the glue that keeps a number of our most vibrant and dynamic organizations committed to and moving toward measurable change. Her commitment, candor, and ability to leverage all of her skills, influence, and resources to redefine what a corporate citizenry is and can be should be a blueprint for other impact-minded professionals who want to do the most good—in their companies, their communities, and most of all, for the defining social issues of our time.

"All of my work," she says, "is done within the confines of larger organizations: a long-standing corporate foundation, a volunteer leadership position of a large giving circle, and board positions of philanthropy-serving organizations. While I must operate within the structures of these organizations, the way I operate is what is important to me.

"I have always believed that in order to advance community needs, no matter what they are, you must operate from a place of trust, friendship, and honesty. To me this seems obvious, but until recently this standard has not been the norm. The power dynamics in philanthropy have always been there, and in order to mitigate them you really have to do the work to dismantle them. I would like to think that I lead by example in these efforts."

And it's Sara's kind of leadership that shines through in the most testing of times. The COVID-19 pandemic has highlighted so many systemic issues in our society. A bright spot in these dark times has ultimately been the recognition by institutional philanthropy that the way it has been traditionally operating is no longer the most effective.

"I have been pleasantly surprised at the quick reaction by most private and community foundations to change the way they do business to be more flexible and equitable in funding and meeting the needs of our communities," Sara says. "Walls that had been erected between philanthropy and the nonprofit sector seemed to fall overnight. Zoom screens seem to be opening conversations where in-person conversations could have never happened. My hope is that we never go back and this trust that has been built in disaster remains."

Yet the bottom line has a much different context in the for-profit world. And with the pandemic wreaking havoc on the revenues, jobs, and services of millions of businesses worldwide, will corporate foundations continue to focus on what is right? Or will they focus on what is convenient?

Sara remains bullish on this progress. She believes that organizations will continue working toward a corporate responsibility that is for justice, equity, diversity, and inclusion and that has seen an unmatched energy and support of civil rights, such as the Black Lives Matter movement. "While philanthropy can play a role in funding programs to reach underserved populations," she says, "more work needs to be done within corporations to recognize bias. A sector-wide commitment I would like to see is for them to become more intentional in bringing women into the conversation. To this end, I worked to create a women's affinity group within my company to start the work of change from the inside out." The success of this group coincided with Sara's own success in another organization that sought to help women and girls of San Diego achieve economic self-sufficiency. That organization was the 150-plus-member-strong giving circle, Women Give San Diego, of which she currently serves as copresident.

"I think giving circles have great potential to democratize philan-thropy," she says. "The giving circle I play a leadership role in allows younger women to become philanthropists at less than the cost of a gym membership per month. Empowering people to look at them-selves as philanthropists when they may not have much disposable income impacts not only the person contributing but the sector as a whole. It makes us all have a feeling of responsibility for each other and levels the playing field of that responsibility dynamic."

With giving circles democratizing philanthropy at the grassroots, what about reforming the higher echelons of institutional philanthropy? What levels of risk should the philanthropic sector be taking right now?

"Any foundation with a substantial endowment should be dipping into that endowment and spending down funds," Sara says. "If not now, when? What are we afraid of? What is the worst-case scenario—you make an investment in a nonprofit and they fold? If business and ven-ture capital were not willing to take risks, the big ideas, products, and technology that have changed society would not have happened."

Sara is right on the money here in this assessment, with legacy fast becoming more a self-serving vanity play that provides a welcome tax break rather than seeing it in person making an immediate impact. Yet it's not surprising given the values and actions of her company's found-ers. "It's all about courageous leadership," she says. "Speaking the truth no matter how uncomfortable. Sticking your neck out and standing up for what is right in both the big things and small things."

A company may not be a person regardless of legal precedent. But if it were, we would be best served by it sharing the outlook, actions, and dedication of folks like Sara Vaz, who is a true civic asset.

CHAPTER SEVEN

Opportunity Rising (and the Consequences of Misunderstanding It)

REEMERGENT TECH AND ITS NEW WAVES OF IMPACT

Tech and the solutions it helps ideate are often years ahead of their time. This is not futurism in the way we use futurism. It's more like an evolving version of a technology adoption curve that was generalized by Everett Rogers from his book *Diffusion of Innovations*. Given that Rogers created this psychographic chart in the early 1960s, a time when customers were generalized across an *x* and a *y* axis in terms of product market share, it should come as no surprise that in our current world of boom and bust, cyclical buying patterns, and targeted algorithms, an argument now exists that this long-lauded chart is out of date and has more ups and downs than a Six Flags roller coaster.

New technology wows us. Heck, little gadgets wow us. We saw it with the internet and smartphones. We now see it with 3D printing, virtual reality, and virtual assistants like Siri, Cortana, and Google Assistant. When something wows us, there is an instant gravitation to it, an insatiable thirst to interpret its many uses and layer it into our work. Then the shine wears off, and the total addressable market narrows to become more a focus on mass adoption and scale.

Take VR for example. It's been around for a while now, yet it isn't ubiquitous in households across the globe. Much of that might be attributed to assuming we were at mass market, when all we were doing was flooding that market with substandard human experiences, coupled with free cardboard headsets.

In the words of a few Mean Girls, "Stop trying to make *fetch* happen." But it wouldn't be wise to write off technology so quickly. With different adaptations and innovations, and together with the right timing and strategy, the right technology can bounce back and far exceed the potential it showed in its first iteration.

One example is the humble QR code. A few years ago, I was asked if we should put those intriguing little black squares, which are arranged somewhat artistically on a white grid, on our business cards. I said no (which shouldn't be held against me through the lens of other predictions made in this book) because it involved folks having to download a reader to scan it. At that point, usage had dropped by around 9.76 million from its market highs of 2011 (approximately 14.5 million). However, the QR code is now cool again, and that's largely because of the timing I mentioned earlier. With COVID-19 calling for contactless options across a range of industries and Apple adding a QR scanner into its iOS 11 update, it means no more third-party scanners. Simply hold up your camera, and you'll be redirected to a restaurant menu, a virtual shopping cart, or a person's LinkedIn account.

Video calls and conferencing have followed a similar trajectory. It started with the pioneering video app Skype, released back in 2003, with more than 600 million worldwide users at its height in 2010. I was one of those users, chatting with friends and family thanks to a webcam. Over the next decade, video calls became more of a nice tool for keeping in touch with friends and family rather than reaching its full potential, which was transforming the very way in which we communicate. More specifically, it didn't reach its potential in revolutionizing the nonprofit sector, the way our funders interacted with its grantees, and the way our nonprofits interacted with those they served.

(As an aside, my father always lifted up the fact that every major advance in tech first featured on *Star Trek*—that included phones, tablets, smart watches, Bluetooth earphones, virtual assistants, and of course video calls. While he secretly hoped to one day take a video call with a Klingon, I doubt he imagined that he would be calling his grandchildren with the use of filters and voice effects.)

On reflection, it was a travesty that our sector didn't realize this opportunity sooner. It's crazy to think that a pandemic would be the thing that pushed back against outdated approaches to work and the traditional office setting.

Don't get me wrong, video conferencing has been forced on us, and in many ways, we became exhausted by it. This was due to the necessity to carry on our work, some way, somehow. But the pandemic has also accelerated the adoption of video conferencing and, effectively, its sustainability. Video conferencing has changed the way we work—and newsflash, we will not be going back to how things were before the pandemic. We should not underestimate the ways in which video conferencing will truly elevate our effectiveness, especially if we understand and use it to its fullest potential. Most of all, it shifts the egregious nature of meetings—the time suck, the power dynamics, the bureaucratic theater, the extra tasks generated to an already impossible workload, and the fact that the information shared could have been sent via email—to a more dynamic, multimodal approach.

For nonprofits, video conferencing is a game changer in the following ways:

- **Cost:** Video conferencing is largely free or inexpensive for an upgraded license. The real cost savings come in the form of office space, with the question being how much square footage you truly need.

- **Accessibility:** Video conferencing opens so. many. doors. Or is it windows? Nonprofits can now connect with donors with limited time and who live across the country, clients who struggle with transportation issues and need just a routine consult can hop on a quick call, and stay-at-home parents who want to go back to work but require workplace flexibility to make it a reality can reengage with, and reignite, their careers.

- **Time:** The frequency of commutes will change in our new normal. The time it takes to walk across campus for a meeting, and the actual length of time of the meeting are all things that can be adjusted to reclaim someone's time to do the real work and advance the mission. We will be laughing in ten years' time about the old days where we sat in traffic for an hour just to come in and interact with three to five people during the day, just to do the exact same painstaking thing eight hours later. That's more time with family, more sleep, and a step toward a real work-life balance.

- **Relevance:** Meetings are often a catchall for a team, and once you enter that meeting you won't be leaving until it finishes. Video meetings can add folks and let folks go depending on the agenda.

- **Transparency:** Transcription, meeting recordings, and the ability to pull statistics on things like amount of time speaking (a telling stat around team dynamics) will help ensure there are no misunderstandings, and minutes will be a clear and concise representation of what was discussed and decided.

- **Multimodal collaboration:** Sharing slides and videos, using the whiteboard feature to brainstorm, and heading to breakout rooms are all terrific examples of using the time we come together constructively. It breaks up the potential monotony of meetings from hierarchy and one-way communication to one of a collaborative and engaging form of participation.

- **Scale:** The traditional event logic where events are capped and success is determined by how many people show up can finally become a thing of the past. Webinars highlight content over participation, and caps and location become irrelevant with rooms now virtual and events able to open up to larger audiences.

And that's just scraping the surface of the immediate future. Zoom will improve; it will listen to user feedback and respond to user demand. It might even be replaced by a better, more intuitive, and more responsive platform, fueled by AI with plug-ins that trigger images upon key words and can offer up definitions, data, and research that could enhance the conversation and capture any action items and assign them instantaneously. Video conferencing has the potential to be one of the biggest communication advances of our time, on par with the phone and TV. And once the frustration and scar tissue of working from home for the past year subside, we would be wise in embracing it as such.

OPPORTUNITY (LISTS) FOR ALL

Philanthropy has a unique vantage point of all the goings-on in the community. Nonprofits see organized philanthropy as a gateway to funding, and businesses, together with government, see philanthropy as a trusted vehicle to convene the social sector on their behalf, bringing with them vetted groups rather than unknown quantities. These are largely misconceptions of how philanthropy works. Then again, money talks and the mere perception of neutral convenorship is a consensus many sectors of our community can deal with.

This view, which philanthropy benefits from, includes knowing about all the events, grants, board vacancies, jobs, and other opportunities that are often only on your radar if you have a robust civic network or have signed up for every nonprofit email imaginable. (Do not try that at home.) However, it is extremely rare to see those opportunities passed on in an unfettered manner, one where they are shared in a way in which membership (either paid or acquired through programming) does not restrict access and where "being in the know" isn't a considering factor.

I'm of the opinion that we can't engage with and recruit new talent to the social sector if we aren't willing to look beyond our current networks and invite new people in. We would be naive to look at those bridges as all the things we take for granted, such as tickets to galas (of which we are always trying to find people to fill seats the day of the event). Instead, an organization (or dynamic individual) should create its own clearinghouse for local career and networking opportunities with the caveat that the majority of events they share are FREE or heavily discounted, the (e)list that shares opportunities is always open, and new members can be recommended and added with no questions asked. This list must be seen as a civic asset more than anything and one devoid of personal and professional assumption. Opportunities should be run much like a waiver wire to ensure it is a fair process.

The genesis of these kinds of lists came when I had the opportunity to host an EU delegation (including elected officials and civic leaders) in collaboration with the San Diego Diplomacy Council, of which I was a board member. In addition to underwriting the event through my Emerging Leaders Fund, I had the privilege of inviting twenty young professionals to participate. It was a truly unique and inspiring event and one where you had to "know" the organizer (me) to attend. The content and caliber of people in the room were amazing; if it had been opened up to a broader audience, it would have inspired more folks to tackle some of our biggest issues head on.

The feedback at the conclusion of this event was about how we should replicate this format more often and how we should also invite folks who are not the main beneficiaries of unique event experiences such as this. This ultimately led to the creation of a listserv very much built on the essence of what I have outlined. This list included subscribers who were civically engaged and plugged into the decision-making trees, influencers of that city, and those who were often sharing opportunities to fill open seats to gala events and other unique opportunities. They are also privy to leadership, job, and funding opportunities that aren't found through a regular online search. They saw a reciprocal benefit to being on the list and thus shared with others accordingly (with the majority being folks they had not even met yet).

In the end we identified the compounding effects of networked privilege (for example, having contacts in organizations that are a result of white privilege and other non-universal advantages), and we found a way to expand our networks in an authentic way rather than a meritocratic one.

That's why the purpose of an opportunity list is to share these opportunities with the view of lifting the careers of everyone on the list (in other words, the people you have worked with, appreciate, and see true leadership qualities in) and connecting the dots across the region for good. It's also a great way to provide a shout-out for folks doing great work so that they could be noticed. I regularly offered to nominate the folks on my list for awards such as the 40 under 40 lists and other flashy vanity awards that look good on a resume. Best of all, I shared the list of all recipients so folks could connect beyond the initial scope of the email. No blind carbon copy (bcc) smoke and mirrors here.

In the end, opportunity lists shouldn't just be geared toward the social sector. Neither should they have a political slant. It should be an authentic email that goes out once in a while, with no obligation to reply or accept the opportunities listed and with the option to opt out at any time without any offense being caused.

Curating such a list also helps build up your personal brand and enhance your networks. Not only can you lift up personal accomplishments of list members, building both rapport and good will with your peers, but you can also push certain events, requests, and viewpoints that you need to be elevated to a broader audience when urgency in driving action is key. It's much like understanding and riding the waves of a Facebook algorithm.

So, go forth and connect your community. Together we can ensure no seat is left empty on whatever "night of nights" is happening in your city this week!

ARE FLAWED METRICS AND GRANTMAKING APPROACHES HOLDING BACK SOCIAL PROGRESS?

Houston, St. Louis, and San Diego are all cities that have been crowned America's Most Charitable City in the past few years as part of the annual charitable cities report by America's largest charity evaluator, Charity Navigator. The report compares the median performance and size of the biggest nonprofits across the nation's thirty largest metro markets and are determined by twenty-one metrics across three distinct rating dimensions of financial, accountability and transparency, and size. (Americans are inherently generous, having given an estimated $449.64 billion to US charities in 2019, despite disincentives resulting from a change to the tax code doubling the standard deduction.) But many organizations that play a vital role in ensuring the health and well-being of our communities still struggle to sustain their employees and day-to-day operations.

What gives? How can we build on these positive giving trends and support a sustainable future for more than 1.5 million nonprofit organizations nationwide?

The first step is to dig deeper into the Charity Navigator criteria, because while the giving trends are favorable, the metrics used are in fact flawed. They are based on the notion that the strongest charities are those that spend minimally on overhead while maximizing dollars to programs. A more balanced approach focused on ROI and positive impact would be a far better adjudicator of nonprofit practices.

For example, administrative expenses in the charitable cities report reflect what percent of its total budget a charity spends on administrative staff and associated overhead. Dividing a charity's average administrative expenses by its average total functional expenses yields this percentage. The lower the number, the more efficient the organization is purported to be. However, while this focus on minimizing "overhead" is intended to promote organizational efficiency, it does not take into account the full costs incurred by many nonprofits to effectively support the causes and communities they serve.

This viewpoint does not necessarily mean we aren't as philanthropic as the record reflects. Many Americans still give their own time, talent, and treasure to nonprofits, with six out of ten households donating to charity in a given year (about seven times as much as continental Europeans) and 77.34 million adults volunteering nearly $167 billion in economic value, according to the Corporation for National and Community Service. Yet gaps in nonprofit capacity and resources can leave a community with gaps in service occurring at a time when many nonprofit leaders report an increase in demand for their organization's services and are confronting workforce development issues.

So how can we devise a holistic approach to philanthropy that starts with the end in mind? What are the outcomes we want to achieve? And what does it really cost to deliver those outcomes?

A growing number of nonprofit and philanthropic leaders across the nation have identified the fact that many nonprofits operate with just enough funding in hand to operate for less than two months—a tenuous proposition for the long-term viability of these organizations and the communities they serve. Even nonprofits that have been successful in establishing seven-figure endowed gifts aren't immune. If their unrestricted cash dries up and all cost-cutting options have been exhausted, that sweet $100,000 gift from last year that only yields $5,000 per year isn't going to save the day. (Unpopular opinion here: Organizations that have a budget of less than $1 million per year and are looking to grow shouldn't focus on planned giving.) Having options is all well and good, but the goal should be upfront gifts. Because at the end of the day, liquidity is nonprofit fuel.

That's why these leaders are supporting both the practical and big-picture cultural shifts needed to change how funds are disbursed to nonprofit organizations. Instead of focusing on reducing nonprofit "overhead," they encourage a focus on outcomes and the role funders want their grant dollars to play in achieving them. Trending structural approaches in the sector that warrant broader dialogue include the following:

- **Organizational Flexibility:** Providing unrestricted funding allows nonprofits to pay the right people to get the job done and have enough in reserve for those unexpected events and "slower" fundraising months. Most importantly, it gives organizations the freedom to explore innovation, improvement, and strategic planning.

- **Grant Renewals:** There is way too much paperwork that comes with grants vis-à-vis how much they are applying for. With micro grants of up to $200 still requiring three pages of information, funders require line-item budget expenditures for new projects that will be funded restricted gifts of $10,000 and ask for a lengthy post-funding report twelve months later. It's time to reassess the process and give nonprofits the twenty-plus hours they spend on average jumping through hoops to get attention.

- **Trust-Based Philanthropy**: Trust is the foundation of any successful partnership. Leaving the organization to get the work done is paramount. If it has successfully made it through the review process, there is no need for quarterly or mid-year updates. Also, trust is shown in how the grant is structured—kudos to those providing unrestricted, multiyear grants!

- **Equity Funding**: The nonprofit sector is going to great lengths to show how woke it is and that it is looking to fund racial, social, and economic justice projects. Now is the time to make this the norm, not just the theme, for this funding cycle. Funders may want to consider a number of approaches, including the following, to be successful in this endeavor:

  o Forming an independent steering committee made of community leaders and subject matter experts that is representative of that community and brings unique personal and professional perspectives to review proposals.

o   Forming authentic and inclusionary partnerships that can include providing successful grantees with further support in the form of mentoring, shared learning, and technical assistance.

o   Creating spaces for fundees to collaborate as strategic partners and thought partners.

o   Knowing when to stand beside grantees and, most importantly, when to get out of the way. Philanthropy has a tendency of showcasing impact and success through its lens and by slapping its logo on it. Avoid this at all costs!

o   Taking risks when tackling systems change. If it fails, review and improve. Never retreat from doing the hard work. Give it more funding and time to be successful if that's what data shows.

o   Listening to your partners, your community, and those whose lives you are seeking to transform. Don't make assumptions on what is needed based on your outrage at the latest Ta-Nehisi Coates piece. Hope to be called in and not called out.

While Giving USA and Charity Navigator data provides reason for optimism and pride, we must continue to keep our energy up when it comes to supporting effective nonprofits. Philanthropy's actions should reflect a genuine community-wide commitment to impactful service delivery. And by changing the way we support nonprofits right now, we can fundamentally improve their ability to achieve our shared goals.

SARAH MORAN

Geeking Out on the Possibilities of Philanthrotech

Missions, moments, movements. Progress, projects, profession.

These are all vastly different terms, but they are all terms that have coalesced over time into a broader descriptor of being a part of social change. No wonder it feels like running on the spot for those who are big-picture thinkers and get shit done. Patience has never been a defining trait of people I admire. But their drive, their candor, and their comfort in who they are and what they bring to the table are.

Sarah Moran, Girl Geek Academy CEO and cofounder, is one of those people. Challenging her limitations and perceptions while challenging the status quo are things that are fluid in her day-to-day work—and sometimes fluid within the context of her current conversation. Our interview for this book was no different, especially given that Sarah's work is not in philanthropy per se. But she is astutely attuned to it, warts and all.

"Even though disruption by 'social entrepreneurship' is what I practice, I wish it weren't framed this way," she said. "Treating social entrepreneurs as folks just 'doing good' detracts from the real need of philanthropy." Sarah is smart, curious, and a triple-box threat, meaning she is adept at navigating issues within the box, can think outside the box, and then can think from an entirely different box. It's like 3D chess but across business, government, and social sectors. "I went to a burger joint recently," she says, "and they have these three jars representing three local charities. And you get a token for buying a burger. You pick which of the three charities to give your token to. But there's only ever the same amount of money being donated: $500, $300, and $200. I hate that approach because people feel like they are giving, but they actually haven't given anything, simply redistributing what's already available. So when someone asks, 'Would you make a donation?' the person thinks, 'I already gave today,' and that's why corporate 'philanthropy' like this, quite frankly, sucks." Sarah's outlook on philanthropy comes from a unique vantage point and at a time when giving is changing under the growing influence of wealthy tech donors. She sees the absurdity of it all through the lens of systems: We are doomed to fail if we constantly repeat our mistakes of leaving large sections of our community behind.

Tech should be the great equalizer of our time with an abundance of opportunity for everyone. But the sector is seeing even deeper inequalities that have been compounded across decades because of the speed of technological evolution. "Before Girl Geek Academy was established," Sarah says, "women-in-tech initiatives were run on a volunteer basis or as charities. This meant women were seen as a charity—when actually what we want is for the structural barriers to be fixed by the organizations that created them, namely big tech, corporations, educational institutions, and, of course, government.

"We are very clearly a business, and we have a strict 'no volunteers' policy. One reason we are set up that way is so that people give their time and money to 'people who need it.' Unfortunately, the market alone will not solve these problems. It created them! So in order to move the needle, we need to be able to apply pressure and accountability to organizations who can structurally solve the problems they perpetrated."

Only 3 percent of the world's venture capital goes to women-led companies, and even less to women of color. "So the whole internet is entirely built and owned by men," Sarah says, "and even if women are working in tech, men are profiting. Venture capitalists are not investing cash in women-led companies. So where else can women go to get the much-needed funds to create technology that solves problems for the world?"

That's where philanthropy could and should come in. How could philanthropy help move the needle in advancing women's representation in tech, from higher education and research through to women founders and board representation?

"Women have been locked out of institutional ways of investing, and while there is promise in impact investing, especially those driven by social change organizations, and whereas crowd equity isn't a donation, it's a way to 'back' causes you care about and problems you want to be solved, there is still a long way to go."

Sarah is undertaking that work by leading a movement to help inspire one million women to get into technology by 2025 and fostering a paradigm shift in the way government, education, young girls, and professional women think about and practice STEM. "We want to know what the internet might look like if there were more women and girls building it," she says. "And that's where philanthropy can be of service. We need a broad portfolio of philanthropic work to make sure all bases are covered, including supporting women in the industry to succeed and lead."

So as a builder, maker, and mentor, what excites Sarah most about the future? "That we might have one," she says.

Who could argue? The future is yet to be written. If we work together to increase the number of women and girls in tech, games, robotics, 3D printing, aviation, drones, and space, then we get to tell the story.

CHAPTER EIGHT

Access and Experience

DESIGN AS A STRATEGY TO ALLEVIATE OUR
SHARED GRANTWRITING ANGST

Often the advancements in the nonprofit sector that have the biggest potential impact are the ones right under our noses that have long been taken for granted. The grant application process falls squarely in this bucket. It is time-consuming, sometimes confusing, and it leaves no room for nuance. It can also be ugly, constructed with little to no input from the end user, and it is essentially a firewall that compounds the power dynamics that continue to exist in philanthropy today. It is a binary process where success is only measured by whether the grant request was successful or not. And because of its multitude of flaws, it's a practice that should warrant more support for its immediate improvement.

A simple recalibration of the application process through a shared sector-wide goal of transparency, accountability, and continual improvement can make the process easier and more informative for both the applicant and the grantor. It is also one way to ensure that all inputs are rewarded in some shape or form.

So what would this entail exactly?

Design Thinking. The first step in improving the grant application process is to unpack all the issues that continue to perpetuate the underlying problems. There is no comprehensive reporting data that truly puts the finger on what is needed, so the following questions will need to be answered:

- What dollar amount is spent by the organization on average to secure a grant (versus the granted amount)? This includes overhead, advertising, CRMs, and other administrative tasks.

131

- How long do staff spend writing a grant application (including research and compiling additional documents, for example)?

- What percentage of grant applications are successful? What is the ratio of success vis-à-vis spending and staff support?

- What are the levels of trust and satisfaction between funders and fundees when it comes to the grant application process?

- What levels of automation currently exist? How open to bias is the review process?

- What feedback do grantors provide to successful applicants? And to unsuccessful applicants?

The list could go on and on.

This would no doubt be a lengthy and cumbersome undertaking and require an independent research body to administer.

Once the findings had been reported, then a committee comprising both funders and representatives from the broader nonprofit sector would need to come together to identify the current design process and review the cognitive, strategic, and practical processes that would need to underpin a "go forward" set of best practices. The sector could potentially provide support through common grant application templates to kick-start the process.

On a side note, another positive step would be to encourage open-source solutions that can automate the process of constructing new grant applications and provide data that continues improving both that and the overall experience. It would be great to have these solutions delivered in ways that are usable for folks of all skills and experience levels, perhaps by using form builders that draw on the success of options like Canva and Wufoo.

UX and UI. UX (user experience) and UI (all the elements that enable interactions for users) are both critical elements to what happens next because grant applications are equal parts intimidating, cumbersome, boring, and aesthetically bad.

A good primer for understanding these fundamentals is that

encountering grant applications that look cool but are difficult to use are examples of great UI and poor UX. Something very easy to use and navigate but that looks terrible is exemplary of great UX and poor UI.

In a world where mortgages can now be approved in a day, why do we continue to operate in a world where we submit a request for quote (RFQ) so we can be invited to fill out a request for proposal (RFP), put together a fifty-page application, prepare for a site visit, and then wait for three months to see if our proposal was successful with little to no feedback? In a new philanthropic utopia where a foundational approach to this proposed full process overhaul has been established (with full board approval!), funders are blessed with a range of options when looking to improve the process.

UI (improving the look and feel of grant applications):

- **Aesthetics:** The most regular piece of feedback on applications is to increase the font size. It doesn't hurt to make it readable and to look good! Also make the look and feel consistent with organizational branding. It's perplexing to know organizations spend $50,000-plus on rebranding and fancy logos yet still send out applications in a black-and-white fillable PDF.

- **An Entirely Online Affair:** Do away with all paper applications. If there are potential equity issues because of connectivity options, host a workshop at a local library or computer lab and have people complete the application then and there with on-site support.

- **Screen Orientation:** The common consensus is that forms are filled out on a computer (desktop or laptop), and while this is predominantly the case, applications still need to adapt for many possible screen orientations.

- **Framing:** Move past leading questions and push-polling tactics that focus on highlighting problems and instead frame the flow and structure around an invitation to provide innovative solutions.

- **Partner Value:** Create strong click or calls to action and processes that foster increased time on your site and with better mission-aligned applications.

- **Video Support:** instead of lengthy supporting documents on how to apply (filing tips), include click-through or pop-up videos that can explain each part of the application with context.

UX (improving the flow and interactions associated with grant applications):

- **Automation:** Ensure your forms are the smartest they can possibly be, pulling information effortlessly from 501(c)(3) documentation, 990s, and other relevant applicant reports together with the auto-population of forms from previous applications.

- **Progress Bars:** On average, applications for $10,000 and above take approximately twenty hours to complete. Let folks know how long the process will take, provide a real-time update on their progress, and avoid any process that has either a timing out function or does not autosave all input to date.

- **Real-Time Support:** Include customer service chatbots to answer any simple FAQs.

- **Smarter Forms:** RFQs should automatically convert to RFPs if the minimum requirements to apply are met. There should be no shortlists. Smart contracts are also on the horizon—using blockchain to execute all facets of a funding agreement from disbursing funds to reporting.

- **Dashboards:** Simplicity in the proposal reviewing stage should include the capacity for peer review to avoid biases (including a timing mechanism to ensure fairness), the ability for the reviewer to see their own progress in reviewing the document, and other methods to ensure the reviewer stays aligned to the mission of the organization and that consistency is applied when assessing proposals.

HX: A Necessary Next Step. HX, or the "human experience," should also be on your radar. This will soon come into focus more in terms of design thinking, with organizations understanding that for all of the advances in technology and for all the effort in automating processes, some folks just crave the human element. It's like the big banks that now run ads to highlight the fact that you will be connected to a real person. We must not lose sight of this. Tech exists to enhance our ability to do great things, not replace them.

Ky Pham from DataHouse Asia sums it up well: "It's not only about finishing your job, it's about how to help others use your deliverable efficiently. This is creating values."

So, when you do your job, make sure you keep in mind the experience of someone who is going to use your outputs:

- When you create the presentation, make sure the audience can see, read, and understand your information easily.

- When you write an email, make sure the receiver can receive your message quickly and clearly.

- When you provide a training, make sure the trainees understand and can perform the task themselves afterward.

"This is why we should always keep HX in mind, to 'satisfy' the other human stakeholders who interact with our outcomes. It's not only about finishing your job, it's about how to help others use your deliverable efficiently." That's what Ky ultimately means about "creating values."

Evaluation Framework. Transparency in evaluation also plays a critical role in the development and continued improvement of organized philanthropy, providing a systematic process of collecting credible data and using it to inform decisions on whether or not funding priorities and those funded projects are advancing the organization's objectives. In this context, a strong evaluation framework can be used to assist funders in understanding the process and to assess the appropriateness and value for money of programs to influence future decision making through a fiscal, impact, and equity lens. A great ROI for the sector would be to include the following:

- **Examples:** Share successful applications each funding cycle to help applicants understand the quality and detail of what is expected. This will help create a much stronger pool of applicants.

- **Data Visualization:** Share the data sourced from applications and reports in a way that is beneficial to the sector and not just how your grants were impactful from a quantitative or ROI perspective.

• **Unfiltered Feedback:** Share examples of both successful and unsuccessful applications. This levels everyone up for future applications and provides priceless feedback on current and future approaches to service delivery.

• **Partnerships:** Is there the potential for expanded or supplementary funding rounds that seek to have applicants partner together if their proposals are similar or have some apparent synergy? Avoiding the competition for resources in favor of bringing our communities together in advancing the common good through novel ideas in solutions and approaches should be something that is cultivated, not overlooked due to rigid, and in many cases, outdated systems.

Ultimately, ensuring that all key stakeholders are involved in this process and are effectively codesigning future improvements will make the grant application process beneficial in some way regardless of the funding outcomes. After all, a grant application should be the beginning of a dynamic new partnership and an opportunity to start conversations about civic solutions, not cull them.

EXPANDING DIGITAL ACCESSIBILITY: THE NEED FOR DISABILITY INCLUSION IN PHILANTHROPY

None of the boards and committees I have served on have been more rewarding than Partnerships With Industry, an organization that has helped more than 12,500 individuals find employment and thrive in stable and safe work environments. Many of the adults assisted by this nonprofit have intellectual or developmental disabilities, and I regularly find myself wondering what has happened to their roles and responsibilities during the pandemic. How many have been affected by organizational shifts to a work-from-home approach? Are their needs being catered to, both from a hardware and software perspective? And that's just looking from a professional perspective in relation to my own. I truly worry about how the livelihoods of these individuals and their families have been affected for the short and long term by this surreal time, especially in a world where people with disabilities account for 12 percent of the US population.

People with disabilities are often the ones who are most underserved and disadvantaged by tech. If we are to stay true to the fact that the internet exists to provide unfettered access to information, then surely all online content, services, and products must garner the same outcomes for people both with and without disability. But the reality is that not everyone receives the same digital experience. According to WebAIM, an organization committed to web accessibility, about 98.1 percent of one million home pages surveyed had at least one Web Content Accessibility Guidelines (WCAG) 2.0 failure, with the average number of errors per home page coming in at 60.9. The most common failures were low-contrast text or empty links, together with missing image text and form input labels.

New tech can be leveraged to advance the common good. But sometimes it's just as important to help folks get back to even, so that their ability to reap the rewards of tech are accelerated from there on in, not exacerbated by it. Philanthropy can do a number of things, including the following, to address these issues and take another step forward toward being more accessible and inclusive for those with disability:

- **Listen:** Engage with the local community about ways to learn more about their needs and how you can support and advocate for their causes more effectively.

- **Fund:** Identify and support innovative programs that can enhance accessibility through technology.

- **Challenge:** Ask all organizations how they intend to address accessibility for clients and partners with disabilities in their grant proposals.

- **Layer:** Add captioning for video presentations and visual indicators in place of audio cues.

- **Focus:** Concentrate on the cognitive, through enhanced UX/UI that presents an uncluttered screen, consistent navigation, and use of plain language over jargon.

- **Review:** A number of free tools exist for you to do a simple review of your current online offerings. Check out the WAVE Web Accessibility Evaluation Tool via WebAIM and the Colour Contrast Analyser from the TPGi, which helps review the legibility of text against the contrast of visual elements. If there are issues, review and update.

- **Highlight:** Global Accessibility Awareness Day exists to get folks talking, thinking, and learning about digital access and inclusion for folks with different disabilities. Supporting this event and having both internal and external programming around it is a great way to raise these issues in an intentional way.

Philanthropy as a whole needs to shift its attitudes and attentions toward disability inclusion across a range of issues and approaches. Getting the tech aspects of that shift correct might play a critical role in speeding up this process toward more inclusive grantmaking and hiring, and exceeding every standard for accessibility.

As a sector, we must do more, especially with critically underfunded support from the government. If you are a funder interested in advancing this work, get involved with the Disability & Philanthropy Forum, which is part of the Presidents' Council on Disability Inclusion in Philanthropy.

Zahirah Mann

The Light on the Hills

When discussing the lens through which she sees the future of philanthropy, Zahirah Mann eloquently paraphrases the actor Tracee Ellis Ross: "There is enough sunshine for everyone." She understands that funding, however limited, can be leveraged to maximize impact and achieve tremendous results. Sunshine serves as the perfect backdrop for Zahirah's work. She's currently leading a strategic initiative at the Ralph M. Parsons Foundation that works with various partners at the local, state, and national levels on issues involving child welfare, and engaging in dynamic collective impact efforts while managing a diverse, responsive grantmaking portfolio that deeply invests in Los Angeles.

With a more than forty-year history, the Ralph M. Parsons Foundation works to improve the well-being of residents in Los Angeles County. Through unrestricted grantmaking in health, human services, education, and civics and culture, it supports organizations that serve vulnerable children and families throughout the more than four thousand square miles that cover the eighty-eight cities and numerous unincorporated areas that make up Los Angeles County.

Drawing on her experiences at United Way of Greater Los Angeles and the Annenberg Foundation, as well as a decade of practice as a public interest attorney addressing systemic issues such as pollution, affordable housing, and public education, Zahirah is uniquely equipped to help foster a healthier and more vibrant community. As community needs change, she adapts her tools; throughout her career she has used law, science, policy, organizing, convening, and now philanthropy.

Zahirah's far-reaching view from her position in philanthropy and her grounding experience in community allows her to understand and lead systems transformation through a range of strategic mechanisms. "We are seeing real shifts in outcomes through collective impact and collaborative efforts," she says. "Together, organizations are able to leverage public and private resources and rethink current systems to achieve better results around big issues like child well-being and homelessness."

Her guiding light is this: "All members of society should have access to the same opportunities and privileges. Whether in the form of racial, economic, or environmental justice—all people should have the same dignified baseline."

One resource that can aid this access is in her own backyard: the glittering Silicon Beach. With more than 10 million people in Los Angeles, Zahirah believes a robust technological infrastructure is one way to make her community more connected, providing opportunity for all.

"The COVID-19 crisis has revealed a disproportionate lack of access to computers, tablets, and reliable internet services," she explains. "These tools are not luxuries, but rather essential resources for communicating, accessing vital information, and fully participating in modern life. Affordable, reliable, high-speed internet access, and the hardware and technological literacy necessary to take advantage of this access, has become necessary for nonprofits to be able to do their work. We see this issue across schools, healthcare systems, and really all areas of life. The door to many rooms is now through a computer screen."

Broadband is transformative. It is changing the way we learn and the way we access essential services. Yet we see the same patterns appearing with basic access. Individuals from underserved neighborhoods are faced with affordability issues, and the government, together with the private sector, prioritizes new infrastructure elsewhere. What Zahirah is effectively saying is that broadband access is also a social justice issue.

If there is one thing Zahirah has learned in her professional career that she would share with emerging leaders in the field, it is that listening is essential to success. "When you listen, pay attention to both what is being said and what is not being said," she says. "Then you can begin to understand someone's real needs. Truly listening takes a number of other skills, such as patience, humility, open-mindedness, and grace, and requires a high degree of social-emotional intelligence, which is the elusive attribute that defines many of our world's greatest leaders. And do not reserve this skill for the few. Listen to everyone, especially the community you are trying to support. Communities know how to solve their own problems. Listen to learn the answers."

We should be listening to these words of wisdom. Zahirah is an absolute star, and I have been truly impressed with her command and understanding of the most critical social issues of our time, especially when called upon to articulate them and their impact in meetings with elected officials both in DC and in the California State Capitol. Her unique sense of poise and purpose stood out to me; when she spoke, you knew it was going to advance the conversation toward a solution when others played around the edges.

This is not a Hollywood overnight success story, either. Zahirah has been putting in years of work and in many ways has been ahead of the curve. Ten years ago, Zahirah cofounded a giving circle focused on investing in projects that support the greater Los Angeles Black community and currently sits on a commission responsible for administering funding to legal service nonprofits throughout the state of California. She was also recently selected to become the next president and CEO at SLATE-Z, a collective impact effort working to revitalize South Los Angeles by moving residents to economic opportunity. SLATE-Z was designated a promise zone under the Obama Administration and has over seventy partners. There is no doubt in my mind that on her current trajectory she will be pulling some very influential and impactful levers of change in the City of Angels in the not-too-distant future, and we should look forward to seeing how this script plays out.

PART THREE

REIMAGINING INSTITUTIONS

CHAPTER NINE

Upsetting the Table

Philanthropy is more predictable, practical, and pragmatic in its approach to change. It's hardly going to advocate for a full revolution or dismantling of the system. But in this current day and age, change is hardly brokered by the timid. New tech and trends aren't going to speed up progress either, especially if we keep the same folks in leadership and celebrate the wins of the status quo.

"We improved the speed of our grantmaking by 20 percent this year," boasts the foundation that hired two new finance staff to help with service delivery.

"We raised $2 million more than we did last year," says the nonprofit that hasn't changed its current programming in three years.

"Congrats to our CEO on being named one of the five hundred most influential figures in the city," exclaims the organization with a fifteen-year CEO who has spent thousands on advertising in business journals for the past five years.

Spin, vanity metrics, and inside baseball have eroded our natural curiosity to challenge current approaches and methods. *Building capacity* is more commonly seen as a fiscal term rather than an investment in the team that does the work. And as we have continually reaffirmed, power dynamics are still rampant in philanthropy and the way we do it.

We are so exhausted that we just accept how it is.

We are so distrustful of politics and systems that we accept that "nothing gets done."

We see large institutions do the same old things (largely without any real scrutiny) because "that's just how they work" and "if it's not broken don't fix it."

What happened to critical thinking? What happened to asking

those stupid questions that leadership encourages us to ask so we can get to the bottom of why things are still the way they are?

Part 3 combines all the major points raised in this book and openly challenges the way we do things by asking, "What if we did it this way instead?" We'll look at the IRS and the US Postal Service and review how nonprofit universities are viable alternatives to private foundations. We'll also see what a national service for volunteering might look like for families looking for relief in the face of rising costs of childcare and education.

Take the discussion about defunding the police as a way to counter police brutality. Looking at this objectively, the theory behind it was an innovative way of thinking about how funding could support policing and safety in a broader yet complementary way, reallocating funds to mental health programs, for example, to support ongoing prevention efforts. With a better narrative, this could have become a quite dynamic national discussion on how to improve both the *protect* and *serve* elements of this important government department.

But this isn't about revolution. It's about an evolution. This isn't about blowing everything up. It's about upsetting the table, changing the cutlery, changing the tablecloth, and serving a different type of wine. Trust me, we will still be talking about the future and our roles in it. We just might be having those conversations with new people and ideating different ways of approaching them.

Some of the new people you will want to invite to the table are Alison Aragon, Erin Barnes, and Seyron Foo, who have been challenging the way philanthropy works and what it stands for, helping build up new leaders, raising funds for new pathways, and fighting for legislative change that helps people's lives, not just their bank accounts. You'll learn more about them and the important work they do in the coming chapters.

SEYRON FOO

Seyron manages the advocacy strategies that advance the Conrad N. Hilton Foundation's programmatic goals on ending chronic homelessness in Los Angeles, supporting transition age youth in foster care, and cultivating successful career pathways to transform the lives of opportunity youth. Previously, Seyron oversaw public policy and government relations at Southern California Grantmakers and Philanthropy California, where he led initiatives that strengthened philanthropy's partnerships with state and local governments. He has experience in various government sectors, including the California Senate Majority Leader's Office and the City of Long Beach. He earned his master's degree in public affairs from Princeton University's School of Public and International Affairs and his bachelor's degree in rhetoric and political science from the University of California, Berkeley.

ALISON ARAGON

Since joining the Play Equity Fund at the LA84 Foundation in 2019 as development associate, Alison has created a donor stewardship plan and a board giving policy and collaborated with Grants and Programs to increase all development functions. She captained the women's golf team at University of California, Santa Cruz, and graduated from the University of San Diego's Master of Arts in Nonprofit Leadership and Management program in 2017 and the Sanford Institute of Philanthropy Fundraising Academy in 2019.

As a first-generation college student, Alison is particularly passionate about access to affordable education and building sustainable social-emotional support systems for youth in Southern California. She has worked at a number of foundations and nonprofits throughout the region, including serving as director of development and communications of the First Tee of San Diego (a role she will be returning to this year), and is currently a member of the Latina Giving Circle and Emerging Practitioners in Philanthropy (EPIP).

ERIN BARNES

As ioby's CEO and cofounder, Erin has led ioby's strategic planning, governance, and fundraising for the last eleven years. Prior to ioby, Erin was an environmental writer with a background in water management. From 2007 to 2008, she was the environmental editor at *Men's Journal* magazine and was a freelance writer on climate change and other environmental issues. From 2003 to 2005, she worked as a community organizer and public information officer at the Save Our Wild Salmon Coalition in Portland, Oregon.

While completing her master of environmental management in water science, economics, and policy at the Yale School of Forestry and Environmental Studies, Erin was a US Department of Education Foreign Language and Area Studies scholar in Portuguese. She did field research on socioeconomic values of water in Goyena, Nicaragua, and the Bolivian and Brazilian Amazon. Her report, "Market Values of the Commercial Fishery on the Madeira River: Calculating the Costs of the Santo Antônio and Jirau Dams to Fishermen in Rondônia, Brasil and Pando-Beni, Bolivia," was published in the *Tropical Resources Institute Journal* in 2007.

Erin also holds a BA in English and American Studies from the University of Virginia. She lives in Brooklyn and serves as board chair of Resource Media. The Rockefeller Foundation awarded Erin and her ioby cofounders Brandon Whitney and Cassie Flynn the 2012 Jane Jacobs Medal for New Technology and Innovation. In April 2018, Erin was selected to join the inaugural class of Obama Fellows.

I may be an empathetic person, but businesses are not people, regardless of legalities to the contrary. So I can't hurt a business's feelings when pushing back on what it does and what it means for our communities. I challenge you to do the same, and to look at the world through its opportunity to be better and do more good, not settle for what is served to us.

Not at this table.

CHAPTER TEN

To Serve and Affect

Hauling Our Government Monoliths into Twenty-First Century Relevance

MORE THAN JUST A TAX DESIGNATION: FIXING
THE ISSUE OF OUR NONPROFIT FACTORY

Face it, everyone in our sector has had this ugly conversation: Are there too many nonprofits?

According to the PNP Staffing Group, the nonprofit sector has grown by more than 20 percent over the past decade. For contrast, the for-profit sector has grown by approximately 2 to 3 percent. Candid also recently released some current key facts on the sector, highlighting that as of December 2019 there are currently 1,729,101 nonprofits registered with the IRS. Most nonprofits are relatively small, with 75 percent having annual revenues of under $100,000.

So is this question one of finances? Or one of service delivery? Of investment or impact?

Saying that we should have fewer nonprofits because of the size of the pie available is an opinion that truly comes from a deficit mindset and uninformed assumptions. You see, 72 percent of revenues come from program services, which highlights a strong demand for services that have obviously become a byproduct of government cuts and under-investment in social services. Also, 18 percent of all nonprofits received a grant from a grantmaker, which indicates from another angle that the majority of nonprofits are indeed needed and most importantly are financially viable, piecing together their budgets from a variety of different sources.

So where's the breakdown? Why do we continue to hang such negativity on the size and scope of nonprofits? It's funny, but what I see is that most of these conversations emanate from urban centers when it's really the smallest states in our union that have the largest per capita of nonprofits for every ten thousand residents. Think Connecticut more than California here.

My take is that the truth has to be found somewhere in the impact of our organizations. But where is the data? What defines impact? Who defines that impact?

This would need a major review and ultimately a resetting of the table, starting with a redefinition of what a nonprofit organization actually is. Because the harshest truth is that it is seen by the IRS as nothing more than a tax designation. However, the harshest truth doesn't necessarily have to mean that this is a depiction of the sector's future.

Nonprofit organizations are the backbone of our society. They are the threads that keep the nation's social fabric together in this most surreal moment in time. And due to their importance to our communities and for our national workforce (being the third largest employer in the country), we would be wise in looking strategically at their future to ensure they remain vibrant and relevant well into the next century.

So what could the next steps possibly be?

A New (or Reconfigured) Federal Department. This could come in the form of a Department for Communities that could finally set a strategic direction for how to develop solutions based on the needs and aspirations of our citizens—neighborhood by neighborhood. The first step would need to be a national review of whatever would fall under this department's purview. This would be a behemoth undertaking. But with a comprehensive and multisector supported approach, we might be able to see the foundations of comprehensive reform that would set our nonprofits up for success rather than setting the majority up for failure, including the following:

- Clearly identifying lanes for organizations, such as identifying and eliminating duplication.

- Establishing new quality standards.

- Creating clear pathways for nonprofits to understand available funding options.

- Identifying which nonprofits should remain, merge, or cease operations (controversy alert!).

- Completely overhauling nonprofit registration.

This is ultimately the crux of my argument and the core of my angst. You know the harsh truth I mentioned earlier? Well, the fact that an organization is registered in a mostly binary fashion, reviewed solely through an application form with no nuance or localized lens, is mind-boggling in this day and age. It's so basic that it was only in January 2020 that prospective nonprofit organizations could submit the 1023 paperwork online. *ONLINE.*

If we are to truly put an end to this question of how many nonprofits are too many, we not only need to reframe it to how many nonprofits are needed, but completely overhaul how the IRS Tax Exempt and Government Entities Division registers a nonprofit.

Now with paperwork being submitted online (and critically the nomination of National Taxonomy of Exempt Entity codes), a fair bit of automation can occur. This will not only decrease human error and speed up the application process but will also provide comprehensive reports based on numerous data sets that will provide a more thorough understanding of a nonprofit's suitability (noting that suitability is very much different from eligibility).

Eligibility should be a baseline for reviews, not the only requirement. Currently, the only prospective organizations whose registrations are rejected have done one or more of the following:

- They sought reinstatement from an initial revocation of status for not filing for three consecutive years.

- They didn't pay the correct registration fee.

- They provided an invalid Employer Identification Number (EIN).

So how can we add more nuance to the process that will ultimately result in a stronger sector?

An Automated Solution. This is a simple process in theory. The IRS has the most comprehensive data set of the nonprofit sector. An appropriate algorithm should be able to digest the information provided by a prospective entity, run it through the system, and identify any of the following:

- Similar organizations already operating in that locale.

- The entity's need based on other data sets such as census reporting.

- Data that highlights alternative revenue ceilings beyond program services.

And the list can go on and on, highlighting the need for established benchmarks for registration and reregistration (which should be automatically processed by tabling your 990s). A multitude of local reports from county governments, chambers of commerce, city councils, community foundations, and other relevant nonprofits and sector associations can also really drill down on the need and demand of a new organization.

Ultimately an IRS officer would need to make a final call. But they would finally be making an informed decision, which would also contribute to rebuilding trust in the sector and in government. (I also recommend that all board members of this prospective organization go through some sort of governance training prior to full acceptance.)

If a prospective organization had been rejected based on these new sets of criteria, a formal response could be provided to the applicant, including details of other local organizations operating in that space and encouraging them to volunteer or support their causes in other ways, ensuring we aren't losing a potential civic asset. If they went to the lengths of creating a nonprofit, then this obvious passion to make a difference in their communities needs to be channeled in a positive way.

(Recommended) Nonprofit Mergers. Building on the multitude of data sets available to government through an application of this nature, another potential benefit might be for the IRS, during its annual reporting, to identify and recommend to organizations potential partners to merge with. Over time, by tracking revenue declines, decreases in budgets and giving, machine learning could identify patterns in what makes a nonprofit close its doors. By identifying these trends in real time, the government may be able to help limit the potential ripple effect that a loss in service, jobs, and personal networks has on a community and its residents. There is also the potential for the government to fund these mergers as a deregulation strategy.

GovTech, a public sector modernization that applies emerging technologies to improve service delivery, is a $400 billion industry. And the way our government operates and services its citizens is something that is in dire need of updating. But getting the basics right—providing a safety net and community support for people to survive and thrive—is essential. We need to acknowledge that this might be better served through our nonprofits at this point, and that they too are in dire need of an update.

CAN PHILANTHROPY SAVE THE UNITED STATES POSTAL SERVICE?

Once social distancing restrictions end, society will return a new "normal." With all of the economic and social upheaval that has followed the coronavirus pandemic, one such normal that has become part of everyone's makeshift routine is collecting the mail.

The USPS delivered the mail come rain or shine during the COVID-19 pandemic. It was deemed an essential service, yet it felt the full brunt of the financial fallout. At one point, the postal service called for an $89 million injection of funding from the federal government or else it risked running out of funds within four months if not propped up accordingly. This only goes to show that its existence isn't guaranteed, despite being enshrined in the Constitution (Article 1, Section 8).

Should the postal service go bankrupt, there would be a number of ramifications for this essential communications channel that provides a public service to the community—and email and its "competitors" would not be able to fix those problems in the short term, if at all.

While there was a groundswell of public support for the government to maintain the USPS through this crisis (even more so than bailouts for airlines and cruise ships that had already received such funding), there was (and still is) also a shared understanding that two prevailing issues are holding the service back. The first was the Postal Accountability and Enhancement Act of 2006, which sought to prefund all of the USPS's projected pension and health benefits through the next seventy-five years (meaning that it put away $5.6 billion per year and was losing $62.4 billion in revenues between 2007 and 2016). The repeal of this act recently passed through the House in a rare bipartisan manner.

The second was that the USPS failed to modernize.

Can You Make a Charitable Gift to the Government? I am truly interested in the modernization of public services and how philanthropy could play a role in catalyzing that change. But before we look at what the future of the USPS might look like by expanding its services to address the most pressing needs in the community, let's answer this question: Can the mechanisms of charitable giving legally be applied to supporting government entities?

The short answer is yes. You can indeed donate right into Uncle Sam's bank account. Way back in 1843, John Spencer, then the treasury secretary, created an account so that "individuals wishing to express their patriotism to the United States" could do so—and still receive the tax deductions that are associated with such gifts. And no, this isn't a well-researched loophole. People actually still give to the government beyond their taxes, in fact donating more than $50 million in the past twenty years. While the majority of these gifts are deemed unrestricted, the statutes of a number of departments allow for restricted gifts that would allow for direct support of expanded services of the USPS.

With that in our back pocket, what services should philanthropy potentially focus on to help the postal service?

Impact and Immediate Advocacy. Firstly, the sector needs to use its collective voice to periodically come out in support of the USPS (including current and possibly future bailouts) using a social sector lens.

Because if the USPS fails in the future there will be huge ramifications for the charitable sector—not only in terms of giving, but also in service delivery and its own support of the sector through food drives, supporting veteran employment (approximately 113,000 or 18 percent of the entire USPS workforce are veterans), and monitoring the well-being of elderly and disabled mail patrons through its Carrier Alert Program.

Postal mail continues to be the most effective way to communicate with current, past, and prospective donors, as well as to receive their donations. All you have to do is look back a few years to when the American Cancer Society paused its direct mail acquisition program. New donors declined 11 percent, and new donor revenue fell by $11.3 million. Over five years, this would have had a projected impact of $29.5 million to the organization. *Imagine what would happen if EVERY nonprofit in the United States was affected by the financial collapse of the USPS. It would be devastating.*

What Kind of Future Does the USPS Have? Postal service reform has also begun to permeate national policy platforms as a response to a perceived need for an extra pillar in our banking sector for those who don't have bank accounts or sufficient accessibility, and as an important response and remedy to egregious payday lending rates. During the 2020 presidential primary season, four candidates from the Democratic Party proposed various options of transforming post offices into financial service centers with the following services:

- small low-cost loans

- payments

- checking and savings accounts to serve the 68 million Americans who don't have bank accounts

- online services

All of the above have numerous pros and cons. Plus, any form of perceived consensus would center on trials for mobile banking options rather than a full rollout of offerings through brick-and-mortar branches (of which there are 31,322).

The majority of concerns focus on loan defaults with high-risk borrowers. So maybe this is where some concerted effort from philanthropy might come into play through impact investing offerings with a loan loss reserve established on the front end to de-risk a possible demonstration project or trial.

If you are not familiar with the term, loan loss reserves are accounting entries banks make to cover estimated losses on loans due to defaults and nonpayment. And through community development financial institutions (CDFIs), there already exist mechanisms for philanthropy to fund financial safety nets, should loans default.

If we adopted some of these approaches we might yield the following benefits sector-wide, highlighted by:

- foundations and investors putting money into unfamiliar markets or products such as postal banking

- philanthropy absorbing the risk of loss and, as a result, helping to convince lenders to reduce interest rates or provide longer loan terms to nonprofit organizations

- strengthening the case to lenders to relax their underwriting criteria in order to lend to individuals or businesses with lower than typical credit profiles

Philanthropy Northwest has a terrific guide on this form of investing, which can be found in this chapter's notes at the end of the book.

So instead of simply privatizing the USPS, it could make both political and policy sense to explore a way to revitalize this service, leveraging a unique physical infrastructure while opening up the funding of such a move to a new type of public-private partnership (PPP) that supports both motivational approaches of financial-first and impact-first investors. A number of other options could be considered, including being a fiscal sponsor for small nonprofits.

Given the current political climate this move would need to be championed at the executive level, meaning that the opportunity for change might come once every four years. It will be interesting to see if the candidates who proposed such measures will be willing to use their political capital to have it become part of a future Democratic

Party platform, especially as the trust in the USPS was eroded given its weaponization (albeit debunked theories) during the 2020 election.

CITY ADVOCATES IN SYNC

Why is it so hard to convene key civic players and organizations to come together authentically and work toward common goals and solutions? Given the number of nonprofits serving our communities, the variety of solutions and programs being initiated across counties and cities to tackle critical needs, and the limited traditional funding sources such as foundations and governments, we have to ask ourselves why there is no centralized local strategy or entity to attract more funding to the social sector in their locales.

Chambers of commerce and regional economic development corporations exist for the benefit of business and growth of the local economy. Yet who out there is fighting for resources to spur innovation, catalyze collaboration, and make our neighborhoods safer, more vibrant, and more prosperous? Community foundations are an obvious place to start, as are United Ways. Even the emerging trend of funders tables, which see collaborative groups formed around specific issues, could bring the sector together in a much more intentional way.

What if small teams existed within a government entity or one of the aforementioned institutions to address this? Their job would be to act as a trusted, impartial convener that would bring together key stakeholders to discuss issues and ideate solutions, help manage these ideas into potential programs, work with the community to assess their potential impact, and then actively seek out funding opportunities on their behalf, whether public, private, or philanthropic.

And why stop there? They could also act as the fiscal sponsor or provide technical assistance where needed, leaving folks on the ground to get the job done and to stay out of the politics.

An example of this approach in action is LA n Sync, which was inspired in part by the Obama administration's Neighborhood Revitalization Initiative and funded by the Annenberg Foundation with the simple mission of maximizing funding that supported strategies to improve the lives of those who resided in Los Angeles County. Over a number of years, a working group grew into an entity that is now housed and funded by the California Community Foundation, bringing in more than $352 million in additional (or found) funding for the region.

By connecting leaders from across a variety of sectors, there lies an opportunity to leverage the talent, resources, and networks of regions in an organized way to support local organizations and ensure the following tasks are moved along in a timely fashion:

- identifying and disseminating information about new funding opportunities

- challenging organizations and service providers to come together to spur new innovations

- proactively attracting and advocating for additional federal and state dollars in a strategic and intentional way

- helping to focus efforts based on consensus-based projects or ones backed by localized research rather than being opportunistic and enabling mission drift for local organizations, or those "in the know"

Creating and funding these positions would see a real return on investment and would be a strong candidate for a dynamic PPP, especially if housed within a mayoral office or innovation department. At the end of the day, if anything should be in sync, it's how we support our frontline nonprofits that are doing much of the heavy triage for the most vulnerable in our communities.

LET'S TALK NATIONAL SERVICE: A "VOLUNTEER BANK" THAT GIVES TO YOU WHEN YOU GIVE BACK

In his proclamation of the 2020 National Volunteer Week, President Donald Trump made some pertinent points regarding the need, impact, and necessity of volunteerism for the country:

- "Civic engagement and volunteer service strengthens the fabric of our Nation and reflects the true heart, spirit, and goodness of America."

• "Our national character is measured by the unity, compassion, and initiative shown by Americans who help others."

• "When friends, neighbors, and strangers unite for a common cause, it demonstrates that we have the power to change lives and improve our world."

Look, these are fantastic ideals that we should strive for. But there's a reason the moniker "the divided states of America" has received so much traction over the past few years, and this is without the complex layers of partisanship and tribalism being applied to it—much of which the forty-fifth president of the United States exploited. But I digress.

The fact is that the quotes attributed to President Trump are largely the standard we wish to see for civic participation regardless of politics. And with all things considered, it should be our post-isolation hope that more people understand, care about, and care for our community. We need a concerted approach to unifying our nation, one that seeks to include those with a just as serious, albeit quieter, loyalty as those who fly the flag or amplify the Pledge of Allegiance: a foundational patriotism rather than a symbolic one, and one where pride is part of our fabric as much as it is espoused in our actions. This can come from a new national service, one that shifts away from the AmeriCorps model and focuses on lifting up parts of the economy.

Pete Buttigieg, the former mayor of South Bend, Indiana, got the most traction for such a plan during his 2020 presidential campaign. He proposed an expansion of AmeriCorps that would include both a Climate Corps and Community Health Corps geared toward younger Americans. His approach was naturally influenced by his military service and municipal success with the Cities of Service program for which South Bend received $25,000 in 2018. Other candidates who leaned toward a service approach as a tool to generationally reconnect and reinvigorate our neighborhoods were Senators Kirsten Gillibrand and Elizabeth Warren and Representatives John Delaney and Seth Moulton. (Oh, and for the record—and for contrast—President Trump consistently proposed to shut down the federal agency that leads volunteering programs, that being the Peace Corps, which was established in 1961 by President John F. Kennedy.)

Regardless of the pros and cons for corps programs, the reason a new national service has not been part of a broader national dialogue beyond being a minor plank in a presidential candidate's platform is that it can't work if it's not transactional. An unpopular opinion you may say, especially given that 77 million adults volunteered in 2018. However, what if we set the bar at a level that was revered the world over and designed to lift up significant parts of our community that were struggling too?

Firstly, you would need to set the table. The good thing here is that there is a universal indicator of which to build some parameters for the sake of constructive ideation. Independent Sector, a national membership organization that represents the broader charitable sector, has calculated that the value of a volunteer hour is $25.43.

Now, say that the government provided a monetary threshold or equivalent that would translate into a mutual benefit for both the volunteer and the organizations they volunteered for. For guesstimate's sake let's say that it is capped at $5,000 per year. That number, divided by volunteer value per hour, equates to $196.62. Divide this figure by eight to reflect each "working day," and that would come in around 24.5 days or, in the simplest terms, volunteering one day every two weeks for twelve months.

This may seem like a steep time commitment for working families and possibly an issue in terms of accessibility. But if the incentives are attractive enough, then so could be the benefits to our society.

What possibilities might we explore?

- **Education:** Instead of full student loan forgiveness, a more pragmatic approach (that could receive bipartisan support) in reducing crippling student debt would be to apply this $5,000 to current or future student loans (perhaps also being applied as a match to 529 accounts).

- **Cash:** Let's make sure that options are afforded to those whom an extra $5,000 would make a tremendous difference. These funds would only be made available to those who sit under the poverty line (or other similar eligibility thresholds) as a straight cash payment. They would also help us tackle one of the most abhorrent issues of a first-world country: the fact that 34 million Americans—including 10.5 million children or 14 percent of the population under eighteen—live in poverty.

- **Childcare:** According to a report in The Atlantic, the current average cost of childcare is $16,000 per child per year, which in some states is more than tuition at a flagship university. In most cases, this would be the second-highest expense for young families after rent. Most people have their children at the midpoint of their careers, so debt-to-income ratios are tighter, and any extra dollars flowing into the household budget could make a huge difference for a number of quality-of-life indicators.

- **Business:** The corporate sector might think of matching these proposed donations via enhanced employee benefits that complement their ongoing corporate social responsibility (CSR) work. This could either copy the traditional approaches of a one-to-one dollar match up to a certain level or opening up new leave options where extra days of service leave are applied to current entitlements. For example, an employee could be granted two days extra leave to volunteer or participate in a board meeting or significant event, with their employer being covered for benefits owed through this volunteer credit.

- **Participatory Budgeting:** Funds could be pooled for the neighborhoods where volunteers reside to be used each year to fund public spending decisions, projects, and improvements. This would also create an engaged and cohesive community that would identify, discuss, and decide where funds are spent in collaboration with their local officials and help repair and build trust in democracy and government.

- **Donation:** When volunteering, most folks naturally gravitate toward organizations they are passionate about. Therefore, an obvious candidate of your accrued volunteer credits would be the organization where you accrued those volunteer hours. Organized philanthropy can also join the party by offering matching gifts to truly leverage impact in its communities.

- **Impact Investments:** Charitable bank accounts could be a potential vehicle for accrued national service credits or funds. This could be in the form of a donor-advised fund (DAF) at a local community foundation or United Way, or alternatively through an online impact portfolio where their funds could be directed to social good projects that could generate a measurable impact with a reinvestable financial return. Doing so would tackle big issues such as reincarceration and preventative healthcare and help create savings in government budgets to be distributed to other areas of need.

The options are endless and should go some way in lessening the burden on government and social sector budgets, while tackling social mobility by giving folks an option to lessen debt, housing stress, and other critical issues that form the base levels of Maslow's hierarchy of needs. It would no doubt also lead to record levels of giving, stronger governance of our nonprofits by attracting more talent to serve on boards and committees, and ultimately what we would all expect from a commitment to an audacious national service such as this: better civil discourse, higher levels of civic participation, and the beginnings of a new, exciting chapter of citizenry of which we can all be proud and feel a part.

SEYRON FOO

Progressively Activating the Levers of Political and Philanthropic Change

Philanthropy plays two critical functions in advocacy and public policy. The first is as a funder of organizations that are proximate to the solutions that affect our communities. In an ecosystem where different special interests have strong representation in city halls, state legislatures, and Congress—among other venues of public policymaking—philanthropy is a crucial partner to organizations that may not have the capacity for advocacy. Funding organizations where solutions are sourced from communities most affected by the issues being advocated for is crucial to advancing public policy.

Secondly, philanthropy has a powerful role in using its voice—strategically deployed and in close coordination with advocates—to open doors, spur innovation, and capture attention. As a part of the civic infrastructure that underpins the fabric of (a frayed) civil society, philanthropy's voice on different public policy issues has the potential to shape the narrative amid increasing noise.

Seyron Foo is someone who is not only breaking through that noise but also creating his own in the process. As an immigrant from Southeast Asia, he is the product of interventionalists and changemakers who saw his penchant and passion for community at an early age. "I'm inspired by my community—and our communities demand it, rightfully so—to make the world a better place," he says.

Seyron isn't another young leader looking through the rose-colored glasses of change. He is dynamic, driven, and engaging, someone who proactively leans into some of the most pressing issues of our generation and strategically goes about piecing together all the key actors, tools, and funding needed to effect informed and intentional change.

163

He understands the need to not only fix the issue on the frontlines but also build a sustainable policy solution around it to ensure that people are protected—and not neglected—as a result of populist approaches and political cycles.

As the vice president of public policy and government relations at Southern California Grantmakers and weaving together the collaborative efforts of the Philanthropy California alliance, Seyron understood the power of connecting grantmakers and public officials in order to strengthen communities and advance local, statewide, and national policy goals. He currently manages the advocacy strategies that advance the Conrad N. Hilton Foundation's programmatic goals on ending chronic homelessness in Los Angeles, supporting transition-age youth in foster care, and cultivating successful career pathways to transform the lives of opportunity youth. He also has experience in various government sectors, including the California senate majority leader's office and the city of Long Beach, which supports the theory that public service of this nature serves as a dynamic baseline for excelling in a career in philanthropy.

"In terms of understanding public policy and systems change, I've found my experience in the legislature essential to navigating through philanthropy's engagement with government," Seyron says. "By knowing how things work in a legislative or agency setting and how decisions are made, you are able to understand the external pressures that policymakers experience, and can plan accordingly when building a case for support."

And while legislative change is where the big dollars and solutions are derived from, Seyron is also attuned to the opportunity for a new social compact to be established through technology and, with it, a potential reaffirmation of our communities' core inclusive values. "We need to be harnessing the incredible energy being generated from civil rights movements such as Black Lives Matter to make sustained change in our communities," he said. "I continue to be inspired by our next generation who are not only mobilizing their communities but also rolling up their sleeves to make change and headway on all fronts, from immigration to environmental justice, trans rights to criminal justice reform."

There's so much we can learn from each other, particularly when we think through how civic engagement may look different and how that civic engagement will affect our civic institutions. Take social media, for example. "Social media has facilitated giving tied to specific stories, and that can grow an organization's budget overnight," Seyron explains. "As the national outcry over the family separation of children and families at the US-Mexico border reached a crescendo, RAICES: The Refugee and Immigrant Center for Education and Legal Services went viral, raising $20 million, nearly tripling their annual operating revenue of $7 million through a Facebook fundraiser. It has also accelerated giving to bail funds across the country in support of social justice advocates who may have been arrested partaking in peaceful civil disobedience. These platforms move dollars quickly and swiftly and can dramatically change the budgets of an organization."

So what's the role of institutional philanthropy in these moments? And what role should it play in advancing equity and opportunity? Seyron, unsurprisingly, is bold and unabashed in his assessment: "Fund organizations led by Black, Indigenous, and people of color (BIPOC). As Echoing Green and Bridgespan studied in their May 2020 report, 'revenues of the Black-led organizations are 24 percent smaller than the revenues of their white-led counterparts, and the unrestricted net assets of the Black-led organizations are 76 percent smaller than their white-led counterparts.' So let's ask ourselves—what are some of our practices in our organization that feed into these barriers to entry?"

It's this self-reflection and personal accountability that ensures Seyron is not only an authentic voice but an effective one too, leaning in to what he sees as a civic duty to lead as a connector, bonding us together from different walks of life to be a force of good. So let's not forget to ground ourselves in the personal work that really sustains the professional piece, and create space for our own reflection to do this work. Like Seyron, we need to be in it for the long haul, because change, as we know, is not an overnight phenomenon.

CHAPTER ELEVEN

Community Building through the Virtues of Infrastructure and Institutions

PHYSIOLOGICAL NEEDS NEED NOT BE A DREAM: LEVERAGING CAPITAL AGAINST THE ODDS

It is said that home ownership is one of the defining traits of achieving the American Dream, with the median net worth of homeowners eighty times larger than renters as per the US Census Bureau. So why is philanthropy not playing a more active role in the fight against poverty and justice by focusing more on housing? Why are socially responsible and conscious investors not being offered a variety of social impact bond opportunities by the government, for example? And why are zip codes still a prevailing indicator in determining one's life outcomes?

Maslow's hierarchy of needs clearly states that the basics of safety and physiological needs are mainly supported by having a roof over our heads. So tackling these issues at the root cause would be a good strategy at the very least—don't you agree? Think of how many housing units you could purchase with the $425 billion-plus of charitable gifts that are made each year.

While this is a very basic Pollyanna generalization of the issue, why is it that we don't bat an eyelid when property developers buy up significant parcels of land, creating master-planned communities based on amenities and aesthetics, yet only in areas that make financial sense for them? Why do we reelect folks who get kickbacks from these developers in return for a more friendly regulatory environment and who give exceptions on projects that require a certain percentage of affordable housing or paying for additional neighborhood improvements as a result of their developments?

166

What is stopping philanthropists or impact investors from buying the land? We have a whole range of options, including a variety of different trust options that could help address the issues of homelessness, gentrification, and cultural significance.

Racial discrimination and residential segregation extend deep into the history of the United States. Slavery and segregation policies across all tiers of government (such as redlining) have had generational effects on poverty, education, and opportunity for Black Americans. The legacies of these housing policies are not accidental, and the ramifications persist with wealth gaps growing to record highs between white and Black Americans. The dream of home ownership is out of reach for so many despite concerted efforts to change this, such as the 1968 Fair Housing Act, the 1974 Equal Credit Opportunity Act, and the 1997 Community Reinvestment Act.

There has never been a better time for philanthropy to enter this market. The sector can help repair a number of current and historical injustices by supporting a regenerative process for our communities, ensuring equity and inclusiveness are a defining part of their funding strategies. This can be achieved in part by a number of financing options existing to leverage new community infrastructure and investment such as:

- **Promise Zones:** Areas of high poverty where the federal government partners with local leaders to increase economic activity, improve educational opportunity, and leverage private investment among other community-identified priorities.

- **Opportunity Zones:** Areas designed to spur growth in designated census tracts through the reinvestment of capital gains into Qualified Opportunity Funds.

- **New Markets Tax Credits:** A mechanism to attract private investment in distressed communities with the goal of incentivizing community development and economic growth.

I have worked with organizations whose work preceded some of these government programs and taken advantage of others, sharing stirring examples of lessons learned and what could be achieved in both instances. The beauty of this example is that it serendipitously inter-sected a specific point of time in both my personal life and professional career.

In 1988, the Jacobs Family Foundation, a traditional grantmaker, became frustrated with the fact that their dollars were only resulting in incremental progress and not the big transformative change they imagined. The family saw that being a place-based funder was the best approach to making a difference. So, they identified and purchased a long-neglected twenty-acre lot in the Diamond Neighborhoods of southeastern San Diego, with the goal of having its residents own the future community assets and become financially sustainable and then having local leaders continue this momentum long after the land was transferred to public ownership thirty years later.

The strategy and community engagement components of this au-dacious project (which were pivotal to its eventual success) fell at the hands of the Jacobs Center for Neighborhood Innovation (JCNI). Part philanthropic steward and part program manager, JCNI was charged with developing the project's newly expanded sixty-acre parcel into a vibrant and economically sustainable destination. They had some big wins right out of the gate. Their successful community development initial public offering (IPO) for Market Creek Plaza, a commercial and cultural center, was the first project of its kind in the US and saw the community invest $500,000 for 20 percent ownership and a further 20 percent owned by the resident-led Neighborhood Unity Foundation.

With all the talk of food deserts in today's philanthropy, it's good to see Market Creek Plaza be the catalyst for the first major grocery store introduced to the area in thirty years and the community's first sit-down restaurants.

This project was ultimately tackling disparities on a multi-generational level.

There were also a number of missteps within the first fifteen years of this project. It's what you might expect in hindsight given how large the undertaking was, but it was synonymous with the dangers of having a large corpus. Basically, JCNI spent more time working within the community, rather than building up the community, still reveling in the establishment of the plaza and ultimately creating a bubble around it. After a period where business and nonprofit turnover increased, almost 100 percent of JCNI's staff were let go to ensure a realignment of goals, an infusion of new leadership, and an accelerated timeline that could still fulfill the Jacobs family's vision and meet the community's expectations before the area was turned back over to the city. There was a real tension in the community around the status of this master plan, and the press was searching for answers.

In 2012, JCNI and Jacobs Family Foundation turned to Reginald Jones to turn it all around. Jones previously led the Steans Family Foundation in Chicago, which had a similar revitalization commitment to the community of North Lawndale in the city's west. After Jones came on board, the community finally got to see what the end game would look like through the Town Center Master Plan, which provides extensive details of how the remaining thirty-seven acres (of sixty) would be transformed to increase jobs, housing, and access to educational and recreational opportunities.

When this master plan was announced, a decade-long dream was also realized for Access Youth Academy, the urban squash and educational program I previously worked for. Access was led by a terrific leadership team that understood what it took to dream big, and then put in the work to get there, no matter what it took. They were like the Rocky of nonprofits, an organization that punched way above its weight and wouldn't give up in the chase of its dreams. And that dream was a new state-of-the-art educational and squash facility, where it could ultimately scale its program to serve hundreds of local families.

But like Rocky, Access had to overcome a few—actually, several— hurdles to get there. It was originally due to have a new facility built on the grounds of a high school in City Heights, a similar community to the one the Jacobs Family identified. Coincidentally, this facility was similarly supported by huge philanthropic investments from Price Philanthropies and the California Endowment and was to be built using funding from the Proposition Z school bond and $2 million in innovation grants through the California Endowment and the Alliance Healthcare Foundation. The project was close to being ratified by the

San Diego Unified School District, only to be shelved due to a change in leadership at the school.

After this initial heartbreak, Price Philanthropies stepped up with the prospect of Access acquiring space in land adjacent to the newly built Copley-Price Family YMCA. The success of the Y, however, was to the detriment of the Access project, with Price deciding that an expansion of the Y was a safer bet for the future of that parcel.

To top it all off, Access then lost a significant chunk of one of the $1 million grants due to the time that had passed between that award and the difficulty in realizing contractual deliverables that would trigger each additional phase of payments. The project was now staring at a potential TKO.

Access needed a new approach, a potential resetting in its way of thinking, a way to exercise the ghosts of plans past. Since I believed (and still do) in the power of symbolism to help mobilize individuals, I sought to do something to get our leadership out of their funk.

First, there was a big acrylic scale model of the proposed facility that took pride of place in our offices and was featured on all of our promotional materials. There was no better focus for this organizational exorcism, and it just had to go. Our executive director loaded it into the back of his car, and we haven't seen it since (and I hope that any curse left with it).

For the next few months it was widely acknowledged that we would not be able to fund the facility from philanthropic dollars, especially since two of the region's biggest funders were already committed to supporting the project and urban squash was a hard sell given the amount of cringeworthy jokes that accompanied opening discussions with new prospects around the differences between the vegetable and the sport. It was agreed that a loan or even long-term rental were alternative options, with the potential location of the facility being expanded from just that of City Heights.

With that last decision, I suggested the alternative of the Diamond Neighborhoods, given my understanding of the area and the goals of the Jacobs family from my previous role at the San Diego Foundation. I reached out to one of JCNI's leadership (who coincidentally sat on the Center for Civic Engagement's advisory body during my time there) and brokered a meeting. Long story short, there was a perfect match between their plans and our offerings, a mutual need that complemented both of our goals, and the fact that we could pay for the land outright, then and there, sealed the deal and saw our inclusion in the master plan fast-tracked.

This was definitely a Rocky 2 victory and not a gut-wrenchingly close Rocky 1, 3, or 6 outcome.

With the donor base of Access, there was no way it was going to run a capital campaign that was fueled primarily by donations. The math just didn't add up. So they scoured the sector for blended funding mechanisms that could help the organization reach the $12 million that was needed to build this forty-thousand-square-foot piece of civic infrastructure. The Access board was comfortable with taking on a loan as one part of the equation, and with it the ability to unlock New Markets Tax Credits, which are effectively incentives for low-income community investments. This turned into a leveraged loan (with favorable terms) in partnership with Civic San Diego, a city-owned nonprofit that describes itself as the entrepreneurial development partner for targeted urban neighborhoods in San Diego.

Access was also the beneficiary of luck and timing. Its shift to southeast San Diego meant it was now situated in a federal Promise Zone. Civic San Diego was struggling to find eligible projects at that time, so it supported this project even though the financing package was far from being realized. And shortly after the funding package was ratified, Civic San Diego saw its power to oversee projects such as these stripped as a result of a court settlement.

But sometimes you make your own luck. And sometimes you have to fight against adversity to forge your own future, very much like the kids that this program supports.

Access has since broken ground on its facility, and I can't wait to see it once it opens. This story can no doubt be a blueprint for other nonprofits looking at innovative ways to scale their offerings, create new revenue streams, and build a permanent home that those they serve can then depend on with a degree of certainty.

The Town Center Master Plan really does embody a cradle-to-career approach. But this wasn't just a bet on a few students to break the cycle. This was more than that. To paraphrase Reginald Jones during a "lunch and learn" he hosted for EPIP members: "We aren't looking at low-income housing for this project, we are looking to build affordable housing so our residents can begin building wealth."

Talk about speaking truth to power. While I understand the need for low-income housing, rent control, density, and similar policies, I never understood why these were pushed as the primary solutions to the housing crisis. Yes, they are part of the solution, but they're not the biggest issue in terms of intersectionality.

I truly hope that JCNI succeeds in its mission, and that the failure to launch in the earlier stages of the project do not hinder the progress and potential impact this philanthropic project may have generationally for thousands of people and their families. Because Reginald is on to something.

Just last year, nineteen families purchased nearly ninety-seven acres of land in Wilkinson County, Georgia, with the aim of creating a safe and supportive city for Black people. At the end of the day, everyone deserves at a bare minimum the ability to feel socially and economically protected, respected, and connected.

Something else that should be considered and nationally debated is the establishment of government-secured, zero-down, zero-interest home loans for Black Americans and others who have been directly affected by racially and politically charged housing policies. This would catalyze new generational wealth and social mobility for currently and historically disenfranchised pillars of our communities. It would also allow folks to climb Maslow's pyramid, as mentioned earlier, engaging more in civic life and seeing more representation and funding as a result of leaning in to things like the census, boards and commissions, and the simple yet powerful act of just showing up.

It's amazing what can be achieved when you don't have to worry about having a roof over your head, whether you are a resident or a non-profit. So let's be more bold like the Jacobs family, more innovative like

Access Youth Academy, and more genuine in our rhetoric to improve the lives of our neighbors.

And guess where we can start? Our country's historical and ongoing housing injustices, since they need to be corrected. If we fix them, the families who have been affected by these policies can begin to heal, grow, and thrive. Now that's the American Dream I know and believe in, and one that should be supported in perpetuity.

NONPROFIT PRIVATE UNIVERSITIES: A PHILANTHROPIC VEHICLE TO DRIVE POLICY, PROJECTS AND PRODUCTS?

For twenty years now, the *Chronicle of Philanthropy* has released its top-fifty philanthropy rankings, which were most recently topped by Michael Bloomberg, who gave $3.3 billion through Bloomberg Philanthropies. Bloomberg has followed much the same approach to charitable giving as other uber philanthropists of the past decade by forming large endowed foundations with a technocratic approach to change. By hiring subject matter experts to lead programs and surrounding them with grant officers, marketing teams, lawyers, and finance staff and forming the best teams money can assemble, this approach is built to deliver real, tangible impact for the issues that most matter to their founders or to tackle large-scale humanitarian efforts to the extent that some governments couldn't dream of achieving because of red tape and short-term populist policies.

However, when you look down that list to number eight and see T. Denny Sanford, the founder of First Premier Bank (who donated more than half a billion dollars in 2019), you'll find that outlier that always seems to break the mold. It's not because of the audacity of his endeavors but because of one of the vehicles with which he chose to deliver his legacy project: National University in San Diego, a private nonprofit university Sanford has given close to half a billion dollars to over the past five years to support the adoption of social emotional learning (SEL) in schools, supporting teacher excellence and inspirational learning from kindergarten through sixth grade, and the elevation of fundraising skills throughout the nonprofit sector.

Sanford Harmony (its flagship SEL program) has already reached eleven million students in all fifty states and across twenty countries and with over sixteen thousand school partners. The curriculum, training, and materials are all provided free of charge and have been adopted by the ten largest districts in the country, including the New York City Department of Education, Los Angeles Unified School District, and Chicago Public Schools. It's no surprise that SEL is now being discussed in Congress as an integral part of a whole-child approach to child development in our schools, championed by former presidential candidates such as Congressman Tim Ryan (who has proposed a bill in the house) and New York City mayor Bill de Blasio. In fact, when signing a memorandum of understanding (MOU) with Sanford Harmony to bring SEL to New York City schools, Mayor de Blasio said, "We couldn't go to the next level without really doubling down on social emotional learning and we have an opportunity to get it right here in the nation's largest city."

But why this time-consuming, expensive approach? Couldn't the donor have just hired a number of high-priced lobbyists to advance this cause? Of course he could have. But those who are successful in business tend to take a business approach to new products, testing it in the market with an initial gift, doubling down on it a few years later with a further $100 million investment, and culminating in another $350 million gift that would see the university tie all these things together with new courses in SEL among other essential offerings, such as nursing and education at heavily subsidized costs.

These programs were an evolution of sorts. After funding the creation of the program's initial curriculum through Arizona State University, Sanford needed a dynamic platform that could scale at a rapid pace, yet be nimble enough to develop the high-profile partnerships needed to elevate it to be regarded as one of the best SEL programs in the market. The forty-year-old, veteran-founded National University and its other affiliates were the perfect fit. Headed up by skilled leader Chancellor Michael Cunningham (who himself had a background in marketing and sales), and with a near eighty-strong marketing team dubbed "the Agency" at its disposal, National University would ultimately house Sanford Harmony, Sanford Inspire, and the Sanford Institute of Philanthropy, choosing to staff the project with former superintendents and talented salespeople from publishers and tech providers in the education space.

So is this a shrewd investment? Firstly, the return on investment on this approach has been almost immediate without having to build the infrastructure a business of this size and scale would require. Secondly, the funding to a nonprofit university is in fact leveraging one of the most underrated educational resources in our community. Let's not forget, too, that almost 30 percent of all US students (3.4 million full-time equivalent students) go through one of the 1,687 private nonprofits operating in this country. And according to the Brookings Institute, they are not only contributing to the nation's educational attainment but also its economic mobility.

Putting aside Ivy League and other top-tier universities that make up the majority of this tertiary category, it's the smaller systems that are leading the charge in the adoption of online course offerings and enabling structural flexibility and inclusion through affordable courses, one-month units (catering to full-time workers, parents, and transitioning veterans), and corporate personalization of courses as a workforce development option. Given the needs of high-tech companies, start-ups, and other skilled contract work, higher education is fast becoming more focused on credentialing to keep up with sector demand.

Beyond the immediate success, reach, and branding of the Sanford Education Programs, the smallest of the three should be of most interest to you. The Sanford Institute of Philanthropy, or SIP as it is more affectionately known, has taken a serious look at how to increase the effectiveness of our nonprofit sector by simply teaching the skills needed to bring in more funding. More funding, more capacity as the theory goes.

SIP was added to the program's portfolio due to Sanford's ongoing experiences with nonprofits nationwide. You can imagine a billionaire receiving plenty of asks and finding a lack of substance to these funding requests. That's why he championed a new "cause selling" method—which has spawned a textbook and professional development course—as a way of attracting more money to the charitable sector as a percentage of GDP.

The substance Sanford sought was in the ask, the story, and the ensuing partnership toward change. That's why cause selling at its core is a relationship-centered, collaborative approach to professional fundraising. According to its website, "It is a model for fundraising that integrates valuable systems from the for-profit realm, with an intense focus on building long-term connections that benefit both the donor and the organization."

SIP's underlying goals, therefore, are in adding value to the philanthropic community by strengthening our frontline fundraisers. And that can't come soon enough, given that they continue to be treated as the professional underclass of our social sector.

That was a big call, hence the need for a new paragraph. Fundraising has never been seen as a real career path, caught in the gray area between program delivery and the extreme pressures of meeting budget, and rarely given sector-wide investment beyond credentialing and a travel or conference budget. But while SIP's methods don't exactly break the mold here, there are plans underway for significant investment in eLearning through LinkedIn, together with partnerships with large nonprofit organizations (such as AFP and Candid) and universities (NOVA Southeastern University, Long Island University and Maricopa Community Colleges, for example), with the latter perhaps opening the door for future undergraduate and graduate degrees.

According to a study by author Penelope Burk, the average fundraiser stays at his or her job for sixteen months before assuming another position. Replacing these professionals doesn't come cheaply, averaging around $127,650 in direct and indirect costs. This needs to change and can only do so with a deeper level of professionalism that can change the narrative of "I got into this line of work by accident" that accompanies any published Q&A with a development professional ever. Ultimately, a master's in fundraising that isn't just a component of an MPA or master's in nonprofit management should be something that our national associations should push for.

So are nonprofit private universities becoming a breeding ground for philanthropists and their legacy projects? It's possible, but many will be watching the future success and impact of this donor's unique approach come 2023, when the current funding agreement concludes, to see whether there is indeed any systemic ROI beyond just reach and teach metrics.

Looking ahead to that end date, let's take a quick look at what might determine whether this project was a success:

- **Expectations:** Did the Sanford Education Programs create lasting change in the way they were intended to (e.g., improved relationships between individuals)?

- **Return on Investment:** Did SIP and the concept of cause selling make a telling impact in nonprofit development?

- **Education:** Did Sanford Education Programs help expand SEL in a substantive way that led to its adoption in curriculums nationwide?

- **Research:** Did the partnerships established by Sanford Education Programs yield substantive research around SEL that informed and guided changes in the educational approaches to SEL?

- **Further Education:** Did National University use the opportunity presented to create a strong educational pipeline to its SEL majors programs?

- **Philanthropic Blueprint:** Was outsourcing this legacy work a more effective way of moving the needle in SEL, rather than tackling the whole-of-child issue in perpetuity?

There are many ways this audacious project could play out, as there were many ways the program could have been set up. Ultimately the win for all involved might be to sell the programs and, with the funds from such a move, coming back to further grow National University and make higher education more accessible to students with ensuing lower fees (mimicking the features of a charitable remainder trust).

Then again, a lot could happen in four years. Changes in leadership and the potential to create an unsustainable model in relation to its rapid growth—fueled by the contractual obligations related to product deliverables in the early stages of scale—are all potential minefields for the program. And that's not taking into account how you "close down" or "end" a program with (on current trends) close to twenty thousand partners, a staff of more than fifty, and one of the best potential pipelines for future revenue the university has outside of its current offerings. Let's also not forget the fact that they have just one donor who ultimately calls the shots.

I'm excited to continue watching how this unique project evolves, as are sector-wide commentators. Could it spur federal funding to support SEL? Could it inspire other philanthropists to donate to National University to leverage more impact? Or could it simply fizzle out and serve as a warning to those questioning traditional approaches that there are only a few viable options available to them to tackle real systems change?

At the end of the day, this approach has to be applauded. It's innovative and goes against the traditional wisdom and models of how big philanthropy is done, and that's how progress is achieved. It makes sense from a business standpoint where a lot of market research, testing, and the ability to pivot are staples of proving your product or vision in the marketplace.

Social emotional learning is an important step to a whole-child approach in education. It also comes at a time when we need it the most, when our civil discourse and trust in our institutions are at all-time lows. The gift that fueled this program was definitely motivated by legacy, understanding that someone's success can help lay a path for millions more. The Sanford Education Programs are a reflection of that vision, and history will ultimately tell if it was a pivotal moment for philanthropy and how it partners with academia.

GETTING IN THE GAME: PROFESSIONAL SPORTS TEAMS AS PHILANTHROPIC ANCHOR INSTITUTIONS

What if a community foundation had tens of thousands of vocal residents volunteering their time every two weeks or so to show their support for their local community representatives? Well, this is a regular occurrence for professional sports teams, and they would do well to realize and leverage this support—coupled with their leadership and influence in their geographical market—to drive a much deeper level of local involvement than simple baseline CSR initiatives that tick the traditional boxes of complementary practices that lift up their core business.

Professional sports teams have long supported their communities. They inspire involvement, drive organizational initiatives in health and accessibility, give back to the grassroots by funding local sporting infrastructure through grants programs, and help leverage extra funds through signed memorabilia and free tickets. But is this enough? Should the next decade see pro sports teams take a more transformational approach to their community engagement? What are the legacies major league owners want to leave behind? And could they use their status and goodwill as a catalyst for the change we desperately need to see in our communities?

Organizations have traditionally been loath to get involved in the politics of the cities they represent. Yet we are starting to see a new generation of owners begin to put their philanthropic dollars and CSR initiatives behind programs that intentionally tackle local systemic issues such as homelessness, access to healthcare, and inclusion. This isn't because of a new strategic plan but because the owners know it's the right thing to do. They understand their team's influence, and they want to make their regions even better places to live. They rightfully see this as their obligation rather than an optional add-on.

So can major league sporting teams (and the thousands of minor league and semi-pro teams that form part of each sports pyramid) become the new beacons of community change? In short, yes. They remain the more positive elements of a city's civic infrastructure, and if we overlook certain shortfalls in the franchise model (teams being able to move cities for example), they can ultimately be more dynamic than other anchor institutions such as community foundations and local United Ways, attracting a much more diverse membership and being much more accessible in the process.

There are a number of innovative new steps that professional and semi-professional sports teams can take if they wish to play a genuine leadership role in their community.

The key here would be to adopt philanthropic and tech trends that can raise awareness, increase impact, and build an authentic relationship with the community in a way that speaks to them both on and off the field.

To bring these options to life, let's use a hypothetical test case with the new Major League Soccer (MLS) franchise Austin FC, which will join the league for the start of the 2021 season. There are four main reasons for this:

1. **Focus:** They will become the first—and only—professional sports team in this major metropolitan city.

2. **Scale:** Austin has a number of internationally renowned annual events, such as Austin City Limits music festival, the Formula 1 United States Grand Prix, and SXSW.

3. **Influence:** It has prominent A-list celebrities on its ownership group.

4. **Alignment:** It understands the importance of local philanthropic endeavors by already announcing the formation of the 4ATX Foundation, a significant level of initial gifts, and a number of funded partnerships with local charities, currently totaling up to $6 million.

(Full disclosure: When I began writing this book I lived in San Diego. Yet due to a number of unplanned circumstances, my family and I ended up in Austin, Texas. Since then I have joined one of Austin FC's supporter groups and purchased season tickets for its inaugural season. My exposure to the team in this way has only served to enhance and reaffirm my initial thoughts on professional sports and its philanthropic endeavors.)

So what might we see from pro sports organizations in the future?

Membership in Perpetuity. Rather than creating more perks and cheap memorabilia to make membership packages more attractive, a percentage of membership fees could be going toward an endowment that will ultimately drive deeper connections with fans and their families over the long term. Funds yielded from each year of this compounding principal can help bolster community investments or cover the operations of the foundation to ensure that this is always a club focus and it isn't absorbed into marketing or external relations. With the right blend of exclusive events that have a charitable focus, this will help keep fans coming back regardless of how the team is doing on the field that season and can play a role in building lifelong supporters across generations.

Donor-Advised Funds (DAF) for Players. With players transferring in and out of professional sports teams and the expenses (and paperwork) involved in setting up a private foundation, a mechanism for more personalized and impactful charitable giving could be established if the charitable arm of the organization is established as a 501(c)(3) and not just a CSR initiative. The club could handle the accounts and provide a great vehicle for players who want to give back more than just participating in scheduled team events and appearances. A great example of this approach can be seen through the charitable work of former San Diego Padres/Boston Red Sox/LA Dodgers player Adrián González, whose foundation is actually a DAF housed at the San Diego Foundation.

Donor-Advised Funds for Supporter Groups. As with the player option mentioned above, supporter groups can pool funds together to support their favorite local causes. The benefits again are based in creating deeper connections with community partners.

Leaning in to Supporter Groups. Supporter groups are a team's ambassador, grassroots champion, and an extension of their standing in the broader community. Many professional teams, however, keep them at arm's length, and new teams (especially those in minor leagues) often dictate the terms. This is a mistake, as supporter groups can really elevate a team's brand by enhancing charitable campaigns and events through their participation.

I have truly marveled at Austin FC's main supporter groups, which include the Austin Anthem and Los Verdes. During the COVID-19 pandemic, a full year before the team would play in the MLS for the first time, these groups have lifted up social issues, collaborated with local small businesses for unique cross-over promotions (including coffee shops, breweries, and social change organizations), and created socially conscious and aware merchandise that is as inclusive as it is on trend. Austin FC understood the power of that and the importance of reflecting the key values, constituencies, and economic drivers of the city, even selling T-shirts in collaboration with local Grammy-nominated artists the Black Pumas, with all proceeds going to local live music venues that have seen their incomes decimated by the pandemic.

Using In-Game/On-Field Tech. With a new stadium for Austin FC on the way and learning from the advances of recent new stadiums nationwide, it would be great to see charitable options built into the in-game experience and general infrastructure of event-day operations. This can include donations through apps and rounding up at concessions, using crowd sentiment analysis for when to make asks via push notifications and on billboards, and using mixed-reality options for messaging, driving empathy and awareness for the club's charitable work.

Leverage Major International Events. There is a certain star quality with new franchises. This is no different with Austin FC, with Matthew McConaughey a partner on the ownership team and serving as its minister of culture, a title he also holds with the University of Texas at Austin. A larger-than-life personality who knows just how and when to hype up his base, McConaughey brought together the supporter groups via Zoom in the summer of 2020 to talk about his vision for game days at the new stadium. I was lucky enough to participate in this exchange, regardless of my surprise that the Oscar winner joined the chat wearing no shirt and a few other people following his lead. He talked about a "hundred-year war" and how the club's very heartbeat could permeate through the energy of a crowd through the use of drums. (Yes, one supporter group exists for this sole purpose—take a bow, La Murga de Austin).

Anyway, fledgling clubs need to be more strategic with their early charitable endeavors and seek to build annual events that will compound over time. Lots of affiliate groups in the area already exist and are broadly supported. But given the pulling power of events such as Austin City Limits, the Formula 1 Grand Prix, and SXSW, there exists a dynamic opportunity to engage with these more established brands and bring awareness to the club and its community work. Events like five-a-side competitions around an issue such as homelessness with visiting celebrities and bands participating is a surefire hit in my eyes.

Tackle Systems Change. As previously mentioned, many organizations shy away from involvement in critical local issues because of the politics as well as the team's broader appeal due to neutrality. However, communities are changing and there are higher expectations for all those that form part of a civic ecosystem. The reality is that clubs are largely respected entities and have the ability to use their influence for good, not just vicariously live through their star players' own commitments to justice.

Examples of this potential new compact with communities are becoming more frequent and can be seen through a number of equity-based programs to encourage more girls to play sports and to support ways to make playing accessible to all regardless of background. Look at the ownership of organizations like the San Diego Padres, who are tackling issues such as homelessness with funding through public-private partnerships and with local service providers. Or the Los Angeles Lakers, who have formally partnered with Game Changer, a California Peace Officer Standards and Training (POST)-accredited law enforcement/community relations program that brings together police and community residents for moderated focus groups to discuss community problems and devise solutions. Once the focus group concludes, participants adjourn to watch a sporting event in order to form more authentic relationships between residents and law enforcement.

Standing for something has far better long-term benefits than any initial blowback from smaller sections of the fan base. Catalyzing civic pride is one thing. Having fans proud of their local team is a priceless commodity.

There is a legitimate lane here for a new actor to play a leading role in our civic life, not just exist as a complementary piece of social infrastructure. Connecting the threads between game day and people day to day is an important endeavor that can be amplified both through technology and by embracing nontraditional approaches to CSR.

As I always say, innovation doesn't have to be new, just new to you. There are plenty of major league franchises that can learn from organized philanthropy and its strategic impact. Heck, it might even be the difference between moving a team to another city or not. Austin FC gets it, and there is a reason it has sold out of its fifteen-thousand-plus season tickets six months in advance of its inaugural season.

ALISON ARAGON

Leveling the playing field for our communities

Earlier in the book, we covered the pay equity gap. But what about the play equity gap?

Sports can enhance the very fabric of our communities, bringing people together on an even playing field irrespective of race, color, creed, ethnic or national origins, gender, marital status, sexuality, disability, or age. It's a true world language, so what better vehicle than the Olympics?

With the 1984 Olympics legacy still impacting the very city that showcased it, and with the growing excitement of it returning some forty-four years later, Alison Aragon of the Play Equity Fund at the LA84 Foundation is working hard to ensure that funding and sustainable solutions are secured to ensure kids of color have access and opportunity to pathways for lifelong well-being.

To Alison, philanthropy is a key component of her career playbook and one she realizes is an action rather than a symbol of community care. It is more about the trust and recognition in our shared humanity—an openness and curiosity to transform how and who our current systems take care of now and into the future. "In a time when everyone is challenged to pivot," she says, "I think philanthropy is dipping its toe in the tides of change. It is not really an institution built to yell 'cannonball' and jump right in, but my favorite funders are questioning the rule books, who wrote them, and how the regulations limit community voice.

"Ultimately we find our truth by opening ourselves to each other. That work has historically been placed on the shoulders of nonprofits and underresourced communities to undertake themselves, but never asked of philanthropic institutions. I think we are beginning to see this

185

shift now, with a shared understanding that real change is built on an exchange and vulnerability of both funders and the communities they are built to support."

Alison sees much of this dialogue emanating from a more localized conversation and democratized approach to giving. She is excited that options exist for people to learn more about their communities, noting that when those participants come of age professionally, they will more likely adopt those grassroots lessons as a way to drive impact where they know (and understand) it will make a difference.

"The most authentic giving, listening, and learning experiences have come from my participation in the Latina Giving Circle," Alison says. "We've created grant cycles from scratch with an accessible application process and meaningful project focus built by members, and I have learned a great deal both personally and professionally by going through two rapid response cycles during COVID-19."

Giving circles are unique and versatile and lack the same structural rigidity as other philanthropic vehicles. This allows them to give rapid-response grants to organizations that don't have the capacity for administrative staff—often keeping them from getting recognized for grant proposals, or even having the opportunity to submit them.

"The first cycle of these rapid-response grants went to groups that did not qualify for the stimulus check funding, recognizing that many immigrant, undocumented, and mixed-status families did not receive the same access to federal and state benefits," Alison explains. "The second round was in partnership with a more established and traditional foundation to fund organizations led by women, supporting Black women and girls, and advancing racial justice in our community. This type of responsive and collective giving is harder the more bureaucratic and higher up the ivory tower you go, but it does seem to be what is needed as we come to terms with the intersectionality of community need."

People like Alison can look at these new trends in philanthropy, then conceptualize and apply them in different sectors and introduce new actors to what giving can accomplish for their communities. It's effectively building a bigger tent for what giving is and means for people and leveraging a following for good.

Unsurprisingly, Alison is interested in the elevated presence of athlete advocacy and the willingness to not only pool funds as teams or cities after large sporting events, but also the willingness to stop the bubbles that exist within professional sports to give space to the larger human rights conversations that need to happen. "Athletes are often seen as superheroes," she says. "So admitting that you are a superhero who is scared to live in America is a big deal. Admitting fear when you are full of uncertainty is exactly the sort of conversation philanthropy needs to be willing to put itself in."

When it comes to philanthropic partnerships with sports teams, honesty with all stakeholders and looking at what a return on investment looks like through the lens of inequity and injustice, rather than how to sell the brand, more tickets, or merchandise, is really where we need to go. This requires a shift away from checkbook-and-confetti-style community philanthropy.

It's also time for sporting bodies and teams to get uncomfortable, and not just because of societal pressures like what occurred with the now Washington Football Team. It's about the organization's proactive searching for growth for both itself and its region. "There is a lot of tradition and legacy in endowment philanthropy," Alison says, "but we must be honest about that history. I respect organizations who are willing to listen to their communities and trust in their shared insights, learnings, and advice, both encouraging and critical."

With the world due to once again turn its gaze back to Los Angeles in anticipation of the Olympics in 2028, let's hope that organizers are listening to emerging leaders like Alison and understanding that play equity is indeed a social justice issue, and that inclusive and participatory philanthropy is the key to a true community-focused legacy. Either way, there is no doubt that Southern California is glad to have Alison on its team.

CHAPTER TWELVE

Social Sector Charrettes

The Time for Efficiency, Effectiveness, and Exploration

THE CASE FOR SILICON CITY HALL: A TECH CLUSTER . . . FOR GOOD.
Have you ever been on a sales or demo call for a tech platform and felt a strange disconnect with its narrative, stats, lingo, and insights? Like it doesn't understand your services or impact and feels it necessary to "techsplain" all of your digital deficiencies? Well, you're not alone. According to NetChange's survey of technology use by nonprofits, only 11 percent of organizations feel their digital strategies are highly effective, which goes to highlight the current digital divide between the adoption and use of tech solutions for both the for-profit and not-for-profit sectors.

Those in the private sector will have you believe that the question is actually whether nonprofits take their systems and services seriously when it comes to digital adoption.

The real question, however, should be whether the products being offered are in fact real solutions to the needs of nonprofits based on cost, capacity, and support.

"Tech for good" in this instance is a misnomer when the product is built by a for-profit entity, with solutions needing to be specifically built with an understanding of—not an assumption or interpretation of—the structure and needs of nonprofit clients front and center. An alarming number of tech companies have strong solutions for business but believe that, with just a couple of tweaks, the addition of a nonprofit sales department and promise of a silver bullet can solve numerous issues for your organization.

Nonprofits need to be stop being seen as an additional vertical through this lens for a number of reasons:

- Scaling operations are polar opposites in the business and nonprofit worlds. If you sell more product, you can drive lower margins and increase revenues. If you are successful in the nonprofit world, you drive up demand for your services, resulting in an increase in your operational costs and then needing to find more revenue streams (namely grants and donations) to meet this new budget reality.

- Nonprofit donors are not the same as venture capitalists (VCs).

- Donors are not the nonprofit's customers.

- Applying a nonprofit discount to an enterprise pricing model is not being charitable. It is still just a tool to drive sales.

- The for-profit sales model is arguably a predatory approach when applied to organizations with revenues of less than $500,000 (which is approximately 88 percent of the 1.5 million nonprofits nationwide, according to the National Council of Nonprofits). These organizations are understaffed and vulnerable to professional pitches centered on a mission and impact ROI and are probably unaware of when they have entered into sophisticated sales funnels when downloading "freemium" content.

Right now, you might be thinking, *But there are nonprofit tech companies building innovative solutions to help organizations tackle today's most critical issues.* And you would be right. Organizations such as Fast Forward, Code for America, NTEN (the Nonprofit Technology Network), and TechSoup are doing stellar work cultivating talent, creating real solutions that help some of our most underserved communities, and acting as a bridge for the digital divide. Plus, more and more nonprofit hubs, coworking spaces, innovative applications of fiscal sponsorship, and social sector accelerators are popping up across every metro city in the land.

However, we should advocate for something much more intentional. Something big and bold. Something that has the potential to help build the capacity of our nonprofit sector in a sustainable way. This something is the establishment of a genuine nonprofit tech cluster here in America.

Think of it as a "Silicon City Hall," tackling the tech needs and intersections of the social sector from government to civil society, from advocacy to service delivery, and everything in between. By bringing together key players and assets and unifying funding where possible, the nonprofit sector can use a tech cluster model to support both the supply and demand sides of the civic tech industry through a dynamic hub, which can also act as an online marketplace that curates tech packages for those organizations. We could then see the following benefits for key actors.

Nonprofit Tech Companies. At the forefront of driving innovation, yet faced with sustainability issues due to the unique nature of their business model, these organizations face a more systemic problem where they have to focus disproportionately on sales over product. A tech cluster with a collaborative leadership model could also help connect solutions to more clients and decrease acquisition costs. Throw in the potential of supplying additional shared support (potentially through employed digital specialists—a resource many nonprofits don't have the luxury of having), and nonprofit tech companies could benefit from more active users, experience higher rates of renewals, and ultimately build a more sustainable sector on the supply side via a strong case statement for increased donor and government support.

Social Change Organizations. People constantly ask me, "What tech should we get? Have you heard of [insert name of technology]? What do you think about it?" The establishment of a nonprofit tech cluster would make the answers to some of these questions more readily available for everyone in philanthropy. In essence, it would democratize civic tech, making a wide variety of tools, plug-ins, and solutions available at more affordable rates and lending itself to yield greater outcomes. Then, through an online marketplace or peer-reviewed platform, organizations would be able to select the most relevant tools to support and execute their strategy.

Government. Beyond nonprofit services, campaigns, and advocacy, the nonprofit sector could also see opportunities to improve civic engagement and civil discourse by working in tandem with organizations seeking to crack into the $400 billion GovTech market (a key partner in delivering real systems change). Governments need to move past the novelty of civic hackathons, clunky apps, and one-off projects (underfunded or through the guise of an open competition) and invest in their own modernization by hiring public servants that can code, analyze the mountains of government data that exist, and either identify or build real solutions that will energize folks to engage in their democracy, provide a transformative way of having them engage in their own governance, or drive better solutions and improved service delivery for their residents.

Plenty of regions would be terrific backdrops for a potential Silicon City Hall. With places like the state of Vermont and (as previously mentioned) Tulsa, Oklahoma, paying remote workers $10,000 to move to their regions, it is possible to move such an ambitious project forward quickly, especially one that has the capacity to help millions of people in a sector that is fast becoming one that cannot meet the growing demand for its services. Oh, and jobs. Thousands of new jobs. And don't forget the investments. This has PPP and impact investing potential written all over it (with the second P being philanthropic of course!).

So let's move out of the valley, leave the beach behind, and march toward city hall!

DONOR-ADVISED FUNDS FLOODING THE SECTOR AND LEAVING TRADITIONAL PLAYERS IN THEIR WAKE

Many eyebrows were raised when the Fidelity Charitable Gift Fund (FCGF) took the top spot in the annual rankings of the nation's largest grantmaking charities a few years back, surpassing United Way Worldwide in private contributions. Fidelity's private contributions are surging up to 20 percent year over year, according to the *Chronicle of*

Philanthropy, but as we know, the FCGF is not your traditional charity. Fueled by donor-advised funds (DAFs), these giving vehicles have signaled a shift in how the wealthy approach their philanthropy.

But we aren't here to discuss current trends. We are here to anticipate new ones. And when it comes to DAFs, the future is through automated online platforms.

Why this direction? Because of three things:

1. The insatiable thirst of the sector to engage millennial donors.

2. The reality that the fees associated with opening and administering DAFs are overinflated.

3. The sector's ripeness for disruption.

When I say *disruption*, I mean further disruption. You see, Fidelity, Schwab Charitable Fund, and the Vanguard Charitable Endowment program were the first to disrupt the sector twenty-five years ago. All spin-offs of established investment companies, they turned these flexible charitable accounts into a multibillion-dollar-a-year funding vehicle that has seen more than a 500 percent increase from 2010.

Why is it that these companies—sorry, I mean charities—were able to outpace other more established institutions, such as community foundations that offered the same options with arguably better outcomes? In short, it was cost. Community foundations charge on average $25,000 to open an account. Fidelity, on the other hand, charged $5,000 until recently decreasing the barriers to entry even further, supporting households that annually donate $2,600 to charity.

DAFs have been one of the most popular philanthropic vehicles around for thirty years. Yet once applied through that elusive millennial lens, they have been traditionally out of reach for younger or limited-capacity donors due to the costs of opening a fund. In the coming years, though, we should see yet another seismic shift in giving, and the catalyst will be mobile apps. DAFs will become commonplace when hybrid corporations understand the marketplace and can open these accounts at substantially lower rates because their software won't need physical locations or bloated numbers of financial, charitable giving, and administrative staff.

With millennials coming of age professionally, DAFs and charitable banking will become more common and accessible, especially when grant recommendations can be made instantly.

And in the not-too-distant future, they will surely be combined with the following:

- AI that will identify compatible charities and trends for users

- more robust dashboards that will show the impact of donors' dollars

- blockchain technology that will track dollars from donation to implementation, increasing trust, transparency, and accountability within the sector

With 87 percent of millennials donating each year, it's time that the traditional actors within the sector anticipate these future trends (not only DAFs but also the technology that supports round-up spending options, administering giving circles, and pooled funds for collective impact) and look at providing flexible alternatives for their charitable giving. Otherwise, they risk becoming stagnant institutions of yesteryear.

MAKE AMERICA GENEROUS AGAIN: TWEAKS FOR A MORE IMPACTFUL #GIVINGTUESDAY

GivingTuesday will be looking to surpass the nearly $2.5 billion it raised as a global movement in its most recent reporting, with year over year stats indeed impressive from what is still a rapidly growing phenomenon:

- $2.47 billion was donated to US nonprofits by a reported 34.8 million people.

- It raised 34 percent more funds on its 2019 record-setting mark.

- It's a true global generosity movement—with organizations across 150 countries benefiting from the event.

With these strong results, why the constant murmur of discontent from the field around the concept of one of the biggest fundraising days on the nonprofit calendar? Let's deconstruct these concerns and highlight the changes we might see over the long term to enhance GivingTuesday's effectiveness moving forward.

Growing Pains? By way of background, GivingTuesday was founded in 2012 as a partnership between the 92nd Street Y and the United Nations Foundation in response to the consumerism of the post-Thanksgiving season. More recently, GivingTuesday formed its own organization and is now led by a foundational partner alumni and former 92nd Street Y director for innovation and social impact, Asha Curran. This is an exciting development for the group and will no doubt reap real benefits for the sector at large, especially with the evolution of the GivingTuesday Data Collaborative, which we'll talk about later.

GivingTuesday is perceived as the antidote to the capitalistic nature of Black Friday and Cyber Monday, and the perfect kickoff to the charitable giving season. You can't argue with these rose-colored glasses. However, is anything more symbolic of how the nonprofit sector is viewed by society than placing this day at the end of a period where people are spending exorbitant amounts of dollars and then countering their materialistic guilt by donating whatever they have left to their favorite charity?

In 2020 (even in a down year due to the COVID-19 pandemic), Americans spent $9 billion on Black Friday and $10.8 billion on Cyber Monday. GivingTuesday, however, raised just a small percentage of that total.

The concerns around GivingTuesday have largely been argued as misplaced, feeding into the old adage of "you only get out what you put in" and routinely countered by those organizations that benefit the most from the event both on the supply and demand side of the equation. As we identify the future impact of GivingTuesday, we first need to acknowledge and address these areas for which enhancements can be adopted to benefit the broader sector.

There Is a Risk in Diluting End of Year Gifts. Twenty-eight percent of nonprofits raise between 26 and 50 fifty percent of their annual funds from their year-end ask. Given that this is the peak giving season, this is when a number of the larger gifts are indeed realized. While existing recurring donors regularly give an additional one-time gift on GivingTuesday and sometimes on multiple occasions, the average gift of up to $130 (the highest number we found on all fundraising platforms), gives insight that this potentially eats into major gifts and that their charitable spend for the day is shared among a number of different organizations. The antidote here is to resist the temptation of adding major gift prospects in email campaigns and focus on small gift and annual fund donors.

Big Charities Remain the Big Winners. Giving is becoming more concentrated at the top with just one hundred charities (0.006 percent) accruing 11 percent of all charitable gifts. Organizations with larger reach, more staff, and vastly bigger advertising budgets are the real whales of this event, able to break through the clutter and scoop up a majority of the new donors. Just type GivingTuesday into any social media site or search engine and see the muscle of these organizations in full force.

The Math Won't Always Add Up. It might seem a little far fetched, but there is a real danger of GivingTuesday becoming the next "golf fundraiser" for small nonprofits. The investment of staff time compared to the amount of funds raised or new donors captured must be seriously reviewed after the conclusion of each campaign. For example, if a combination of staff members spent sixty hours on the entire campaign—meetings, time spent cultivating donors, and media opportunities—and the day yielded $1,500, then was it worthwhile from both a tangible (wages, additional advertising spend) and intangible (time, volunteer support, and outreach) perspective? And no, social media vanity metrics should not be a defining indicator of success.

An Abundance of Opportunity. GivingTuesday will continue to grow as a global movement. But if it is to reach a transformational phase that could see the realization of a sector-wide dream of giving increasing to 3 percent of GDP, then it should consider the following tweaks to its offerings and approach:

- **Expand its Organization:** As mentioned, this year saw a formal entity created to add a level of professionalism and focus to what in essence was simply an idea to encourage more people to do good. Although this organization has just formed, hopefully it will seek to recruit regional volunteer organizers to cultivate and train nonprofits in advance of each GivingTuesday, developing a number of strategic partnerships to accelerate growth and expand reach and empower these groups to organically grow the movement through a localized lens (think #ILGive and #GivingTuesdayCA).

- **Leverage Impact:** It would be great to see GivingTuesday bring on a number of development staff to link up with philanthropic and corporate partners to develop a pooled fund. This annual fund would in essence act as a matching gift and, if weighted against the size of organization, could provide an amazing incentive for both donors and nonprofits to participate.

- **Provide Additional Tools:** Currently the main tools shared in support of GivingTuesday are logos and shareable social media images together with a blog that highlights hints and tips for a successful campaign. It would be great to see GivingTuesday build out its own fundraising platform that would be offered at no cost to organizations, charge no transaction fees, and drive more internal data sets to help fuel the research and reporting of its new Giving Lab. This way, the annual event is more transparent and accountable—free of conflicts of interest from tech companies in the space that can use the day to develop a pipeline of new nonprofit customers.

- **Continue to Democratize Data:** The Giving Lab and its Data Commons (the data it collects from its partners, and how it digests and communicates its findings) should be built on a foundational commitment to the principles of data philanthropy, creating a true repository for partners to share data sets and for individuals and groups to use it for the betterment of our sector and the communities they serve. Spin-off events including hackathons and XPRIZE-esque challenges would also be a fantastic complement and asset for the new Giving Lab and its ensuing goals.

- **Avoid Easy Gains and Gimmicks:** It is tempting for any new organization to expand its reach quickly using a number of vanity metrics. They make for very fine infographics! One of those is always the value of volunteer time, and there might be a natural gravitation to adding giving the gift of time and talent as a new pillar to its mission. This will help GivingTuesday focus on the giving side and play a supporting role in existing infrastructure such as National Volunteer Week. (Oh, and don't get me started on the #ThankYouWednesday approach to bookend the campaign. Let's keep to a higher standard of stewardship.)

- **CHANGE THE DATE!** Ungrouping the event from the consumerism surrounding the festive season (Black Friday, Cyber Monday, and the annual sales around holiday gifts) and taking into account the peaks and troughs of giving across the calendar year could provide a catalytic effect to those months where giving is traditionally lower with a new influx of funding when it's needed the most. If this occurs, we might see the universal buy-in needed to take this movement to the next level.

  GivingTuesday arguably has the name recognition to make a successful shift in the month this event falls on too. A separate day of global giving that acted as an emergency response to COVID-19, #GivingTuesdayNow, was a tremendous success, raising $503 million in online donations in the US alone. These results lead me to believe a shift in the main event can be an overwhelming success.

The GivingTuesday movement should continue to evolve in the coming years now that it has the organizational infrastructure in place and leadership talent to help it grow with a renewed focus on the end consumers. Given that this event is now a staple of the fundraising landscape—leveraging over $1 billion in donations for the organizations that have plugged in to the movement—its success should be a foregone conclusion if managed correctly. If it can also figure out a way to navigate the possibility of a plateauing landscape in the wake of new tax laws and crack the code on millennial giving in the face of a massive transfer of generational wealth, then it will go down in history as one of the biggest conduits to America's generosity in our lifetime.

Whichever way you look at it, GivingTuesday has been an unquestioned success. The idea behind it has connected more donors to causes they care about and pump-primed the sector to support our nonprofits in delivering essential services for and on behalf of communities the world over.

ERIN BARNES

Crowdsourcing Power, Passion, and Participation for Our Communities

Volunteering is the ultimate exercise in democracy. You vote in elections once a year, but when you volunteer, you vote every day about the kind of community you want to live in. —Marjorie Moore

Getting out the community "vote" is essentially an everyday necessity for the vast majority of our nonprofits, schools, and sports clubs. But we often overlook the smaller "micro" actions of individuals at the neighborhood level, as well as the potential of supporting them to build on these initial forays into civic life and become the courageous leaders many folks are looking for to break through the gridlock and polarization of current elected leadership.

"A healthy democracy is all about how we show up where we live, work, play, and pray," says Erin Barnes, ioby's CEO and cofounder. "It's the ability to move past our informal networks and cross that threshold of being a member or our community to one where we are an active and informed citizen. It's the individuals, not the institutions, that have true collective power, and we need to start showing up as our full selves, as mothers, fathers, workers, and neighbors if we are to reclaim our identities for good and unite communities in an authentic, engaging, and dynamic way." Erin is quick to reiterate that ioby (an abbreviation for *in our backyards*) isn't your typical crowdfunding platform. "ioby stands for taking care of each other, for civic participation, and for trusting neighbors to know what's best for the neighborhood," she says. "We give local leaders the ability to crowdfund the resources they need to build real, lasting change from the ground up, making our neighborhoods more sustainable, healthier, greener, more livable, and more fun."

Through her work at ioby, Erin has been helping recalibrate how

199

people identify with civic participation for the last eleven years. "Our platform was born with the intention of encouraging and educating people to support environmental work where they live," she said. "Global issues are important, but they're also at such a huge scale that it can be easy to feel overwhelmed, and to overlook your own backyard. For example, someone planting trees in their neighborhood might see it as a beautification project rather than helping the environment, and if we could help folks identify with the nuances and the broader effects of those small efforts, and see it as part of a bigger journey, then we might activate new and important voices for a lifetime."

It was during Superstorm Sandy in 2012, however, that ioby saw that community resilience was intersectional in nature and that moving beyond the lens of just environmentally focused initiatives was needed to ensure New York could continue to thrive regardless of what issues confronted it. Over the next few years ioby continued to grow and evolve into how we see it today, as a conduit for change, a community and crowdfunding coach, and, in essence, a full-service civic toolbox for those with a great idea and the energy and commitment to see it become a reality.

"Across the US, local residents know best how issues like poverty, health, education, and the environment affect them," says Erin, "and they can have the best ideas for addressing them. But neighborhood-scale change is often dismissed as unimportant or small, so these citizen problem-solvers remain under-resourced and untapped, preventing the kind of concrete improvements, community cohesion, and long-term stewardship that, in aggregate, their efforts could bring."

It came as no surprise that in 2018 Erin was selected to join the inaugural class of Obama Fellows, recognized by President and Mrs. Obama for ioby's work in leading the next wave of civic innovation in America. That innovation is continuing to scale in places with historic disinvestment. Field offices are now located in five cities across the country and supported by community organizers who are helping identify and support locally driven change through new leaders, and importantly new leaders of color and those from Indigenous American nations.

"Leaders of color continue to struggle to secure funding and support," says Erin, "especially as we continue to see a heavy racial bias in philanthropy. While we can see many institutions dealing with a crisis of conscience in the wake of George Floyd's murder, there are still a large number of transformational ideas that remain overlooked or rejected out of hand through an outdated and rigid approach to grantmaking.

"A lot of philanthropy is geared toward outcomes, but we here at ioby interpret that differently. With about half of our projects being BIPOC-led, we place more attention on the leader and how they see themselves and their service in their community, and become emboldened to speak up when it matters." This approach is driving real change, especially at the municipal level, understanding that this is where innovations can be applied with a stronger understanding of need, empathy, and pride, and lending itself to the old adage that "what starts here, changes the world." We can also accelerate these approaches to start moving money into the community and in a much more fluid way.

"It was only a few years ago that giving money to leaders of color was seen as radical, and that funding grassroots groups was too risky," says Erin. "But we've seen in our experience that these groups are actually safe bets on positive civic change. And if there is anything that the pandemic showed us, it's that providing direct cash assistance is bringing about the change we want to see in our neighborhoods.

"Disbursement models are going to change, crowdfunding is going to evolve, and organizations are going to show bold leadership, fiscally sponsoring new projects and groups to de-risk the injection of resources to support them, rather than what's happening now where organizations have typically shied away from the exposure in fear of not getting future funding themselves."

The winds of change are beginning to roar into the sector. Inspirational mobilizers like Erin are helping to amplify the impact of our newly engaged civic assets and with an unapologetic commitment to building up the civic muscle of those long omitted from decision making and their capacity to help push against the status quo.

GLOBAL PHILANTHROPY

A Shared Future Beyond Our Bubble

The year 2020 was surreal the world over. Yet while the COVID-19 pandemic in some ways exposed the systems and arguable decline in what America is and what it stands for, other countries rallied through with strong leadership and a collective spirit that sought to protect their brothers and sisters both figuratively and literally.

I look back on this year, this election, and the countless messages from my friends and family back home in Australia saying, "What's going on over there? It might be time for you to come home now." If they are seeing something is amiss, why can't we? And why can't we move forward with a new purpose and camaraderie that is geared to rebuilding the very fabric of our country, not just those industries that have either moved overseas or just aren't financially viable anymore?

This may offer a less-than-positive view of the future for the United States, and while it brings instant thoughts of that memorable scene in the first episode of Alan Sorkin's *The Newsroom* where Jeff Daniels's character sought to drop the mic and rattle off a whole bunch of statistics as to why the country wasn't the best country in the world anymore, there is no other country I could see make such a stellar comeback both politically and economically. Sorkin nailed this possible global renaissance in ways I just can't, so here was that part of the script in all its unabridged glory:

> We stood up for what was right. We fought for moral reason. We passed laws, struck down laws, for moral reason. We waged wars on poverty, not on poor people. We sacrificed, we cared about our neighbors, we put our money where our mouths were and we never beat our chest. We built great, big things, made ungodly

202

technological advances, explored the universe, cured diseases, and we cultivated the world's greatest artists AND the world's greatest economy. We reached for the stars, acted like men. We aspired to intelligence, we didn't belittle it. It didn't make us feel inferior. We didn't identify ourselves by who we voted for in the last election and we didn't scare so easy. We were able to be all these things and do all these things because we were informed ... by great men, men who were revered. First step in solving any problem is recognizing there is one. America is not the greatest country in the world anymore.

America has provided me and my family an abundance of opportunity. If I didn't move to the US I would never have forged a career in philanthropy and I sure as hell wouldn't have written this book. But coming here via both England and Australia, I am served by the ability to look critically at current practices and look back at my experiences on how other countries have approached the same issues.

What I'm pitching here is that philanthropy in the United States— despite this country being the pioneer of the field, despite all of the amazing work it has done, and despite of all the impact it has had— must be more open to other approaches to advancing the common good, looking outside of its inherent bubble and realizing that other countries might have something to offer. That means looking to see what trends and approaches are working, listening to alternative strategies rather than dictating perceived best practices, and showing a willingness to collaborate on global issues such as ocean conservation, natural disasters, and realizing new trends (for example, social impact bonds originated in the UK a decade ago).

It's time to take stock of what has been shared in this book thus far and look outward in regard to how philanthropy is helping transform communities. To do this, let's learn about the advances and approaches of Australia and Saudi Arabia from a philanthropic perspective through the thoughts and experiences of Krystian Seibert and Laila Bukhari. While there are still some obvious similarities, I'm sure you will be inspired by what is going on outside of our immediate view and ultimately hopeful about the ability of philanthropy to link arms across continents to tackle some of the travesties that continue to plague our communities.

It won't be long until Krystian and Laila will be making waves here in the US given their deep knowledge, strong and established US networks, and of course their passion for change. They truly are representative of a new dynamic and diverse global philanthropic community, ones that are savvy enough to establish foundations in the US to leverage the support of expatriates, yet smart enough to learn from our mistakes. Let's hope our next generation helps steer the country away from the potential of another gilded age and instead toward an age where progress and partnerships see our neighbors as collaborators with a common set of goals and values, not just people who happen to be in our backyard.

THE COMPATIBILITY OF CHANGE: ADOPTING AND ADAPTING TO (AMERICAN) PHILANTHROPY TRENDS

I always try to stay authentic in my voice, even though it's a hybrid of the three unique chapters of my life. (By that, I mean living in England, then Australia, and now the United States.) It's an identity struggle whenever someone asks me where I'm from. I start with, "Well . . ." and then deliver an abridged version of my background in less than fifteen seconds.

It has also caused me to hedge bets on my career, knowing that I have an abundance of opportunity ahead, but a home and a support base to catch me should our family ever decide to move back.

We have flirted with that idea, and philanthropy would be the ideal landing spot. But due to the relatively small footprint the sector has in Australia and the fact that the structures that make philanthropy so dynamic and engaging in the United States aren't necessarily compatible there, I play the part of interested bystander, watching the evolution of the Australian sector and periodically connecting with my former peers who are now senators, state premiers, and leading voices across a number of social movements, encouraging them to think about new approaches to social change and touching that third rail of tax reform.

A number of amazing leaders from Australia are also featured in this book, many of whom work with American companies and thought leaders. It was only natural to look deeper at the future of philanthropy in Australia and take a refreshing break from all of the thoughts and ideas whirling through our heads around on how to make America's sector more effective and more just—and quite frankly, to look outside the bubble and realize that we are more connected than ever and that we could learn a thing or two from what others are doing and vice versa.

As a quick primer here, let's go over some statistics that reflect the most up-to-date research currently available on giving in both countries.

In 2015–16, an estimated 14.9 million Australian adults (80.8 percent) gave in total AUD $12.5 billion to charities and NFP organizations over twelve months. The average donation was AUD $764.08 and median donation AUD $200. The specific source for this is the individual giving study conducted as part of Giving Australia 2016. The Giving USA report in 2019 saw giving by individuals total an estimated USD $292.09 billion.

Based on 2018 data, Australian charities received AUD $10.5 billion in donations and bequests. The total income for charities from all activities was AUD $155.4 billion, so donations and bequests account for 6.64 percent. Note that this is only charities, while Giving Australia includes other not-for-profit organizations as well. Total income from these same sources in America totaled USD $427.71 billion.

According to the Australian Charities and Not-for-Profits Commission (ACNC), in terms of organized philanthropy, or as they say down under, "structured philanthropy"—which commonly includes "charitable trusts," as well as so-called "private" and "public" ancillary funds—the value of giving from such structures in 2016, commonly referred to as "grantmaking" within the not-for-profit sector, amounted to AUD $1.53 billion. When compared with the total income of Australian charities, which in 2016 amounted to AUD $150.58 billion, grantmaking from structured philanthropy may seem rather insignificant.

Also, as reported by the ACNC, government funding of charities amounted to AUD $61.35 billion during the same period. Grantmaking from structured philanthropy may seem even less significant when compared with the total expenditure of the Australian government, which amounted to AUD \$447.8 billion in 2016–17 as stated in its 2018–19 federal budget.

I won't apply too much context due to the vastly different structures. But I will note that giving in America is becoming indicative of a new gilded age, one where any tinkering with philanthropic vehicles is largely benefiting the richest individuals of our society.

Although charity was around long before the country's federation (with the Benevolent Society existing since 1813), Australia has the opportunity to weave it more intentionally into the very fabric of its society, one that is personified already through "mateship" and a strong tradition of civic engagement through nonprofits, sports clubs, and other associations. The problem is a blurring of the lines and whether academia, government, and the nonprofit sector can indeed work as a cohesive unit, understand their roles and lanes, and have that united front instill confidence in the public.

Philanthropy can be better; we all get that. And it's going to take an interdisciplinary and multisector approach to get there. The two major driving forces are academia and government, which in this approach effectively become the cause and effect. On the one hand academia is theorizing what the future might be and researching its effectiveness. These findings and independently drawn recommendations and conclusions are then put out to lawmakers and the social sector for debate, discussion, and then (ideally) captured in the form of new legislation that closes loopholes or outdated provisions and expands on current regulations to allow new processes to be codified and opened for broader adoption, new programs, and funding.

This is happening on one side, but there is definitely a disconnect between elected officials and the role and potential of philanthropy. I have witnessed it many times during my visits to Congress and California's State Capitol as well as through my work in the Australian Federal Parliament.

So how do we bridge this gap moving forward?

I wanted to speak with someone who has worked within all of these structures but comes from outside of the bubble of American philanthropy with a vastly different ecosystem in which to operate. That's why I was thrilled that Krystian Seibert, an industry fellow at the Centre for Social Impact at Swinburne University of Technology in Melbourne, Australia, was happy to share his thoughts with me.

When I lived and worked in Australia, I saw charity mainly as an arm for celebrities and sports stars. Organized philanthropy such as community foundations were more like nonprofits than anchor institutions, and large family foundations weren't that prevalent as Australia is a relatively new country in the greater scheme of things, only becoming a federation in 1901. So there are no industry pioneers that endowed much of their wealth such as the Fords, Rockefellers, and Waltons who now represent traditional philanthropy.

This might also explain why I see an underlying discomfort in its role in society, especially when large personal gifts from mining magnates are met with skepticism, and almost demonized for circumventing government policy.

Having now lived in the United States for a decade, I'm always intrigued to see the evolution of philanthropy in Australia, knowing that it is in the unique position to adopt vehicles and approaches from other countries more swiftly than we can. Philanthropy in Australia can also benefit from the rapid globalization of the past few decades, as we begin to see an increasing number of prominent universities (and charities with global footprints) creating foundations in America to take advantage of gifts from those who have moved there and become extremely successful.

I have great hope that Australia can be a blueprint for a "new philanthropy," one that works in tandem with government to create a more dynamic tax code and culture that spurs a new golden generation of giving. And what better person to ideate with than Krystian, who has worked in government, as head of Philanthropy Australia's policy advocacy work (where he still retains an advisory role), and now as an academic and a leading voice in the sector. He is also working toward his PhD on the regulation of structured philanthropy, specifically looking at why foundations are subject to regulation by the state. It's going to be concerned with not only theory but also the perceptions of policymakers, regulators, philanthropists, and foundation staff.

Australia's philanthropy ethos has its own distinction but is also loosely centered on the United States structurally and the UK culturally, with the notion of using private wealth for public good. The nuance around that is what folks in the field are trying to work out, and it is that underlying tension mentioned earlier.

There can be a view that government is needed to provide the solutions to all our most pressing problems. Yet government doesn't have a monopoly when it comes to delivering a just and equitable society, and government is not some neutral force when different ideologies pull the levers of change at different times.

When asked about his current feelings toward philanthropy and the nonprofit sector at large, Krystian gave a nod to his optimistic nature, noting that they both play a vital role as part of the fabric of civil society, in that vital space between the individual and the state, between the fully private and the fully public. "In the case of philanthropy," he says, "particularly in Australia, I've seen over the past few years a real willingness to be introspective and reflective, focusing on understanding where philanthropy is now, thinking about where it needs to go, and a willingness to confront difficult questions, and have what may be difficult discussions. But I've also seen areas where there are the right words being said about how philanthropic practice needs to change, but they still need to be 'matched by action.' So while our progress is encouraging, there is still much more to be done."

Academia. Academia may be a much more significant actor in the field of philanthropy than many would give credit for. They are much more than a good place to fall back on for a partner and venue for your next event. They are a diverse community of scholars, educators, and practice leaders that strengthens our field through nonprofit and philanthropic research and often through a localized or niche lens, which is critical for the reflection of our sector that Krystian mentioned.

Academia has a very important and essential role in this regard:

- **Research:** It supports the building of an evidence base about what works and what doesn't, helps identify and conceptualize challenges and problems, and analyzes and articulates ways of responding to those challenges and problems.

- **Teaching:** It builds the capacity of the people working in the social sector, with impact only being as good as the people who lead it. It helps cultivate knowledge and skills among current and future leaders, translating research into practical applications. But it's also a two-way process—academics learn from students too, and it helps with the evolution of thinking and best practice.

- **Engagement:** Academia has an important public engagement role—helping the community, government, and others understand the nature of philanthropy and nonprofits. It can provide expert advice to governments, grounded in evidence and working in partnership with those in the sector. It can also be a critical friend to philanthropy and nonprofits, observing, commenting, scrutinizing, and critiquing—ideally based on evidence and informed by practice and not just theory.

Noting that last point, it's important that academia's contribution is not only grounded in theory but also in practice. That's why Krystian uses a term I like to describe his role: a "pracademic." He likens his work to being a bridge between academia and practice, especially when his work is where different sectors and disciplines intersect.

To understand this work in regard to the core components identified above, let's employ the "pracademic" approach so that you can see a career in this line of work rather than "fall into it":

- **Research:** Krystian seeks to understand the nature of the sector, the challenges it confronts, and opportunities available to it. "I have a particular interest in the policy and regulatory framework for the sector," he says. "But my interest is not limited to this. My work is grounded in practice, and whatever work I do, I aim for it to make a meaningful contribution to how the sector evolves to be more effective and impactful. Personally, I have little time for abstract debates which are divorced from reality, though I also appreciate that such debate can be valuable. It's just not my focus in my work as a 'pracademic.'"

- **Teaching:** As part of Swinburne University of Technology's Master of Social Impact program, Krystian teaches a number of units focused on philanthropy and the nonprofit sector and also areas such as corporate social responsibility and accountability. "Teaching is a vital part of my work, because the philanthropic and nonprofit sectors are only as good as the people working within them," he says. "And equipping the next generation of sector leaders with the knowledge and skills to be effective in their work is absolutely critical work that I take very seriously. But I also don't see teaching as merely me imparting my knowledge. It's not a one-way exchange, but rather a curated learning journey where students learn from me, I learn from them, we learn from guest speakers sharing practical expertise and experience, and as we move along on this journey we all learn together."

- **Engagement:** "I am very engaged in policy debates in relation to the philanthropic and nonprofit sector," Krystian says. "And as mentioned previously, I have a particular interest, also expertise, in relation to the policy and regulatory framework for the sector. I think this is important work, because a well-designed policy and regulatory framework for the sector is essential to its effectiveness and impact. It doesn't just come down to tax exemptions and things like that, but also the ability of the sector to achieve change through approaches such as advocacy and collaboration with government, for example.

  "In terms of this work, in addition to my role at Swinburne University of Technology I am also a policy adviser to Philanthropy Australia, where I support the work of the team, thereby providing strategic advice in relation to its policy advocacy activities. As part of my engagement work, I also do quite a lot of public engagement such as media interviews and contributing articles to sector and other publications."

Take note of the latter part. We really need to start seeing new faces in academia that understand the importance of branding their work to make it more appealing to the field. Sharing expertise with a broader audience and helping grow the understanding of philanthropy and the nonprofit sector must become a more important aspect of an academic's work.

Government. I am quite vocal about the role of government in philanthropy and how government needs to become more informed, more

210

connected, and more engaged with the sector moving forward. This isn't just in defined partnerships, but also in a shared spirit of advancing civil society.

Beyond their shared language, America and Australia are different in a multitude of ways. This also stems from philanthropy in the form of structural barriers at both the donation and disbursement ends of charity. So if there was one piece of legislative change to help make philanthropy more effective, what would it be?

Krystian suggests that "a requirement that foundations contribute a small portion of their annual grantmaking toward organizations focused on scrutinizing philanthropy. I'm not talking about a large amount, but perhaps 1 to 2 percent of the annual amount of funds which are granted (so a foundation which grants $1 million would need to contribute $10–$20,000). The funds would be contributed to a body (perhaps a foundation itself) which would then grant them out in the form of general operating support and also project specific grants to organizations and individuals."

Not the sexiest answer, but it's indicative of the need to build up trust in the sector as a partner rather than a way to circumvent accepted standards of how to operate within the community. It's the very definition of "fair dinkum" (which, to those unfamiliar with this Australian term, is used to emphasize the truth of something).

One of the benefits of philanthropy is that it isn't accountable in the same way that government and business is. This means that it can, in theory, be more flexible and nimbler. However, as Krystian explains, "I think there is a need to 'invest in accountability,' in terms of funding organizations and individuals to critique and scrutinize philanthropy, which I believe would help make philanthropy better, provided it's constructive and evidence based."

Pushing this to the forefront will obviously need a healthy dose of policy formulation and advocacy for it. Public policy is starting to become more important in the US, with philanthropy finally beginning to understand its unique position and voice in our communities.

Krystian mentions here that "I think philanthropy has a vital role to play in advocacy and public policy. When I was working full-time with Philanthropy Australia, one of the pieces of work I led was to encourage our members and the field at large to more actively engage and fund in this space.

"I think we need to be realistic about government and its limitations, and must be careful not to adopt a naive or overly idealistic view of its ability to address all the problems we face as a society. But I still firmly believe in the power of good government. Many of our social and environmental challenges can only be solved through changes in policy and practice by government—such an approach to systemic change is based on not only seeking to address the symptoms of problems, but also their causes."

That holistic approach will no doubt need to also include advocacy by nonprofit partners who have a vital role in not only pushing for change but also holding governments to account. To enhance their voice, however, they will need to be supported through funding and targeted research, which can be ably provided by philanthropy as an additional way of contributing to democracy.

Krystian explains, "I may not always agree with the advocacy, but I think in a pluralistic democracy, there are many voices and ideas in the debate, and the interplay of these voices and ideas, the tension between them and also the tension with government, is by and large a good thing. However, I don't think philanthropy should be able to fund partisan advocacy and campaigning (and I also don't think that charitable nonprofits should engage in such activities), but provided advocacy furthers a charitable purpose and is not partisan, I see no need for further restrictions and limits."

It is important that the social sector hold governments to account. However, the inevitable tension that comes through the lack of understanding mentioned earlier can be navigated through strategic collaboration. As Krystian explained during our conversation, there are positive aspects to strategic collaboration between government and philanthropy such as foundations prototyping new programs and approaches or co-investing in new ways of achieving impact.

Two particular examples of cross-sector collaboration in

Australia showed great promise and could be a template for new public-philanthropic partnerships:

1. **The Maranguka Justice Reinvestment Strategy:** This Indigenous-led initiative adopts a different approach to addressing crime, incarceration, and disadvantage in the remote community of Bourke in the state of New South Wales. It won the 2019 Best Large Grant award in the Australian Philanthropy Awards and is now attracting government investment.

2. **The Our Place model:** This new approach to education, first started in Doveton, a suburb in the outer east of Melbourne, has experienced high levels of disadvantage. A partnership between government and philanthropy, it is now being expanded to other locations across Victoria.

Successful projects like this really shine a light on how philanthropy can catalyze change and be the delta between a program being given the green light or not. The sector might be best served by identifying them and leveraging their local representatives or the appropriate government minister. Let's be proactive rather than wait for the false funding idol of an election to gaze its eyes on our sector once every four years.

Corporate Social Responsibility. I would be remiss if I at least didn't mention the for-profit sector, and the rationale for this may surprise you:

Krystian states that "our economic model is under strain, there are major issues with precarious work, a sizable class of 'working poor,' and I think a move towards democracy in the workplace through employee representation on company boards could shift corporate practices in a way that can help address some of these issues."

That democracy, according to Krystian, should come through mandating employee representation on company boards above a certain size, with employee directors chosen democratically. "I'm not necessarily talking about a majority of directors being employees, though I do like such cooperative models, but at least one to two directors on each board should be. It's not particularly revolutionary; rather, it's an incremental change, and I'd challenge somebody to put up a credible argument why this is a bad idea." While we are seeing positive shifts in corporate governance (for example, a recognition that maximizing shareholder value is not the only responsibility of company directors), one could argue that as major generators of a company's wealth, its employees should have some sort of decision-making power when it comes to the ongoing direction of the company.

Krystian goes on to add, "I think that the group of people from which company directors are generally drawn is too narrow, and employee directors would provide new and different perspectives that would add immense value and ensure that companies truly do take broader factors when making decisions. We often talk about the importance of democracy in our societies, but somehow think that it's all right for there to be no democracy in the workplace. We also talk about a 'crisis of democracy' in countries like the US and Australia, with lower engagement, growing cynicism, and distrust. Perhaps part of tackling this crisis is to inject democracy into other parts of our society, so that people can see its benefits in the places they spend a lot of the waking time, to see it literally at work!"

Having staff on your leadership group also will instill a sense of pride in the organizations that struggle to manifest in decisions of those without accountability to their peers on the shop floor, as it were. The small choices they make, especially around corporate giving, will add another layer of empathy and understanding to a company's response to the needs of the communities in which they live and work.

Civic Participation. While scrutiny of philanthropy can raise difficult questions for the sector, it is an important form of accountability and can also help make the sector better and more responsive. The role of sector media, broader mainstream media, the scholarly community, commentators, and others in this respect is important.

When Krystian spoke with me, he also shared concerns about some of the generalizations made as part of this scrutiny, that can magnify the negative and minimize the positive. "I am concerned that when scrutinizing or critiquing philanthropy, some commentators compare the reality of philanthropy with the ideal of government, for example, which is an unfair and unrealistic comparison in my view," he says. "We need to compare the reality of philanthropy with the reality of government." Government can be and often is a force for good and positive change. Yet despite being democratically accountable in places such as the US and Australia (unlike philanthropy), governments also make bad decisions and, most recently in the height of a populist approach, decisions that appeal to one demographic at the expense of another.

"I don't agree that government is some sort of ideal form of collective action," Krystian says. "I think it's a very important and indeed vital form of collective action, and many of our social and environmental challenges can only be solved through changes in policy and practice by government. But governments can also be rather detached from citizens, and accountable in theory but not always in practice."

The role of collective action outside of government, which represents a broader conception of democratic participation, is also vital. Philanthropy—big and small philanthropy—is a key part of that. It doesn't mean that philanthropy is perfect, or that it won't do bad things (or things which we would regard as bad).

"Of course, the role of nonprofits in that regard is also absolutely vital," Krystian says. "And in some ways they could be regarded as the air that fills the lungs of democracy. And philanthropy, when 'done right,' should be about helping the lungs of democracy fill with that air.

"In relation to the nonprofit sector, I think its role and value is more important than ever. Whilst it may be a cliché, our societies really are at a crossroads. Issues may be different in different countries, but the nonprofit sector has a vital role as an agent for change, a facilitator of debate and collective action, a means for a diverse range of people to shape responses to societal challenges." The nonprofit sector has a number of challenges, especially in the face of a "shrinking space for civil society" in some parts of the world, how it maintains its sense of direction and purpose in the context of a "marketized" society (and often while operating within market contexts itself), and its resilience as it buffets up against government, funders, and others. The decline in civic participation in some countries also has implications for the sector, and while

Australia has compulsory voting, nonprofits need to consciously think about how they can involve and engage more people in their processes and activities, and in new ways.

There is a vital role for philanthropy as a facilitator for citizen action. Empowering residents and the groups of which they are members of to come together, build coalitions, experiment, innovate, and hold others accountable (including government and business) will see a whole new energy for change.

The Future of Philanthropy in Australia. The future of philanthropy, especially if realized through the predictions made throughout this book, will more than likely be implemented in tandem globally. It'll be a plug-and-play mechanism for enhancing the impact and effectiveness of existing structures rather than the arduous task of either reforming or legislating wholescale change (which is never a perfect remedy). I asked Krystian about the new ways of giving that he feels have the most potential to make an impact in our sector.

"I think that participatory grantmaking has lots of potential," he says. "It helps democratize philanthropy, and places decision-making power in the hands of communities and those with lived experience."

But as with most things so far, there is a lot of talk, and agreement about its benefits, but little action. "I tend to think we should be adopting an 'if not, why not' approach to participatory grantmaking in the case of larger foundations," Krystian says. "If they aren't doing it for at least a portion of their grantmaking, why not? What's stopping them?"

That's a fair point through the lens of perpetuity, and one that begs the question: What levels of risk should the philanthropic sector be taking right now?

"I think one of the key roles for philanthropy is to provide 'risk capital for social change' and to fund organizations to experiment with innovative new approaches to addressing social and environmental issues," Krystian says. "I think that fulfilling this 'discovery' role (as Stanford Professor Rob Reich describes it) is important for philanthropy to maintain its legitimacy within society and it's an important function for philanthropy within a democracy."

That being said, there's no balanced level of risk that philanthropy "should" be taking. Sometimes a community group needs a new shed to store equipment, and a foundation may contribute the funds for that. It's not risky or innovative—but it's important for the group, and more broadly, in supporting grassroots civil society. We must remember to not dismiss this as less important or ineffective due to the size and scope, but rather recognize that different organizations and causes have different needs, and philanthropy needs to be responsive to this nuance.

Krystian continues, "However, I do think that philanthropy needs to also pivot more towards empowering others to take risks. What I mean by this is that it would be good to see more funding provided as general operating support, which organizations can decide for themselves how to use.

"I am a fan of a strategic approach to philanthropy, which in its simplest form means that some thought is put into philanthropy, how and what it funds, and why—but at the same time, I worry that we can overthink and overcomplicate philanthropy. We can create too narrow and specific grants programs, with processes involving multiple hoops to jump through in order to receive a grant, with multiple levels of decision-making that nonprofits must negotiate, and burdening them with having to engage with funders who may want to be very hands on, when that just makes life more difficult for the nonprofits. That doesn't mean that we shouldn't have engaged funders, because I think sensitive and thoughtful funders can and do provide real benefits through their engagement—but at the same time, sometimes a hands-off approach is better."

It's important to pause and think about that last point and realize there is a bit more depth to it. This hands-off approach is part of a much larger and ongoing conversation about trust-based philanthropy and having philanthropic institutions challenge their own underlying assumptions about their corpus and approach to spending. Ultimately the hard work will come in this phase of reflection and regeneration, which will hopefully then drive an approach that is as simple, transparent, inclusive, and accountable as possible.

Since coming into the world of philanthropy around seven years ago,

Krystian has been pivotal in elevating and accelerating the conversation of organized philanthropy in Australia. While he realizes the barriers to entry are high due to the limited number of foundations and the jobs that go with it, he has a very similar mindset to what was highlighted in this third part of the book, understanding that there are a number of complementary roles that prepare you for a career in this field, those being government and nonprofits.

"I am excited by the people in philanthropy and the nonprofit sector," Krystian says, "because they are part of shaping the future. Whether they are people I work with in the sector, or students, I am just so impressed by their passion and desire to build a better world. It's one of the things that actually attracted me to working in the sector in the first place, wanting to work alongside these people."

I'm also excited about the future for Australian philanthropy, even though it's currently from afar. Other US folks reading this might be inspired, and served well, by plying their trade over there too, especially as the fundraising profession matures in higher education and other globally focused charities that have a presence in the region. All I know is that those currently working in the social sector in Australia will play a big role in reimagining a world that works for all of us, and understand that philanthropy has a supporting role in creating that shared future.

A SAUDI VISION OF PHILANTHROPY THROUGH THE LENS OF FAITH AND FINANCE

For a country built upon Islamic foundations—including *zakat* (the obligation an individual has to donate a certain percentage of wealth each year to charity), which by Quaranic ranking is next after *salat* (prayer) in importance—it is only natural that philanthropy in Saudi Arabia would grow exponentially. It is very much part of a citizen's identity, and together with the encouragement of giving through Islam (*sadaqah*), there is a strong mandate for the giving of one's time, talent, and treasure.

Generally, what is happening in Saudi Arabia is a fascinating case study for organized philanthropy. And while much of the structural elements of endowment building and the establishment of foundations

218

largely mimics that of America, the religious, state, and issue-specific elements that make up the sector—in some cases meaning a royal decree to formalize nonprofit organizations—together with the rapid growth, education, and globalization of the region makes it a key actor in each nation's ongoing success.

In an *Alliance* magazine feature on Saudi Arabian philanthropy, a consultant field trip provided the following insights into the Kingdom's overarching ecosystem.

The use of endowment funds to fund philanthropic organizations was the most innovative practice seen during the field trip. Foundations in several areas (including poor rural ones) have endowed shopping areas, residential buildings, pharmacies, clinics, and so forth using the income generated from such investment to cover administrative and program expenses. Also, *zakat* funding, which normally consists of simple handouts, is being made contingent on its use for specific purposes such as children, health, or education needs, which also builds awareness among recipients of these priorities.

In addition, according to a study conducted by researchers at Harvard Kennedy School's Hauser Institute with funding from Swiss bank UBS, nearly three quarters of philanthropic foundations in the Middle East are concentrated in Saudi Arabia. These resources are also highly concentrated in certain areas with education as the most popular area for investment globally.

Lots of cultural assumptions are made about Saudi Arabia. Yet with a deeper dive, we can see that changes in attitudes around women, youth, and education in places like Saudi Arabia have coincided with philanthropy playing a bigger role in the country's development. This coincides with around thirty new universities being built in the past decade or so (twenty-four of them being public institutions, with 70 percent of students studying in the fields of humanities and social sciences), more than a third of the population younger than twenty-five, and in just one generation having transformed its citizenry from one of the highest illiteracy rates (60 percent) in the world to one of the highest literacy rates (95 percent).

And while oil has indeed fueled this growth, the region is looking to tech and tourism (among other sectors) to sustain its growth and also continue its trajectory. The majority of the top ten countries with the highest internet penetration rates are Gulf nations. They have one of the highest mobile phone subscriptions in the world, and—this should come as no surprise—Arabic is the fastest growing language on social media channels such as Twitter.

What all this points to is a shift from fossil fuel dependency to an intentional shift to a new digital economy, and new voices leading that charge.

This direction is underpinned by the Saudi Vision 2030, a strategic framework to reduce Saudi Arabia's dependence on oil; diversify its economy with the development of new tech and finance services, companies, and products; and accelerate the development of its public sector service such as health, education, and tourism. Another key goal is promoting a more modern image of the Kingdom at large, one that is seen and respected as a key economic and digital player on a global scale.

We are already witnessing the benefits of this shift. One of those success stories belongs to Laila Bukhari, whose star has risen in the tech field, formerly through Microsoft and now through Cognizant. Laila works to create better digital experiences for the advancement of the financial sector (specifically), and our global community (generally), including the nonprofit sector, so they can realize their full potential and scale. She also helped draft the Y20 Communique (under the future fit track) as part of the Saudi delegation for this year's G20 Y20 working group, where she focused on creating and negotiating youth-centric policies on the future of work, the future of skills, and entrepreneurship, along with the G20 youth delegates.

The communique was published on October 17, 2020, at the end of the public Y20 Summit and signed on by a representative of the G20 chair, Custodian of the Two Holy Mosques, King Salman bin Abdulaziz Al Saud, and was formally shared at the G20 Summit in November 2020.

While Laila's values see philanthropy foundationally as a lifeline for more distributed good, she also sees it as a key element in advancing the quality of human life. And with that, she is crystal clear on where it should be focusing: female representation.

"Over the past decade, nonprofits such as the US-based AnitaB.org foundation, the National Center for Women and Information Technology (NCWIT), and Women in Technology International have amplified their call to action for more diversity and inclusion of females within the tech sector," Laila explains. "I believe there's been progress when it comes to entry- and mid-level female representation, but more work remains to be done when it comes to advancement all the way up to the C-suite and board level. This can be achieved if the sector as a whole advocates for equal pay and generous maternity and caretaker leave, advises on establishing institutionalized sponsorship for emerging female leaders (using targeted research), and supports more upskilling and reskilling initiatives when it comes to technical certifications aimed at females who are looking to pivot into the tech field or advance within it."

Laila is leading from the front in this regard and also leveraging tech to make it happen in a transformative and transparent way. "I'm proud of the digital skills training advocacy, which is at the core of the Cognizant US Foundation's work to help equip young talent with the needed technical skills for employment," she says. "And while I see philanthropy as a force of change, tackling issues that may have not been addressed and helping to improve the lives of those affected by it, I believe it can be incorporated more into company cultures, schools, and community service from an earlier age."

Education, automation, and enabling others to "see their future" through augmented reality also seem to make up key parts in Laila's recipe for success and change, with entrepreneurs also seeing the advantages of moving to what is an emerging innovation hub. "Philanthropy should be leaning more into technology in nontraditional ways," she says, "including further exploring how data modeling and augmented reality can help the philanthropic sector, highlighting impact and progress where there are gaps and helping the Kingdom achieve its 2030 vision through a digital transformation any advanced economy would be proud of."

Laila identified augmented reality, AI, and machine learning together with robotic process automation (RPA) as the keys to unlocking a new decade of impact, especially by complementing the current push for a new digital economy that is underpinned by a boom in financial technology (fintech) start-ups, strategically funded by the Kingdom.

"I believe that fintechs, along with new mobile payment apps, as well as social media, have introduced new 'donation channels' to individuals passionate about supporting philanthropic causes," she says. "Moreover, AI and data visualization have also opened the door for more transparency when it comes to highlighting impact by numbers to donors and spawned amazing collaborations such as the ID2020 Alliance—a global public-private partnership dedicated to aiding the 1.1 billion people around the world who lack any legal form of identity. This is a collaboration between Microsoft, Accenture, and Avanade on a blockchain-based identity prototype on Microsoft Azure."

It's these big goals that have Laila thinking about big-ticket items such as a universal global minimum wage, how to further digitize current services, and ways both she and her female peers can espouse all the traits of courageous leadership, especially when this ambitious country is still navigating exponential cultural transformation with the entire world watching.

"To me, authenticity, resilience, ambition, and commitment to the purpose you're working toward and the people you lead are hallmarks of my work to date," she says. "I'm excited about the possibility for more innovation and more positive impact for advancement for both my country and the global community and hope that the world will turn its gaze to Saudi Arabia not only as a partner, but a leader for imagining what our world could be."

With innovative and inclusive leaders like Laila leading the charge, and with their trajectory coinciding with a generational wealth transfer the likes of which has never been seen before, it's time to move past the differences and move toward the commonalities, and our shared goals for the future of humanity.

PART FOUR

THE DECADE OF DISRUPTION

CHAPTER THIRTEEN

Do We Even Need a Table?

I have framed these four pillar introductions around expanding the voices and seats at the table and discussing how we can reset and upset the table to ensure those new voices are in a position to contribute, lead, and not be tokenized. But the reality is, do we even need a table?

If anything, this book—together with the societal upheaval of the coronavirus pandemic, Black Lives Matter movement, and the 2020 presidential election—makes the case that the formal approaches to our work, how our communities function, and the potential for them to rise out of this civic malaise are all in our hands, not in the hands of those we have long accepted to be in positions of power.

The formal symbolism of a table has always been that of the boardroom, where the big decisions are made, and a place we aspire to take our careers. But that's just part of the out-of-date narrative of a meritocracy, one that overlooks the real issues of our communities and rewards capability not ability, regardless of what the true definition reads.

Tech has the potential to level the playing field and to level up its participants. It provides the tools and capacity for folks to build solutions that just weren't possible a decade ago and gives people, groups, and governments the chance to create a new future if they are not currently excited about the one they are seeing unfold.

We should be taking an interest in how tech works and how it can improve the world, moving from consumer to producer. And we should come to the understanding that we need to seize the opportunity and see tech for good, not become tech for the few.

We are already seeing what the consequences might be if we do not create "lanes" for the successful integration of tech into our daily lives. These include a consolidation of wealth and power, a loss of freedom in the form of data monitoring and manipulation, and all the damage tech has caused our democracy, intentional or not.

The social sector has a big role to play here. That's why we outline the need to look at the ethics of technological advances from both policy and psychological standpoints before we turn to the potential impact of technology. And that's where things get really interesting.

This was by far my favorite part of the book to write. It allowed me to see what was out there on the horizon and imagine what could be, purely looking at impact rather than monetary benefits and envisioning the future of work not as an option, but as necessary shifts.

Those emerging leaders highlighted for this final pillar have been in the engine rooms of this change, building the policy landscape, developing the tech, and fast-tracking new approaches and solutions through big philanthropic investments.

As you read the remaining chapters, you'll learn more about the work of Laura Tomasko, Efrem Bycer, and Ruby Bolaria-Shifrin, as well as what values drive them. Most importantly, you'll discover how they are in your corner fighting for a better tomorrow.

LAURA TOMASKO

Laura is a policy program manager for the Center on Nonprofits and Philanthropy at the Urban Institute. She oversees work on charitable giving and impact investing and ensures Urban's research is widely used by practitioners, advocates, and policymakers. Before joining Urban, Laura was an associate program officer at the Bill & Melinda Gates Foundation, where she managed a portfolio of grants focused on building policy and data capacity for the philanthropic sector. During the Obama administration, she served as a senior policy advisor for social innovation on the White House Domestic Policy Council and deputy associate director for public engagement on the Council on Environmental Quality. Laura previously held positions at national philanthropy associations—the Council on Foundations, and Grantmakers for Effective Organizations—as well as community-based organizations Central New York Community Foundation and the Children's Aid Society.

EFREM BYCER

Efrem is a cross-sector leader focused on making our economy and society more equitable. He's currently a member of LinkedIn's Public Policy and Economic Graph team, where he leads a set of partnerships with government agencies and civic organizations to help connect workers to economic opportunity, particularly through job training and reemployment services. Prior to joining LinkedIn, Efrem led Code for America's efforts to help governments better leverage agile software development and user-centered design to support their economic and workforce development efforts. He has more than a decade of experience working at the intersection of economic development, workforce development, civic engagement, digital government, and public sector innovation. He has a BS in urban and regional studies from Cornell University and an MPA from the Maxwell School of Syracuse University.

RUBY BOLARIA-SHIFRIN

Ruby manages the housing affordability program at the Chan Zuckerberg Initiative (CZI). Partnership for the Bay's Future is CZI's biggest housing investment to date. Prior to CZI, she worked in real estate development, managing multifamily mixed-income development projects in San Francisco for Fivepoint (formerly Lennar Urban) and has experience in commercial real estate at JLL. Ruby also worked internationally at the Housing Department in Johannesburg, South Africa, where she managed an in situ upgrading pilot project. She started her career in environmental, public health, and social justice nonprofits as an organizer. She holds a BA in politics from the University of California, Santa Cruz and a master's of urban and regional planning from the University of California, Los Angeles.

The decade of disruption, as I call it, is based in a real reality, not just a virtual one. Much of what will be highlighted and ideated in the following pages will become mainstream by 2030, including smart contracts, 3D printing, and machine learning. And while I don't quite speculate things such as flying cars becoming the new fleet vehicles for Meals on Wheels, I'll throw a few wildcards in there that might catch fire in their first iteration.

Change is coming. So rather than have it forced upon us, we should make the necessary moves and adjustments to let it help our work take flight. But let's not forget that we are also people, not machines, and that we must take time for our own well-being if we are to be the champions of the future I know we can all be. That's why we end the book with Beth Kanter providing that much needed pause and reflection. Burnout is real, and computers aren't the only ones that can fry their circuits.

CHAPTER FOURTEEN

Curating a Modern Ecosystem

EVEN SYSTEMS BUILT AND DESIGNED TO DO GOOD HAVE IMPLICIT BIASES
In 2018 I joined the Philanthropy California delegation in Washington, DC, for Foundations on the Hill, a two-day convening of hundreds of foundation leaders meeting with Congress to discuss issues of critical importance to philanthropy. The highlight was meeting then-junior senator from California Kamala Harris, whose office in the Hart Senate Office Building was one of the most photographed, given its proximity to the entrance and the large sign outside stating "dreamers are welcome here." About fifteen of us were piled into the office that day, with the majority being CEOs of our states' regional associations and other prominent family foundations. Unsurprisingly, we all had a focused issue to raise with the future vice president of the United States.

We all sat around a large table when the senator came in. After the pleasantries exchanged by way of introductions, she launched right into what was obviously troubling her at that time: the issues with implicit bias being intertwined in the coding of new technologies.

Most of our delegation were taken aback, whereas my eyes lit up. This was a leader who got it and saw philanthropy as a key player in tackling the issue.

Raising philanthropy's awareness and understanding of unconscious bias allows us to rethink and retool the ways and means of how we tackle key processes, structures, and relationships. We often talk a lot about the value of inclusion, but even though we may as individuals have great intentions to be equitable and inclusive on a conscious level, our unconscious beliefs can get in the way of us actually tackling inclusiveness and equity in the ways that we know we are capable as a sector.

Tech has a role to play in navigating implicit bias and has done so already with lasting effects. Some of the stories that have increased my awareness of these issues include research that used computers to screen hundreds of thousands of books for key descriptors around white and Black people and their characters. What it found were dominant trends among both the positive and negative (and you can do the math on that one). These findings, delivered in a workshop through the Opportunity Agenda (a social justice communication lab out of New York), spurred me to think more critically about and further analyze storytelling and history in the United States. They have also shifted my perspectives and attitudes and helped me articulate and challenge my own narratives around critical moments of our past.

But where tech can improve our understanding, there needs to be a broader discussion and exploration around the legal, ethical, and economic impact of these advancements on society. For instance, the failed AI project from Amazon had been building programs to review job applicants' resumes, with the aim of identifying top talent and revolutionizing the hiring process. A year later, it was found that the new system was reviewing candidates in a gender-biased way. Basically, Amazon's computer models were trained to vet applicants by observing patterns in resumes submitted to the company over a ten-year period. For an industry that wasn't exactly diverse, being male became the identified dominant requisite of the ideal candidates. It also actively penalized resumes via this learned methodology by concluding the word *women's* was not a good thing. This meant that graduates of all-women's colleges and captains of the women's STEM or robotics clubs were unfairly downgraded, things that no doubt would've made Senator Harris's blood boil.

Moving forward, it is ethically irresponsible to focus only on what tech can do for society. It's just as important to ask what it should (and should not) do, and important to instill a fail-safe in our design thinking immediately.

Tech—and more specifically AI and other reinforced learning paradigms—is at the forefront of our thinking and future planning. And while tech does many things faster and more efficiently than humans can alone, there are lingering ethical and societal implications to consider.

For example, how can we ensure that AI is beneficial and not detrimental to human progress? What unintended consequences are we overlooking by developing technology that can potentially be manipulated and misused? The goal of new sophisticated systems and applications has to be the need to create technologies that both protect and improve our world.

Technology by itself isn't good or bad, but it's also not neutral. It reflects the biases of the people who design, train, and use it. If any one of us who was there for that conversation in DC took anything away from it, it was that we needed to better understand what changes these new technologies would bring, predict how those changes would unfold, and mitigate the harms or unintended consequences they could cause while still leveraging their benefits—and we still need to do all of this today.

Philanthropy should be looking to partner and fund academia to help address this generational conundrum. A program I work with and am happy showcasing (via my own bias) is at the University of Texas at Austin and its Good Systems initiative, which is establishing a framework for evaluating, developing, implementing, and regulating AI-based technologies so they reflect human values at their core.

AI is changing the way we live and work—often, for the better—but it has the potential to be harmful in ways we fail to predict. Designing AI technologies that benefit society is a noble challenge all pillars of our society and economy should be looking at, including the social sector, despite how daunting it may seem.

R&D AND OPEN DATA: A REPOSITORY FOR PHILANTHROPIC KNOWLEDGE, LESSONS, AND LEANINGS

I still remember walking into the storage cupboard of the San Diego Foundation in my first week of working in the philanthropic sector and seeing a vast array of unlabeled and sealed-up boxes creating a floor-to-ceiling mosaic of all the shades of that distinctive cardboard-box brown. The shades were either darkened from dust or from their prior location sitting in front of a window next to someone's desk. These boxes, I realized, contained some of the most original, rich, and curated data available to our local region. They contained hundreds of copies of *Our Greater San Diego Vision*, which was a visioning document that surveyed over thirty thousand residents and provided a number of rec-ommendations across four key indicators—jobs and the economy, cul-tural and community amenities, housing, environment, mobility and the cost of living, and education and learning. This was given the catchy acronym of WELL (Work, Enjoy, Live, and Learn) and forged a new path for the foundation into the world of civic engagement.

And it did, for a few years—until it failed to launch and was shuf-fled into the marketing arm of the organization to be kept out of the community spotlight. This was pretty much symbolic of the number of reports sitting in that cupboard that I was motivated to give a second lease on life to. You see, foundations—for all of their funds, scope, influ-ence, and potential—have a penchant for sticking their logo on almost anything, getting that dopamine hit of organizational relevance from their community and sending out an accompanying media release to prove that they are at the forefront of all civic trends.

It could be oh-so-different. Imagine an entity that was patient and understood its ability to forge consensus–based and collaborative long-term change through playing what is a long term game. Imagine a foundation using that report as a catalyst for a one- to three-year con-versation about that change and helping educate, create awareness for, and execute on its findings and recommendations.

You see, there was a reason why those reports were sitting in those boxes. They had run their immediate course instead of their actual course. The ROI of that report was not fully exhausted across the spec-trum of the social sector. Nor was it part of any strategic plan where any element of accountability for its success was present.

It would be great to see the establishment of a philanthropic watch-dog or an entity that grades the effectiveness of reports across a number of metrics, such as the extent to where they are disseminated, and the leveraged impact of its findings from the community.

Qualitative and quantitative examples of this include whether they are cited in media and academic papers, whether core data sets are highlighted in grant applications, or if its finding were basis for a policy change in government.

Reports aren't helping anyone by sitting on a shelf. Access to and the adoption of research and data are some of the most underused assets a nonprofit organization can have at its disposal.

If you invest the time and resources into creating research reports that address critical civic needs, you should fully exhaust that content in a variety of ways:

- **Distribution:** Don't just have copies of the report sitting on a card table at your events as a prop. Send copies to local elected officials and organizations that are tackling the issues head on. This includes both businesses and nonprofit organizations.

- **Engage:** Create a monthly or quarterly "Solution Series" that convenes leaders and the community to discuss the issues and recommendations contained within the report in an intentional way. Build momentum that can lead to commitments of action.

- **Accessibility:** Include a downloadable copy (that isn't protected by passwords or restricted by membership levels) in a prominent and easily locatable space on your website. Include print-on-demand options too!

- **Content Creation:** A hundred-page report can generate so much content that it could easily pump-prime your social media channels for a year. Cut it up into blog posts, coauthor them for a new viewpoint, create videos, build a six-episode themed podcast—the choices are endless.

Issue Lab, which is part of the Candid umbrella, is a good example of this. It collects, collates, and makes available for free through its website close to 30,000 publications and reports from more than 7,500 organizations. This is all through a simple search bar and is supported by its Open for Good campaign, a concerted push for foundations to share their reports, findings, and ultimately their knowledge for the benefit of both the field and the communities they serve. This is a learning tool first and foremost, because—as Issue Lab aptly puts it—"we can all learn from each other especially the inputs and outputs associated with more than $5 billion in grants going out the door each and every year." Issue Lab also created the foundational elements of a similar searchable library (named Knowledge Center) at the Barr Foundation, which could prove an important blueprint for broader community-based data repositories.

While philanthropy can and should be leading from the front on this one by making all its reports and evaluations public, the sector should also be seeking opportunities to partner with cities that ultimately possess the mother lode of data for folks to utilize for the common good.

Some of the larger cities are tackling this issue with open data portals to spark innovation and better inform decision-making. However, the Sunlight Foundation, an organization that fights for transparency through the utilization of civic tech and open data to "enable more complete, equitable, and effective democratic participation," finds that out of the more than one hundred cities, countries, and states that now have open data policies across twenty key areas, only around three dozen of those governments' efforts have resulted in wins for their communities.

It would be good to see a broader discussion around this from key players with the goal of moving beyond the token hackathons and student app-building initiatives.

Granted, these initiatives are cute and engaging, but they are not tackling the biggest issues head on or building solutions that the community can use beyond it being packaged commercially by some local start-up.

Matthew Taylor, CEO of the Royal Society for the Arts in London and former chief advisor on political strategy to Prime Minister Tony Blair sums it up perfectly when he mentions that "cities must think like a system and act like an entrepreneur."

This quote became a cornerstone of *The New Localism*, a book by Bruce Katz and Jeremy Nowak, which looks into how cities can thrive in the age of populism.

Ultimately, we shouldn't just make the data available, because that is just the most basic of baseline metrics. Instead, we must actively dive into it through research and development teams on the council payroll, actively seeking research grants to support these efforts and have that dedicated team build new efficiencies that make our cities better. It's that simple.

IMMERSE YOURSELF IN THE NEW EMPATHY MACHINE

Nonprofits and associations are beginning to use virtual reality, augmented reality, 360-degree video, and other innovative storytelling vehicles to help advance their missions with some encouraging results. So how far away is the charitable sector from using VR as a legitimate communications and fundraising tool? Well, it's still in its infancy and only truly available to the largest charities in the world due to the costs involved with creating original content. These costs can easily exceed six figures, so expectations will need to be refocused over the coming years from the traditional lens of return on investment to that of a return on immersion. This will require the foresight (and goodwill) of first movers in this space to continue to increase awareness of VR in marketing and fundraising, and ultimately share their results to help more organizations (both charities and production houses) become more comfortable utilizing these lived experiences for the common good.

In particular, VR will likely help shape the following nonprofit staples through 2025.

Conferences. At least 75 percent of large nonprofit conferences will probably have some form of VR component for use by attendees. This will range from simple VR booths to expose attendees to these computer-simulated realities to breakout sessions discussing the possibilities of VR's future use. (Maybe some will even provide a complimentary headset upon check-in!) Content shown will mainly be replicated, not original. Yet it will drive conversations and persuade attendees to purchase VR hardware for their own private use.

Gala Events and One-Off Fundraising/Campaign Events. Given that VR is still relatively new in terms of mainstream commercialization, creating special events around these unique virtual experiences is allowing charities to reap rewards in real time and provide out-of-the-box thinking to highlight stories of impact and combat major donor fatigue. Event managers who can successfully execute the use of VR and weave it into the experience rather than simply adding it on because it's a cool trend will see their clients yield significant benefits. The leading example of this experiential approach is Pencils of Promise, which created a sixteen-foot replica of a Ghanaian classroom to set the scene for its Wall Street gala. It ended up raising $1.9 million at one of its star-studded events with just a ninety-second video. In the next couple of years, a number of events will likely become even more innovative with their use of VR with the possibility of a single event or multiday conference able to raise $5 million or more.

Major Gifts. Examples of major gift projections being surpassed by up to 70 percent have been reported by UN-backed conferences using VR for donors to highlight the devastation in Syria. It was also found that one in six people pledged donations after participating in that same experience—double the normal rate. Similarly, a donor who recently visited the office of charity: water and had already committed to giving $60,000 watched a VR film on its work in Africa and was so moved by the story that he gave $400,000 instead.

These outcomes should not be underestimated. The sector (or academia) should embark on significant research projects to help fundraisers understand the empathy triggers, motivations, and power of immersive experiences of major donors. Currently VR/AR is driving a $150 billion industry, and it's safe to assume that a VR headset will one day take pride of place in a number of nonprofit CEOs' offices for when that all-important request comes.

Activism. With major elections in the US every two years, VR campaign videos will eventually be released to highlight key policy issues and drive donations toward engagement efforts. Organizations such as Amnesty International and the International Rescue Committee are leading the way on linking virtual content that communicates their missions and current work both locally and globally. It's also being taken to the streets through innovative grassroots engagement tactics.

A great example of this is Amnesty International launching a Virtual Reality Aleppo campaign in three major UK cities to amplify the effectiveness of its traditional street-fundraisers messages. This campaign used refurbished smartphones and basic VR headgear and took viewers on a tour of the war-ravaged Syrian city of Aleppo, one hundred kilometers south of the Turkish border, to highlight the impact caused by barrel bombs.

Fundraisers and door-to-door canvassers won't just be drawing you in for a conversation with loaded salutations and a disarming smile. They will also be equipped to spark your curiosity with immersive hardware.

Industry and Foundational Support. There are huge equity disparities within nonprofits that are just being exacerbated by access to this technology. The top 10 percent of charities have large teams of communications and fundraising staff as well as the budgets to execute. Smaller nonprofits that often are doing the hard work on the ground and have truly inspiring stories to share are more concerned with raising enough money to keep the lights on than taking on the risk and costs associated with creating a VR experience for its limited donor base.

To help close this gap, major national foundations should expand or create grant opportunities that will allow for smaller organizations to create VR content. This could also come in the form of partnerships with major companies and platforms such as Oculus VR, Samsung Gear, and HTC Vive to help partner VR production companies with impactful nonprofits, which have already explored this approach through their VR for Good and 360 Bootcamp programs.

"Telling your story" has always been at the forefront of advice given to nonprofits. Now the sector has a new tool to add to its fundraising arsenal and assist in its ongoing narrative. It is one thing to read and contextualize impact but quite another when you can see the real difference your donation makes to a person's life, through their eyes, and understanding (to a point) the harsh realities that are sometimes all too easy to ignore.

The VR industry understands that adoption and conversion will be driven from the outside in and that VR won't flourish in the social sector without its intervention and ongoing commitment. And while we are still in a holding pattern of VR exploration and awareness in the nonprofit world, there is no doubt that we are ready to conceptualize truly impactful and innovative uses of the medium and bring these conversations from online speculation to fleshed-out campaigns.

Perhaps you, too, can imagine other outcomes of using VR, such as visualizing data in new ways, assisting in disaster response by transporting lawmakers and funders to "ground zero," having supporters "walk" around a proposed new building for an upcoming capital campaign, training for health and safety, and volunteer and employee onboarding. The reality for this tech is that anything in the physical setting can be mimicked in a virtual setting—and simply knowing that should help you dream of the next big thing.

LAURA TOMASKO

Informing a New Attitude to Philanthropic Power

Laura Tomasko is, in my view, well-positioned to think about strategic shifts in philanthropy. Her philanthropic experience comes from past positions in grantmaking at the Bill & Melinda Gates Foundation and a community foundation, as well as sector-building roles at two philanthropy infrastructure organizations, including the Council on Foundations. She currently works at the Urban Institute, where she focuses on nonprofits, philanthropy, and impact investing.

Many funders use data to inform grantmaking decisions and evaluate the effectiveness of a particular program or organization. But do they think critically about where those data come from and what purpose they serve?

"When it comes to setting strategy or determining which organizations to support," Laura says, "funders have an opportunity to bring new voices to the decision-making table. All too often, academic and professional experience outweighs lived experience. Funders who are concerned about this dynamic can adjust hiring practices to prioritize lived experience and integrate participatory grantmaking principles into decision-making processes so that people with lived experience have a voice at the table."

Laura recognizes how current funding practices compound historical and current inequities, privilege, and power dynamics in the sector. "There's a lot of focus in the sector on achieving scale and supporting evidence-backed interventions," she says. "I think it's important to pair that goal with critical thinking about the extent to which systemic racism and bias might have created conditions that enable some organizations to grow and build evidence of success and others to stay afloat with few resources. Did the larger organizations have leaders who gained expertise through academic training and professional experience, with strong networks in philanthropy that enabled them to secure grants for evaluations? If given the same access to funding and evaluation, would the programs at less well-resourced organizations demonstrate similar or greater effectiveness?"

She goes on to say this: "When making grantmaking decisions, funders who want to support organizations likely to achieve program-matic objectives would be wise to consider organizations that might have fewer resources and little to no formal evaluations, but whose leaders come from the community they serve. These leaders know what might work from lived experience and have the knowledge and trust of the community to bring about change. Funding within established networks can perpetuate inequities by overlooking community leaders and solutions that derive from that lived experience."

Beyond the traditional grantmaking processes, data plays a key role in evaluating the effectiveness of a grant or an organization. Laura be-lieves funders should think less about data as a tool for compliance and punitive action against organizations that have not achieved certain projections, and more as a tool for evaluation and to support an organi-zation's learning, growth, and storytelling capacity.

"We want grantmakers to recognize the ways that data can empower their grantees to thrive while also acknowledging the flaws and limits of data," she says. "When gathering data to evaluate effectiveness, think about who pays for the assessment, who determines the research ques-tions, and what information is available and collected and by whom. All of these factors influence the data that ultimately helps determine the effectiveness of a program or grant. And who benefits from the data? Do the data collection efforts burden grantees and ultimately not benefit the organization itself? Or do they empower organizations to evaluate and improve programs, as well as equipping them with infor-mation to tell their story to their stakeholders?"

And it's not just the data that the sector should reflect on. Phil-anthropic funders should consider how well they are engaging with government to advance their mission. Both public policy development and implementation can help philanthropic funders in their strategic approach to change. And there are many ways beyond lobbying to engage in the policymaking process.

During her time in the Obama administration, Laura served as a senior policy advisor for social innovation in the White House Domestic Policy Council and deputy associate director for public engagement at the Council on Environmental Quality, which gave her a unique insight into how philanthropy could be more effective in its advocacy efforts.

"Often, philanthropic funders think of policy change as the domain of the legislative branch, but should not overlook opportunities on the executive side," she says. "Many philanthropic and public sector funders are trying to achieve similar objectives, and it makes sense for the two sectors to find opportunities to share information, coordinate, and partner when appropriate. Foundations interested in aligning their work with government should figure out which government agencies are working on policies that affect their charitable goals and develop relationships with those officials. They should participate in stakeholder engagement opportunities such as attending meetings, writing letters, and commenting on proposed rules. Foundations can also identify ways to assist grantees in applying for public funds. And when there's high alignment between government and philanthropic priorities, foundations can seek opportunities to align their grantmaking to complement government initiatives and grants."

As helpful as Laura thinks it can be for foundations to partner with government, she cautions policymakers and government officials to remember that philanthropy cannot and should not replace government funding. "Let's not forget that philanthropic dollars are just a drop in the ocean of trillion-dollar government budgets and they are not there to make up for budget cuts and shortfalls," she said.

Beyond data and partnerships with the public sector, Laura explained what we might see from the sector in the coming decade. "Rather than drawing a bright line between individual giving and institutional philanthropy," she says, "I imagine we will see more funds and philanthropic initiatives that look different from the traditional private foundation structure. We might see more opportunities for donors at different wealth levels and institutions of various sizes and legal structures to pool philanthropic resources to support common goals.

"The COVID-19 crisis has opened the eyes of many to the benefits of giving direct cash to individuals in need. This is greatly enabled by online giving platforms, app-based payment platforms, and new technologies yet to be created, which I imagine will continue to facilitate direct giving over the coming decade. And while there will continue to be nonprofit intermediaries that administer direct cash giving (along with the opportunity for foundations to make grants and individual givers to receive a tax deduction for the small segment of taxpayers eligible for the charitable deduction), many individuals will happily give directly without the possibility of a tax benefit."

Most critically, Laura hopes that in the coming decade the sector addresses its own issues of power, privilege, and racial justice. "The philanthropic sector plays a key role in exacerbating many of the inequities it also aims to ameliorate," she says. "Ten years from now, will we look back on this moment—the confluence of a pandemic and movement for racial justice—and say this was a watershed moment for the sector? That it caused philanthropy to think about ways to share power and reduce the gatekeeping that has often prioritized white privilege over lived experience in hiring and grantmaking decisions? I would like to say I'm hopeful, but there's a lot we need to do to get there."

CHAPTER FIFTEEN

Feed the Machines

WHAT IF MACHINES SHOWED US OUR APPROACHES TO SOLVING SOCIETY'S BIGGEST ISSUES WERE WRONG?

For all the talk of big data, how many nonprofits, foundations, and national associations truly have the capacity to use it in a way that could find innovative new ways to tackle some of the most critical issues of our time? This might be the case for larger foundations sitting on billion-dollar endowments. But even then, they are focused on larger ROI in developing countries or newer industries where they can move the needle.

As we continue to see rapid growth in this digital age, small to medium organizations continue to double down on the status quo with limited capacity software supporting a glut of program managers, marcom staff, and grant officers with visualization tools that simply highlight the problem through a more focused lens.

This is a missed opportunity given that tech exists now that can identify new patterns that could determine a totally different approach to solving the issues people have dedicated their careers to within these organizations.

The origins of explaining big data were not initially applied as a term as they are today, but more of an adjective on how to tackle a problem. This drift in interpretation has ultimately affected the social sector's approach, with folks selectively using data sets to reaffirm their own symbolic reasoning and process in solving a particular problem.

So what could our social sector do to revamp its approaches and create breakthrough solutions by using new tech to tackle more localized and socially entrenched issues such as poverty, homelessness, and health care access? In short, it might be time we moved this work to a machine.

Not in its entirety, of course, because networks can only show patterns and not the answers. However, machines can digest big data sets in a way that can be blind to regular wisdom, politics, and personalities, grouping it in simple ways that might help folks see the issue in a new light and ask new questions that might catalyze alternative approaches.

What would this entail? First, you would need to build a new machine environment to enable deep learning, more than likely a cloud–based approach with something such as Google Colaboratory or Amazon Machine Images (AMIs). Then it's time to start coding and implementing your own deep learning models.

Let's be realistic, though. That is probably beyond a regular nonprofit's capability and something a much larger actor would need to take on in collaboration with those organizations to help provide a clearinghouse for multiple data sets and additional layers of privacy and integrity. (More on that later in this book.) If you're new to machine learning, a far better use of your time would be to simply begin to understand it in basic terms, become comfortable with speaking about it both internally and externally, and looking at how it could be applied to your organization's future impact.

Machine Learning in Practice. With that in mind, let's talk about what some outcomes might look like using homelessness as an example. This issue, and the effects of its intersectionality, provides rich, robust, and diverse data sets, including (but not limited to) the following:

- decades of data across local, state, and federal jurisdictions

- a number of approaches to tackling the issue

- thousands of associated nonprofit entities supporting those affected

- more than 500,000 homeless individuals who have ended up on the streets for a variety of reasons

(If you're interested in a more nuanced—albeit dated—primer to using data to understand homelessness, you can find it at the HUD website, which is included in the notes section at the back of this book.)

The goal here would be to feed large, clean data sets into the deep learning model and allow it to find meaning in connections that are not easy to see. This will lead to unnamed groupings regardless of current classifications (e.g., chronic, episodic, transitional, and hidden) with no blind spots or bias, which would then be available for decision-makers to digest and use in ways that could be applicable to addressing the issues in new ways (or help reaffirm the current direction). The outcomes that these patterns can generate should hopefully lead to us having a tool that can be a real X factor in identifying indicators such as why people become homeless in the first place and the key to having folks transition away from it.

Let's highlight this by using a regression analysis example:

> **Dependent variable** (outcome)—likelihood of being homeless
> **Independent variable** (predictors)—sanitary items or small monetary amounts charged to a credit card before rent was due

Machine learning can analyze patterns that would be extremely hard and time consuming to identify if done by an analyst. In the example above, it could detect a pattern between homelessness and life essentials being purchased in a certain way or in a certain clustered time frame. A mechanism could then be built that would trigger a flag for an at-risk individual to receive immediate outreach and support that in turn could save someone from becoming yet another statistic on our streets.

The Need for New Structures. For all the potential of machine learning, this is where it becomes difficult to foresee its immediate uses, because introducing new tech such as this would mean a fundamental shift in how the nonprofit sector operates, including:

- **Staffing:** Organizations will need to start recruiting data scientists and perhaps provide more dollars for organizers and public policy specialists to analyze new data patterns and shift laws, regulations, and public perceptions in their areas of focus. Data scientists apply a range of skills and methods to explore data, and experiment to find new stories and see beyond current insights, providing informative reports to management (and other key stakeholders where appropriate) to make decisions.

- **Collaboration:** Again, it is highly unlikely smaller nonprofits would have the capacity to drive these efforts even though they stand to yield the best ROI from any potential findings. Therefore, collaboration would be a necessity. There would initially be issues associated with trust and privacy. But if organizations, governments, or any other key stakeholders were willing to enter into legal agreements with specific entities to share their data, it would make these sector-wide outputs far more effective.

- **National accountability:** An independent body or consortium of national organizations would need to exist to make sure any machine learning model that impacts a large intersectional social issue is free from bias and that the patterns it identifies are part of an open and transparent process.

- **Funding:** Homelessness is a funding area that is largely driven by empathy for those affected. Apart from organizations such as Funders Together to End Homelessness (which is looking at systems, structure, policy, and capacity), smaller, location–based gifts are predominantly enabling service providers to triage the problem on the front lines rather than providing the capacity to tackle the problem at large. If data is more readily available for funders to understand some of the root causes at a more nuanced level, philanthropists could then look more strategically at the problem in tandem with curbing the short-term effects.

- **Fuel new investment:** Machine learning also has the potential to fast-track new trends like impact investing, helping to identify new trends that can save governments money and generate a return on investment for nontraditional funders.

This generation-defining technology has the ability to tackle some of the biggest issues of our time. And over the next few years, it will become more readily available for future-focused groups that truly want to solve these existential problems. Philanthropy has a big role to play in bringing machine learning into the mainstream, whether that be through direct funding, advocating for or supporting public philanthropic partnerships that use it to inform and de-risk large-scale investment, or simply by being a trusted vehicle for its reporting (think community foundations, economic development corporations, and industry groups).

Machine learning will be a welcome addition to the social sector's tool kit and shall be able to operate free of systems bias. Remember, the models explain that patterns exist or are occurring but not why they occur. That's an important part of the narrative. (It's important to note that machine learning will never fully replace the work. Subject matter experts will always need to interpret the data from a humanized perspective.)

So, let's not be afraid of investing in things that may challenge our thinking and our approach, and let's reinvent the missions of our organizations so that they can be more successful and profitable for decades to come.

SMART CONTRACTS AND THE AUTOMATED REVOLUTION OF GRANTMAKING

Blockchain and bitcoin are arguably the most talked-about things in tech right now, with rising interest in public discourse. But the concept of smart contracts is the one that needs to be an immediate focus of research, trials, and implementation for the philanthropic sector.

These self-executable contracts have the capacity to revolutionize the sector in a plethora of ways, including grant reporting, best practices in transparency, and organizational productivity.

And to be frank, this kind of technology is a great example of what is needed to ensure that the power dynamics between funders and nonprofit recipients disappear in the joint pursuit of community change and impact.

What Are Smart Contracts? Imagine the contents of a regular grant agreement redrawn in computer code and executed automatically when the terms of that agreement have been completed, thus triggering the full execution of that contract and releasing funds to the grantee. This would be a smart contract in the context of a nonprofit grant agreement.

To keep things simple: the "contract" effectively receives and distributes assets. There is no intermediary and there is no two-month delay from the day your organization learns it has been successful in a funding round to receiving those important funds. (You're not bitter, though, right?) An automated and trackable process for clearing and settlement ensures that this form of contract is truly transparent and conflict-free. It will clearly define the rules and penalties up front and automatically enforce these obligations (including the triggers needed for distribution) of multiyear funding agreements and returning the money to the donor in cases of noncompliance.

Operational Benefits for Donor-Grantees. The appeal to donors is pretty self-explanatory, but the benefits for nonprofit productivity (which we all know carries a monetary value) include the potential for the following:

- shortening grant application times, since a letter of intent can pre-populate a full proposal rather than create unnecessary duplication

- speeding up the grants process from acceptance to remittance, such as uploading attachments, calculating budgets, sending complete contracts, signing contracts, and then distributing funds all online

- providing the scaffolding for a simple funding renewal process

- scanning uploaded metrics and inputs to provide simple and informative end-of-grant reports

Is It Time for Social Impact Bonds to Become a True Force for Change?
These benefits will free up considerable time for both parties but are more operational than revolutionary. So in terms of the big picture, the application of blockchains like these will really help social impact bonds take off as a legitimate public-private-philanthropic approach to solving some of society's biggest and most systemic issues. As of late 2020, there were at least sixty social-impact bonds active in fifteen

countries, with those currently running in the US having an average deal size of around $10 million.

But with research from the Center for Public Impact saying that investors think social-impact bonds below $15 million don't justify their costs, can advances in the evaluation phase of pay-for-success models—and in fact you will be effectively eliminating the need for an intermediary to analyze returns—be the spark for smaller, more innovative programs that can help build confidence in the process and attract larger donations?

And let's not forget that, despite all the benefits of weaving smart contracts into nonprofit grant cycles, the potential cons are clearly evident but can be overcome as this technology matures.

Current Issues for the Application of Nonprofit Blockchains. The first issue is that blockchain has the potential to exacerbate the skewed power dynamics that already exist within the sector.

With all the upside that transparency brings, if the contracts still focus on restricting gifts to programmatic outcomes rather than seeking a balance in supporting the capacity of nonprofits to invest in the deliverables and drive real outcomes, then this is just another way of nickel-and-diming the line items of our nonprofit organizations (which are constantly thinking about keeping the lights on rather than given the space to do essential work for our most vulnerable people).

Another worrying trend is that due to the technical nature of blockchains, the narrative around nonprofit applications is being driven by business and not in tandem with the voices in the sector they wish to impact. This will lead to general assumptions that will always fall on the funder side of the equation—due to the higher likelihood that this will be their customer base—and leave the potential for a compounding effect on issues of full cost as mentioned above. This is not exactly helped by the majority of commentary on this tech looking at the potential of other industries and often neglecting to discuss nonprofits as a viable market, leaving a vacuum for blockchains to focus on the flow of cryptocurrencies as a funding alternative and missing the point of where change in the third sector is sorely needed. We must continue to be patient in waiting for the right tech solutions, rather than fast-tracking those that show promise but might end up being the wrong ones.

All of the webinars and sales pitches for blockchain in the nonprofit and philanthropy world I have seen have surprisingly focused on the most extreme cases of fraud from rogues in the sector and make misguided assumptions about best practices in the field. However, nonprofits can't just be run like the private sector, and not all nonprofits are created equal.

It is important for funders to recognize that organizational effectiveness for their nonprofit partners can come in a variety of different ways. Hopefully technology like the blockchain and smart contracts are used to lift the burden of onerous tasks, reporting structures, and capacity constraints while in return delivering real impact and the outcomes the donors set out to achieve. After all, everyone will be contractually obligated to do so!

ASKS OF THE FUTURE: SELLING BROWSING DATA TO FUEL ARTIFICIAL INTELLIGENCE

AI will eventually become your best development asset, perhaps even your new director. It will provide more accurate prospect data, reduce missed opportunities, and make automated messages feel human. In addition, the future of fundraising will see systems that identify and understand in real time when a potential donor is primed to be asked to give. This request could be delivered online via a bot, or an alert could be sent to an organization's representative to realize the gift in person. Regardless of how this happens, we should expect big things from this game-changing technology.

So how would AI work? Think wealth-research platforms such as Donor Lead or Wealth Engine on steroids. All of the publicly available information on prospects such as previous charitable giving, political donations, business interests, and real estate absorbed into one platform and layered with their browsing history to add more context and personalization. New donor "psychology" profiles would then be created. Once fused with AI, this would become a dynamic process where the understanding of that donor's interests, passions, and motivations would become even more refined each time they log on to the internet.

The catalyst for this future can be drawn back to the recent congressional repeal of historic FCC-installed privacy protections, which gives internet service providers (ISPs) an easier path to collecting and selling your web browsing info and app usage. But it's not the repeal that will set the wheels in motion for this revolution in donor cultivation. Instead, it will be the inevitable pushback from consumers wanting to take back control of their own data, especially in a world where their digital footprint has real monetary worth for business, yet they do not share in its inherent value. Legislation could then be introduced (or the Supreme Court could rule in favor of an individual or group) that will duly recognize the private ownership of an individual's digital activities, actions, and communications. Once people are in control of their data then they will then be in a position to sell these unique data sets themselves. This is when things get disproportionately interesting and valuable. But let's be honest—you won't be making tens of thousands of dollars from all those hours you browsed Etsy and E! News.

Personal data marketplaces will soon become commonplace online and will facilitate the selling of data to interested parties, which will then feed these platforms of the future. These marketplaces are now popping up online (platforms such as DataCoup and CitizenMe) but are not at a stage of maturation where individuals are partnered with retailers, banks, or your local nonprofit. But imagine a place where your bank accounts, social media, and Windows or Chrome extensions are linked via an application programming interface (API) to generate your own unique profile. Then, using this profile, you will learn what your data says about you and have the ability to choose what and who you want to sell your information to.

So how is this data going to be turned into a system that generates more effective asks? In the end, it boils down to the donor's psychology. What truly motivates them to give? When they log on to the net to donate, do they go straight to a nonprofit's page and click through to the supporters tab? Or do they click through to a charity's website after reading an article about a local pet shelter? Everything leading up to a gift will be an essential part of building a donor's profile in the future.

AI has the ability to be a 24/7 observer of these key motivators while they occur in real time and will prompt those all-important asks when they see common patterns and previous triggers align with past giving history. Systems will then anticipate with a fairly high degree of certainty whether that donor is ready to give or is in a "persuadable state" and then execute in ways that are premeditated by the organization's overarching fundraising strategy (for example, asking for a small or main gift or an event ticket or event sponsorship). The probability of a successful ask will also be compounded in the positive when targeting millennials, who are historically more likely to take action online. In the latest *Consumer Email Habits Report* commissioned by Campaign Monitor, the study found that "personalized marketing makes an email an even more powerful tool for this demographic, that is quick to make an impulsive donation to a nonprofit—an impossible task to achieve without the data necessary to create relevant campaigns at scale."

While the introduction of AI to fundraising will be revolutionary in itself—and has begun in earnest with companies such as the Futurus Group and Gravyty—programs will inevitably become smarter, more predictive, and more responsive with the constant growth of online giving and all the data that precedes (and follows) that gift. The possibilities are endless, and in the end it might be AI that helps us crack the code for two of the sector's longest-running conundrums—increasing charitable giving above 3 percent of GDP and engaging the next generation of philanthropy.

DYNAMIC DISCOURSE: HOW CHATBOTS AND VIRTUAL ASSISTANTS CAN STREAMLINE GIVING

We live in a world where the predisposed narrative is that we are available to work 24/7 and that exempt status equates to completing the work regardless of the time it takes (complete with the increasing top-down organizational pressures as a result of shareholder expectations and the passive-aggressive management styles that exploit it)—and that if we cannot meet these requirements, we either are not up to the job or can be replaced.

Balance is important here, but should not be defined. Everyone's circumstances are different. However, we must agree at some point that if tech is layered into our day-to-day practices to help drive more efficiency and "free up more time" to do more productive work, then this reclaimed time should be used to move the needle; undertake larger projects that require a deeper level of research, strategy, and time to execute; and ensure that time isn't backfilled with more mundane tasks that occur as a result of being understaffed, underprepared, or both.

Nonprofits have a complicated relationship with this approach. For-profits push for higher outputs to maximize economies of scale and revenues, whereas nonprofits sometimes have to work longer hours due to the critical need of their services knowing that lives sometimes might literally be at stake.

So where are the pain points? And what are the available solutions?

The answers are obvious from a nonprofit standpoint: administrative tasks and fundraising. The solutions, however, are not so obvious. Options that are affordable, engaging, easy to use, and personalized exist right now, yet they are universally undervalued and underused.

The options I'm talking about are chatbots and virtual assistants. They can provide value and improve your donors' and clients' experience on the front end and duly free up your time on the back end. And while you might find them intrusive at first, since they occupy prime real estate on your screen or pop up over that key piece of information you were seeking, a recent Usabilla report showed that 70 percent of respondents said they have already used chatbots and 60 percent of those who hadn't said they would feel comfortable doing so. Folks may prefer to speak to a human, but it's clear that they would be happy advancing their query in order to save time.

Chatbots. What is a chatbot anyway? In short, it's a simple program that facilitates diverse conversations with single-line responses. In its more complex forms, it uses AI to interact with users through advanced

Future Philanthropy

simulated conversations that facilitate customer service, capture data, and route requests to the right destination.

It's not hard to envision what that might look like and ideate how it could be useful for your organization—and that's not including using the data to improve service delivery by seeing the statistics, patterns, and pathways most commonly used and enhancing those processes accordingly. "Work smarter, not harder," is the relevant adage here.

An example of working smarter is leveraging tech that exists, yet might not be commonplace in your nonprofit toolbox. Did you know that more than 300,000 chatbots were being used on Facebook in 2018? A number of website builders also offer chatbot plug-ins and apps for free. The market size of these tools is projected to grow from $2.6 billion to $9.4 billion by 2024, meaning a compounding growth rate of nearly 30 percent.

The great news here is that this is affordable, ranging from a free, functional option through to software platforms and agencies at the very top end.

It also has the potential for high ROI, especially if used for the following:

- **Lead generation:** Chatbots can ask contextually relevant questions that identify and move prospects along the giving process and, with the right keyword triggers, respond in a way that directs them to a gift officer or to register their details in some intentional way.

- **Lead qualification:** Again, layering in qualifying questions prior to the system forwarding a lead to a staff member can help automate the entry points for donor cultivation. It will only be a matter of time before this all syncs up with wealth-screening platforms and relevant CRM data to ensure donors and volunteers are not falling through the cracks.

- **Donor conversion:** There is a reason nonprofits have their donation button placed prominently on their home page (and every other page thereafter). It's to ensure that someone looking to make a gift there and then can get to where they want in the most efficient way possible and with minimal clicks. Optimization is key

254

to conversion here, and that little prompt from the bottom right corner of your screen could make all the difference. Your bot would be programmed in this instance to assist browsing, and with smarter AI, recognize IP patterns and behavior to personalize the experience with every visit. This is one application of sales conversion that should be replicated for nonprofits.

As you can see, chatbots are great options to optimize administrative tasks and increase staff capacity. However, they are ultimately geared toward serving the organization rather than the donor. User experience is something that can be conceptualized and tested, but it will never be truly user-oriented, given the motivations for creating it in the first place.

Virtual Assistants. Virtual assistants foster a more dynamic discourse and are geared toward understanding the user rather than a simple request. They also warrant the sector's attention, given that the Smart Audio Report showed one out of six people own a smart speaker, and Perficient Digital found that voice is the number-two choice for mobile search behind browsers. This tech already has the capacity to donate to your favorite charity (especially if linked to Amazon Pay, for example), but that is hardly revolutionary or something that you can influence. So what's the hook?

There is no doubt you can thread the needle between mission and messaging by creating new Alexa skills that can help inform donors on your work. Let's say you were a popular education nonprofit. You could build a skill that answers the questions of "Alexa, how many first-generation college students from Cleveland graduated this year?" and then a curated answer could be "According to X Youth Academy, 105 students from Cleveland were the first of their family to graduate college in 2019." This is a great way to inform donors and build awareness of your nonprofit's services and impact.

Coding and scripting these skills are pretty simple, with Amazon providing tutorials and supplying code samples tailored to various skill levels. Just imagine creating an Alexa skill for your events calendar and prompting your supporters to add a reminder to RSVP, or creating a skill that connects them to their member of Congress when you are lobbying for more funding, all without ever having to press a button.

Treat yourself to some important skills too. For instance, a CEO could provide each staff member with an Echo Dot or Google Home so that just prior to a donor call they can ask, "Google what was the last contract report for John Smith?" or "When does Jane Smith's pledge conclude?" You can also add donor engagement notes directly to your CRM without having to type a thing!

If the services don't currently exist through your expensive CRM or fundraising platforms, then experiment with simple coding assignments. It will make your office more dynamic, more connected, and increase its capacity—given that this is really just setting up a set of rules. The only limit here is your imagination.

OUT OF THE FOG: THE IMPORTANCE OF DATA
IN TACKLING GLOBAL DISASTERS

Should we have been legitimately freaked out, or was the COVID-19 pandemic being exaggerated?

While those were largely rhetorical questions, many people I know and respect have a way of dealing with things like this. They look at the data available to them to make informed decisions. The problem with this, however, is that the data was incomplete and highly suspect in the earlier months of the outbreak.

Some of the countries most affected have had leaders who were more focused on controlling the narrative than helping their citizens. Beyond that, nearly universally, there are systemic problems in getting the data. For example, as of late March 2020, California had conducted 77,800 tests, which meant that 99.8 percent of the state hadn't been tested. Of those 77,800 tests, 57,400 were pending results. At that rate, they weren't expected to be completed for another month.

Was California an outlier in this case? Who knows? Very few states were even reporting backlogs at that point.

As we continued to develop a deeper understanding of the virus itself, our scientists were racing to find a vaccine. At the same time, while we isolated ourselves at home, we grew more and more frustrated with significant gaps in information, inconsistent reporting, or other barriers that made it nearly impossible to accurately understand what was going on.

To put it simply: *We were operating in a data fog,* and one that wasn't clearing anytime soon, given that tested cases only represented hospitalizations at that point. We were undercounting, and that's a trailing measure.

With fast-tracked vaccines taking around a year to produce and have approved, how can we ensure that future flu seasons (which will now include COVID-19) are not ones that will see a worldwide impact of some $5 trillion-plus, a global depression, 20 percent unemployment, and the loss of tens of thousands of people?

How does philanthropy help play a role in guiding folks out of the fog and support the infrastructure we need to combat issues like this in the future?

Bold Investments. Big philanthropy needs a seismic shift in its approach: tackle systems, focus on long-term investments, go big, and be bold. Endowments are there to help de-risk innovation and help seed future solutions. Research, solutions, and mitigation strategies need to be funded. Triage is an expensive business to be in, and the costs of inaction far outweigh the costs of action. For example, as a result of investments in research at the University of Texas, its lab has since identified the spike protein in coronaviruses that attaches to and infects human cells (a critical first step toward vaccine development). The lab's Frontera supercomputer has also become a key resource within a new high-performance computing consortium that provided researchers worldwide with massive computing resources to help understand, model, predict, and help combat the virus.

Disaster Funding. A number of emergency funds were created in response to the devastating effects of the pandemic to local economies. Fundraising for these disaster funds should remain an annual effort, and a set of protocols established to activate the funds when further disaster

257

recovery and rebuilding efforts are needed. Philanthropy should start being proactive on this front by funding shared staffing resources as a community resilience endeavor, helping drive disaster risk reduction, prevention and management measures, and informing and coordinating responses—before and in the event of a disaster.

Disaster Analytics. Following on from our previous discussion about machine learning, this approach is transforming science in ways that motivate new theories and provide critical feedback patterns in the face of real-world problems, unlocking new ways to achieve societal impact. Funding this work, especially in the disaster analytics domain, will mean that data, physics-based modeling, and high-performance computing will help predict disaster better and enable mitigation and response.

Advocacy. Philanthropy standing arm in arm with its nonprofit partners had a big victory within the $2 trillion economic stimulus package by successfully lobbying Congress to have provisions taken out of the bill that would have excluded nonprofits that receive Medicaid funding from accessing hundreds of billions of dollars in assistance to small businesses. The next step has to be to lobby for more investment in public health, the Centers for Disease Control and Prevention, National Institutes of Health, and expanded health-care coverage.

Our communities are still hurting, and our social fabric is being stretched in unimaginable ways. With an increased demand for food, shelter, and other basic necessities compounded by a decline in donations, revenues, and reduction in force on the social services side, we need to ensure that we are better prepared for events like the COVID-19 pandemic, no matter how inconceivable they may be in magnitude. This future preparation should be underpinned by quality data and fortified by strong leadership.

The fog eventually lifts. Let this test of our resolve inspire us to strive for a clearer, safer, and healthier future.

EFREM BYCER

The Standard Bearer of Civic Tech

Technology is a double-edged sword in the impact space. On one side, it is required to achieve a level of scale where the number of people served can grow exponentially without commensurate increases in cost to serve. However, scale shouldn't always be the goal. Not all programs, especially ones in which the human touch is required, are meant to scale. Too many philanthropists fashion themselves as venture capitalists who can achieve "hockey stick" growth in terms of impact. That might be a nice story to tell at your business school reunion, but it doesn't necessarily guarantee the long-term impact outlined in the mission statement.

Efrem Bycer, a cross-sector leader whose career stretches across government, nonprofit, and the private sector, has seen the promise and pitfalls of technology deployed in the spirit of social impact. "I never thought that I'd work in tech," he said. "In fact, I thought my entire career would be in government and nonprofits helping make government work better and the economy more fair, not thinking that tech could in fact help achieve those objectives. How wrong I was."

When Efrem was in college and graduate school, he had hoped to land a job in economic development. "When I finally did," he explains, "the work was everything I had hoped for: dynamic, complex, cross-sector, and multi-faceted. I got to work with San Diego's most innovative companies, cross paths with national and international thought leaders, and provide insight to policymakers. But I also saw firsthand some of the inequities in how the world works for large, well-funded businesses and the small businesses that struggle to get by."

Many of Efrem's concerns were in his observations around how business was "done." In particular, he noticed how an army of consultants, lawyers, bankers, and commercial real estate leaders ensure their clients' (large corporations) interests were well represented in their work and that those challenges were top of mind when meeting with government officials.

"To some extent, this made sense since these corporations were the region's largest employers and delivered far-reaching economic impacts," Efrem says. "We were quick to help large employers navigate complex bureaucratic processes (i.e., permitting), but left small businesses on their own or to rely on less well-connected organizations for support. I came to realize that in addition to the power dynamics that existed between large and small businesses, another major issue at hand was that these processes were so complex in the first place. And when I went deeper to understand why it was so challenging to engage with government, I learned so much of it had to do with the technology governments rely on to serve the public and, in this case, businesses."

Efrem understands that tech isn't the silver bullet and has a downside. "At the end of the day," he says, "technology is a bunch of 1s and 0s strung together. Building technology almost always requires a set of blinders that block out the true complexity of the problem you're trying to solve in order to build an app that can do something, and the costs of those tradeoffs can be significant."

The relentless focus needed to build a piece of technology that works even at solving a small piece of the original problem means the problem has to be oversimplified into a set of distinct and unrelated boxes that can be checked off when new code is pushed live. This is a feature, not a bug, of tech development.

Philanthropy can and should look at when tech can help solve a problem, but only if it puts the role tech can play within the greater, more complete context of the challenge. The sector must also insist that empathy for the end user, beneficiary, customer, client, or whatever more humane term is used to describe the person on the other end, is paramount.

But many nonprofits are similar experts in the audiences they work with. Rather than tell these organizations to join the twenty-first century and build some app that the intended audience won't use and no one can support long-term, philanthropy can be better spent uplifting this expertise and pushing for other nonprofits, philanthropists, companies, and governments to actually meet the needs of people served by the organizations in their portfolio. In doing so, the sector must also be prepared to challenge existing power dynamics, including those that have historically given philanthropists the power they wield today.

Efrem shares these views, which are also shaped by his eagerness to learn more about how governments built and brought technology to deliver public services and engage the public. "That led me to Code for America, a nonprofit hell-bent on making government work better for those who need it most by bringing the principles of user-centered technology and agile software development to bear," he explains. "We didn't build technology for government and the people it served; we built it with them. At CfA, I launched the Economic Development team, a group focused on helping governments better deliver small business and workforce development services.

"Working directly with governments and technologists, I saw first-hand the promise of technology-driven service delivery, as well as the potential risks. I saw how Code for America's GetCalFresh product radically simplified the process for applying for the Supplemental Nutrition Assistance Program (SNAP) in California, eventually accounting for more than 70 percent of the SNAP applications filed during the pandemic. On the economic development front, I witnessed how new small business portals built by Code for America Fellows with the cities of Long Beach and Syracuse catalyzed further innovative thinking by dedicated public servants and fostered better relationships with the business community."

It was also at CfA that Efrem would see that corporations such as LinkedIn worked with government agencies to increase the likelihood that someone on unemployment insurance would get back to work before their unemployment insurance benefit expired. Their focus on the latter would eventually bring Efrem to LinkedIn, which has the capabilities to work at scale alongside and with government to connect people to economic opportunity. And it should come as no surprise that working there would have him excited to see how philanthropy can play a complementary role in investing in people's careers.

"I've been following the growth of income-share agreements," Efrem says, "and I see promise, assuming these financial vehicles don't follow the same extractive path of student loans. Philanthropy could be well positioned here by putting its corpus to work where impact and returns align, providing more patient capital than market-rate investors would otherwise be comfortable with and also bringing wraparound money and services that actually help people complete their training. If more than half of Americans can't easily withstand a $400 surprise expense (and that was pre-pandemic), this is an area where philanthropy can step in.

"Building really impactful, effective technology takes more than coding skills. It requires the product team to internalize the issues faced by users who they identify as real people. They effectively leverage user research to bring the voice of the user into every decision and work carefully to ensure that the person on the other end of the application has a positive experience and emotive experience throughout their use of the tool. They took the time to understand the greater context in which they were working to find the right moment for a tech intervention. In many ways, the technology itself isn't all that complicated. The complexity lies in building within the context."

And here, amid these challenges, is where philanthropy can play a role. Rather than fund technology for technology's sake, philanthropy can focus on raising up the voices of organizations that have been doing this work for years to help the technologists develop greater empathy for the people they hope to help. It can focus on building upon what works.

It's not that philanthropy should avoid technology. Rather, philanthropy should consider how tech can help solve a problem in the larger context of the challenge. Philanthropy must also insist on empathy for the end user.

At its worst, philanthropy is a vain exercise in legacy-building or using money to wield power over how others without the money do their work. It attempts to give a radical makeover to years, decades, or generations of exploitative behavior not by confronting that reality but by reinforcing it. It forsakes its mission in favor of self-preservation. It only further concentrates power rather than working toward true empowerment.

At its best, however, philanthropy represents a person's care for future generations of people they'll never know. It demonstrates caring for fellow people and puts money and credibility behind ideas that would never otherwise have a chance. It contributes to the democratization of economic mobility, power, and influence. This kind of philanthropy exemplifies human generosity and the capacity to think beyond one's self.

Efrem represents philanthropy at its best. His work, values, and approach will ensure that people are seen, counted, and engaged as a necessity and not just as an end user. In the end philanthropy can and must be a force for good, putting resources behind all the tools, including technology, that can yield impact. After all, we need an all-of-the-above approach to solving issues of income inequality, racial justice, unequal concentration of political power, and climate change.

CHAPTER SIXTEEN

Wishful Thinking?
Or Worth Waiting For?

NOT ALL THINGS TURN TO GOLD: HOW CRYPTOCURRENCY FITS INTO THE FUNDRAISING LANDSCAPE

The impact of bitcoin and other cryptocurrency donations as a transformative source of charity over the short- to mid-term is negligible (hence why it is discussed separately from blockchain and smart contract uses and applications). I hope I'm proven wrong, because the idea of a new digital currency that is highly transparent with additional layers of security in a globalized economy is a really exciting proposition, especially given the impact it could have in philanthropy.

What's more exciting in the currency space as it relates to substantive giving, I think, is the launch of the Donation Dollar in Australia, the world's first legal tender designed to be donated. The Royal Australian Mint created a Donation Dollar for every Australian, creating twenty-five million reminders to donate. It's better than the potential of donating 1/1187th of a bitcoin, but I digress.

At its height in January 2021, bitcoin was trading more than USD $40,000 (just missing the opportunity to peak at the perfect moment for year-end giving, might I add).

However, after it reaches new highs it has historically lost between a quarter or half of its value in the months following, this high being no different. The volatility only goes to show that the world isn't totally sold on something that doesn't have any intrinsic value and that scarcity and the fear of missing out (FOMO) are a potent mix used to great effect by those who are set to benefit the most by an increased demand.

A few people I know personally got caught up in the hysteria of it all a few years back and either lost a lot of money or were swindled out of a lot of money. Social media only helped build up this house of cards, reaffirming the dangers of any get-rich-quick schemes.

For all of these reasons, I won't talk about cryptocurrency at great length. But I wanted to acknowledge that organizations such as Silicon Valley Community Foundation, Square, and UNICEF are advancing grant programs in this space. This is also complemented by $3 million in investments in Cornell; University of California, Berkeley; and the University of Maryland by the National Science Foundation to conduct wide-ranging research into the pain points of the current ecosystem.

I was also intrigued by the Pineapple Fund, which in 2018 saw an anonymous donor gift $55 million to sixty nonprofit groups via Reddit, of all things. (This is not to be confused with the Banana Fund, which was found to be a crypto-crowdfunding Ponzi scheme.) Gifts ranged from $50,000 all the way to $5 million and included the ACLU, charity: water, and Pencils of Promise, to name but a few.

The Giving Block was an organization that emanated from this process. It researched and followed up with many of the funds recipients to ascertain the experience and effectiveness of the process. It's worth going to their website and reading their findings if that's an avenue you want to pursue.

However, the philanthropy sector (especially smaller nonprofits) should not actively source cryptocurrency as a gift. If you do receive it, your organization should be set up in a way to receive it and then sell it that very same day. That includes doing your due diligence by looking up previous transactions on the blockchain to make sure it isn't linked (past or present) to anything potentially nefarious and creating a bitcoin wallet to accept and trade the asset, which, like stock, is tax deductible at the fair market value it is donated at.

If a potential donor wants to use cryptocurrency, they will mention it to you as an option. Trust me on that one. Cryptocurrency is also a good candidate for a blended gift option. If you're open to receiving it, write this option into the gift acceptance policy posted on your organization's website, tagged appropriately so visitors can find it. Don't have a big bitcoin logo on your front page. You're just occupying space that could be used to share stories of impact.

CIVIC SOLUTIONS BEYOND THE BINARY: CAN QUANTUM HELP SOLVE SOCIETY'S BIGGEST ILLS?

Despite all the benefits that machine learning can yield for addressing some of the most critical social issues of our time (e.g., homelessness, poverty, climate change), an even more powerful computational option is waiting in the wings. Quantum computing, according to recent predictions from IBM, will be commercially viable in the next five years. It's an extremely hard concept to come to grips with, let alone see its immediate impact for the social sector. But once it becomes mainstream, it will have major benefits and ramifications for society, accelerating the industries that intersect a commitment to lifting up our communities for the common good.

It felt outlandish to write that last statement, since it sounds vague and is full of buzzwords. But as I mentioned earlier, it's like advancing to playing a 3D-chess master after you have had some beginner's luck at Uno.

I have the privilege of working in the same department as renowned theoretical computer scientist Scott Aaronson, whose primary research areas are quantum computing and computational complexity theory. On the other hand, I am but a humble fundraiser who has to have a baseline knowledge of our work in order to update and connect our alumni with opportunities to support it. It was relayed to me in the nicest of terms that if I wanted to get a grasp on quantum computing, the best thing was to read the 101 articles contained on Scott's blog. I read them five times each and had questions—all the questions.

Quantum computing is no joke and is receiving a lot of attention. In short it is a system that can be in multiple states at the same time, moving beyond the binary values of the computing we currently understand and enhancing how information is stored and processed at a subatomic level. I won't get more technical here, other than to say that where machine learning identified patterns in large batches of data sets, quantum computers will be able to run problems multiple times, giving a number of possible outcomes and providing a higher probability and confidence level in the best answer provided. It's like Dr. Strange seeing only one way to win out of fourteen million other scenarios in *Avengers: Infinity War*.

Now that this technology is moving out of university labs with heavy government and business investment, there are a lot of opportunities for the social sector to benefit from its introduction to the mainstream:

- **Endowments:** Quantum computing will be a CIO's dream with assistance in determining the strongest portfolio options through an immense level of cross-tabulation of assets with interconnective dependencies. Now can we please raise that 5 percent payout?

- **Security:** The current state of (and approach to) cyber security within the nonprofit sector is truly alarming. On the day I was initially working on this chapter, Blackbaud, one of the world's largest fundraising and management software companies, had a major data security breach. Not only do nonprofits lack even the most basic software to combat potential threats, but they also lack basic policies in which they handle sensitive information and what to do in the result of an attack. So while quantum computing can help with identifying issues of fraud, it will make all modern cryptography obsolete, which will require a rebuild of all encryption algorithms in quantum. That's one massive overhaul, and one where we can reestablish a baseline level and bring everyone up to it.

- **Marketing:** This would predominantly be an optimization thing, such as enhancing the algorithmic decision-making of which ad to show a user. With the help of quantum computing, your organization hopefully won't be competing on GivingTuesday with an extended Cyber Monday offer for a master class coaching package on how to fundraise.

Again, the best case uses of this technology will likely be led by government or big philanthropy in crunching large and varied data sets to such a transformative level that it could provide the key to some of the most innovative social solutions of our lifetime and with a level of confidence that could transcend politics and personal influence.

Quantum computing will be a real wild card for our sector. While I don't quite agree with the global VP of IBM Research's predictions of its imminent rise or commercial viability, and despite the compounding acceleration of technology (I mean, we are still rocking out VR experiences that are unrelated to our work at nonprofit conferences, so we are hardly going to conjure up solutions to tackle fake news, childhood obesity, or water scarcity issues), we should be really excited about the fifth generation of computers and their overwhelming potential to improve the quality of options, applications, and outcomes for our communities at a generationally transcendent level.

AN ADDED DIMENSION FOR SERVICE DELIVERY

It's not just the online and virtual technologies that will be used in the future by nonprofits and change agents alike. Physical products that assist organizations in their mission and service delivery and potentially improve their bottom lines through revenue generation will become commonplace when the costs of acquiring large-scale 3D printers come down through advances in the technology and of course via scale.

There are myriad uses for the tech too, from small desktop printers to industrial-sized printers that could play a role in housing affordability and the mobility of nonprofits beyond the confines of their walls. Think arts and education as great sectors to disrupt in this instance. For example, advocates of this tech are calling 3D printers in education the "TV on the rolling stand" of our incoming generations of students. Imagine printing a skeleton, piece by piece, for biology or creating a model of each element of the periodic table during chemistry. It really has the ability to revolutionize teaching and inspire careers in the jobs of tomorrow that will have some element of STEM attached to them.

While 3D printing is not commonplace in the stereotypical nonprofits we have probably worked for or volunteered at, there are already some truly game-changing applications for this tech.

The Hand Foundation is building free prosthetic hands for children, and the organization New Story has been working in Bolivia, Haiti, and Mexico to transform blighted favelas with the construction of six-hundred-square-foot homes for less than $4,000, with plans in the future to build an entire community of around one hundred homes in El Salvador.

It's not hard to see a future where workshops equipped with large printers tackling these kinds of issues exist in a children's hospital or at a local Habitat for Humanity, especially when printing patterns and designs will be widely available for download or purchase. It's also not beyond comprehension that whatever you can think of to assist you in your work can be "printed," which is a truly exciting proposition, especially when viewed through the lens of global scale and potential impact in emerging and remote countries. So regardless of the size or scope of your organization, you can use 3D printing in a wide range of ways.

Programs. Through the construction of new homes, 3D printing can help tackle issues such as homelessness and housing affordability. Leading philanthropic institutions are pushing a housing-first approach to solving the homeless crisis, with homes touted to be built within twenty-four hours and costing less than $4,000 to make. This could be the key to unlocking a new future for those who have fallen through the cracks or been victims of our system.

Austin, Texas (where I currently live), is the home of 3D-printing company Icon, which in 2018 created a 350-square-foot tiny house that cost $10,000 to build within two days. Given that the printer wasn't running at full speed and Icon has since closed a Series A funding round of $35 million, there is no doubt they will be pioneering a new era of construction that will accelerate conversations around new solutions across the sector. All of these 3D-printed buildings will probably be LEED certified, which will also make for an attractive proposition for something that could be commonplace by 2030.

Given the price points and the fact that companies will no doubt scale 3D printing to build bigger and better structures, we could possibly see a boom in first-home ownership, a new generation of wealth building, and a strengthening and expansion of the middle class. Not to mention the racial justice connotations it will have, as mentioned earlier in this book. In short, this technology could have a variety of different applications for programming in a nonprofit context. But for now, take some time to ideate how it might work in your own organization. This is a future where if you can dream it, then you can make it. It's wild if you truly think about it.

Events and Stewardship. Using 3D printing for events and other engagements could be one of the most fun ways to advance your cause, drive deeper donor and volunteer connections, and drive awareness of your work. One of the coolest things I have been a part of was recreating a retiring CEO's office as the main focal point for her farewell party. The concept was well received, but the members who were there for the party didn't have to move the entire thing there and back!

Imagine replicating a classroom or your own CEO's office, building a sculpture around a defining moment or person in the organization's history, creating name tags for a gala dinner, or even creating a fountain pen to symbolize the signing of a new endowed scholarship. Again, the possibilities are endless, but the personalization and meaning can be displayed in ways that have not been possible in the past or can't be hastily arranged by a quick visit to Hobby Lobby.

Commercialization. To be successful in the future, nonprofits should diversify their budgets to include new and passive revenue streams that will enable them to be more dynamic and sustainable. If anything, the pandemic has shown how fragile the sector is. Using 3D printing to build widgets on site or consumer goods that directly funnel funds back into programs or frontline services shouldn't be seen as a stretch. Heck, Goodwill is built on that approach, and other workforce development organizations apply the same methodology. When I sat on the board of Partnerships With Industry, a disability employment agency, many of the jobs were on site and involved widgets and other unique, one-off tasks that automation could never replace. So not only could you produce essential consumer goods or unique items for your clientele, but you could also employ folks who are underemployed or otherwise challenged in finding traditional employment.

Community Response. With an ever-increasing spate of natural disasters, civil unrest, and a volatile economy that have only been exposed and exacerbated by the coronavirus pandemic, the need to activate people and business to support governments in supporting and rebuilding communities beyond a cash donation or "hopes and prayers" is driving a new focus on disaster planning, mitigation, and response.

The pandemic showed us two things. First, our systems were wildly underprepared for the virus, seeing ventilators, PPE, and even sanitizer being in short supply. The second part was more inspiring and a common effect of incidents that reach the level of emergency: Folks stepped up and helped fill an urgent need. Breweries and distilleries converted their operations to make sanitizer. Equipment manufacturers shifted their focus of production to facemasks and ventilators, and tech start-ups pivoted to create new contract-tracing apps.

An example of this comes from my previous neighborhood of Scripps Ranch in San Diego, whose civic association made a call to residents with 3D printers to create face shield holders for first responders via a design they had on file. The simple headgear shield took six to seven hours to make, with volunteers then attaching the transparent sheets and bands. Yet they still managed to source and distribute hundreds of them to areas of urgent need. It really was one of those rallying calls that restore your faith in humanity, especially with doctors, nurses, and paramedics taking photos and sharing their thanks online.

In the future it would be wise for state emergency departments to create a list of organizations with 3D-printing capabilities (perhaps even providing equipment in advance to preferred partners) that could be called upon during an emergency, and then provided with the digital files to begin creating items of biggest need. This of course can be supported by donations that come in to be used for rapid-response grants.

Also, the costs of 3D printing are lowering as the technology's processes and capabilities are being improved with each iteration.

In the future, we will see greener outcomes versus the traditional manufacturing options, including new energy efficiencies achieved across the production, distribution, and waste management processes.

This will be an attractive opportunity for both impact investors and major gift prospects.

It is something not to be ignored: 3D printing will become a mainstream technology and probably expand its capacity and capabilities, including the use of metals, automations, and new product development. Opportunities abound, and the sector should be proactive around it.

Organizations should apply for funding for printers, and funders should have the foresight of its potential ROI by making awards to nonprofits seeking these tangible goods, since they will directly benefit our communities in a potentially more dynamic, affordable, and environmentally conscious way.

MULTIPLE LAYERS OF LEARNING: RAPID IDEATION RECIPES FOR NONPROFIT APPLICATION

Earlier we touched on machine learning and its potential impacts on how we identify, understand, and formulate possible solutions for the future. However, it would be a critical oversight to overlook the vast number of applications and nuances that exist under its broader umbrella of understanding.

Again, it's not necessary to dwell on these subsets of AI right now, but they do lend themselves to something truly important: the understanding that they exist, the knowledge that they will likely be introduced more intentionally into our work over the coming decade, and the fun of thinking about the future—not just from a science fiction perspective, but from an actual scientific perspective.

You may have heard of rapid prototyping as a mechanism to try out and improve products in real time. It's about thinking out loud and iterating and evaluating it in real time to ultimately generate a better outcome. Rapid ideation is a spin on this and built on the premise that ideas can grow beyond constraint if those participating are encouraged to think freely, quickly, and without judgement. In short, you build big ideas (the content for a book manuscript, for instance) in a short amount of time (in this case, before its deadline to your editor).

To help with further imagining the future of philanthropy, I did some of my own rapid ideation after identifying a number of research areas that have not yet permeated from academia into commercialized nonprofit tech products just yet. Here are my quick-fire predictions for how science can continue to change our sector for the better.

Explainable AI. For all of the models and results that can be generated or computed by AI, if we can't understand or interpret that data, then what's the point, right? The techniques of explainable AI—methods that help develop interpretable, high-confidence solutions that can be understood by humans—will be essential in breaking down how the AI came to that decision, especially if its replication can lead to solving big systemic issues or if it will be needed to force legislative change. It's also about trust, and that's what is at the core of the majority of nonprofit partnerships. Organizations like the FrameWorks Institute, which has studied how people think and talk about numerous social issues for the past twenty years, could work together with other prominent think tanks to be our sector's interpreters and knowledge brokers around artificially generated solutions and provide additional commentary on their validity based on levels of confidence.

Graphics and Visualization. This is an easy one. Just imagine typing in a script or various data sets and seeing them come to life. This tech, which generates images with the aid of machine learning, already exists in a number of platforms, website builders, and design sites such as Canva and any advanced logo generator out there. Expect them to be even better and more relevant in the next five years, and finally retiring the generic symbols such as a tree with many leaves or two hands holding a heart as the default graphic to anything relating to philanthropy.

Large-Scale Machine Learning. At some point, a future mega donor is bound to invest the requisite amount of money (upwards of quarter of a billion dollars) into a new supercomputer that will have some sort of data philanthropy component, processing high-volume, open-ended data sets and releasing RFPs from nonprofits to help compute new answers to some of the biggest social issues of our time. Organizations would also be able to use the computer for their own independent research, which would be facilitated through in-kind donations and public-private partnerships. This could become the engine room for new research reporting for the social sector. We would then be able to understand the real ROI on social impact initiatives and ultimately see a new era of impact investment.

Natural Language. Language is ultimately our method of communication. So it's only natural (excuse the pun) to ensure that our systems are engaged in two-way dialogue with us in a structured and conventional way. In a hyperconnected world where we communicate from person to person, person to machine, and machine to machine, the processing by computers needs to make sense of our languages in a way that is valuable.

The benefits of this technology are endless.

It will help people with immigration issues in countries where their first language is different from that of their new home; identify biases in historical documents, general automation, and large-scale analysis; and prioritize user feedback such as an advocacy group pushing for change.

And that's just for starters.

Recommender Systems. This is a widely understood and applied technology in commercial applications. Think of sponsored ads, or the "people you may know" functions on Facebook and LinkedIn. This will also permeate into the nonprofit world, with prospect identification and general fundraising campaigns together with employee training and education being the primary beneficiaries of these particular fundamentals of machine learning.

Robotics. It's a pretty safe bet that more robotic applications will layer into our day-to-day roles over the coming years.

However, intelligent machines won't be a blanket replacement for current roles in nonprofit organizations. Instead, they could enhance service delivery, like stocking more packages per hour at food pantries.

Drones could even be used to distribute aid in natural disasters.

Robots may actually be the answer to service delivery scale, which is totally out of whack compared to that of the for-profit sector. And the list goes on.

Vision. Computer vision, in which computers are trained to interpret and understand digital images and videos, will see rapid growth in the commercial space.

You may have already seen the video of the Amazon Go store where you walk inside, just grab your items, and are charged upon exit. The Amazon Echo Look is another interesting piece of tech that hasn't really taken off yet. But once it does, it could be used for arts and culture nonprofits looking to curate installations or assist in theater planning. Using its depth-sensing camera and other add-ons, it can build on and around the image taken.

Image recognition is also pervasive in the financial sector, classifying, capturing, and authenticating documents such as checks. This is a simple tool that can be used by HR and facilities management across the nonprofit sector. And with the COVID-19 pandemic sure to change some of our practices in the future, computer vision will undoubtedly fuel a more sophisticated and contactless service delivery.

Wireless Communication. With broadband falling short of having a universal FTTP (fiber to the premises), it is important that we continue to seek advances in wireless communication technology. A key component in ensuring our nonprofits have stronger network reliability together with faster downloads and connectivity is 5G. It's important given the sensitivities around their donor and client information. It will also provide the backbone for the onboarding of powerful new advances in AI, the InternetofThings (IoT), and mixed-use and virtual reality.

While there are many other research areas in the scientific field of machine learning, many are mathematical and computational in nature. They all complement the broader uses, but given that this section is probably stretching the 101 nature of this book, it's important to continue to excite the social sector as to what is possible, not spoon-feed it potential false idols. If you're interested in those possibilities and are looking at a way to convert the jargon into water-cooler talk, check out the glossary of terms at the back of this book.

RUBY BOLARIA-SHIFRIN

Accelerating Philanthropic Efforts to De-Risk Housing Innovation

"Everyone has a relationship to housing," Ruby Bolaria-Shifrin says with an assertive blend of optimism and empathy. She is the director of the Housing Affordability Program at the Chan Zuckerberg Initiative (CZI) and previously worked in real estate development as a project manager for multifamily mixed-income development projects in San Francisco. And she is in a unique position to help philanthropy overcome its reluctance to wade into an issue that is effectively the linchpin to stability for individuals and families alike: housing affordability, or (more importantly) understanding the differences between capital-A housing affordability versus that of affordable housing.

"Housing is capital intensive," she continues, "and it's hard to scale physical things, especially with escalating fixed costs and no real innovation in this space over the past century. It's no wonder philanthropy doesn't want to touch what is fast becoming one of the biggest issues of our generation."

Ruby lives in the Bay Area and has witnessed firsthand the skyrocketing costs of housing, dwindling housing supply, and limited tenant protections that led to deepening inequities that were bred from this unsustainable situation. So she's been searching for answers through new investments and new approaches such as impact investing.

"We must start prioritizing equity as an investment strategy, noting that it affects all people across the income spectrum," Ruby says. "However, it's difficult to thread the needle of what we look for in our portfolio partnerships, because while there are lots of players in the space, many are not able to deliver cost savings directly to lower income families."

An example of the partnerships that Ruby and CZI are looking at can be seen with a recent $500,000 investment in indieDwell, an Idaho company that constructs affordable and sustainable homes from old shipping containers. "Everyone deserves a safe, stable, affordable place to call home," Ruby says, "which is why CZI supports innovative efforts to improve housing affordability and champion equitable access for all. We see these kinds of strategic program investments as a way to jump-start new thinking and new models that can help close the widening gap between urgent housing needs through a three-P frame—production, preservation, and protection. We need to produce more housing, preserve existing housing and communities, and protect people in place."

Ruby sees the potential in innovative companies to do the work as well as certain funding mechanisms that are now becoming more mainstream in a bid to free up more capital and unlock traditional bank loans such as funding loan loss reserves, guaranteeing nonprofit capital loans, and also real estate investment trusts. Partnership for the Bay's Future is the biggest CZI investment to date, a collaborative regional effort to increase housing production and preservation and ensure vibrant communities of racial equity and economic inclusion. CZI seeded the $500 million fund with $40 million first-loss capital. The ethos of the fund is centered on collaboration and combined investment capital and grant funding to support policy change to expand and protect up to 175,000 households over the next five years and preserve and produce more than 8,000 homes over the next five to ten years. The partnership launched with other philanthropy, tech, advocates, and business partners in 2018. CZI's first-loss capital acted to de-risk the fund for other funders, including institutional investors like First Republic Bank, to join.

Shared equity models, like the ones mentioned earlier that formed part of the Jacobs Center project, and organizations like Landed that are effectively helping educators and other professional frontline professionals live near the communities they serve, are also options that are gaining traction in the field.

"We need to really move hearts and minds on this issue, correct the historical wrongs of past housing policies, and embrace new technologies, innovations, and funding options to move from a scarcity of housing to one of abundance, and where savings derived from this progress is passed on to consumers in an equitable way," says Ruby.

CZI, along with other large foundations and corporate giving initiatives, has enormous power to convene these conversations as well as address the tensions between major actors on both the supply and demand sides and, more importantly, the communities that are driving the change and need funder investment and solidarity to enact solutions.

"We believe in supporting both innovative models and partnerships and good old-fashioned advocacy," says Ruby. "Supporting organizing, ballot measures, and legislative fights is still relatively innovative for philanthropy, so imagine what we could do together if we all engaged in this way!"

She goes on to say, "In the end it's about trust, and acknowledging your power, while being tolerant to risk and the expectations that come with tackling the defining issues of our time. It's always a work in progress, but one where progress is happening every day."

CHAPTER SEVENTEEN

What Will Your Future Be?

I hope that, thanks to this book, you've learned more about what trends you should be thinking about.

Even more so, I hope you'll use what you've learned as a catalyst to think about and discuss what new technologies and approaches can be applied to help you drive new solutions and impact in your work and community. Ideating about the future is a healthy exercise and should make change less intimidating.

I encourage you to take calculated risks to accelerate change rather than be bogged down in the day-to-day operations of your organization.

Courageous leadership is needed now more than ever. *Future Philanthropy* provides the blueprint for our social sector to lead with conviction in new and innovative ways, and I hope you are willing to take that first step in this new direction or—if you have already dipped your toe in the pool—to jump right in. The water is lovely.

Of course, that's not always possible. So if you can lead, lead. If you can contribute, contribute. If you can connect folks to opportunity, connect them.

Your word is also important. If you are committed to change you must commit yourself to that change. Put ideas into action, and don't be afraid of stepping up to be counted.

Seek challenges, ask to be challenged. Don't be scared to take that four-year course because you're twenty-eight and by the time you're done you'll be thirty-two. Whether you take the course or not, in four years' time, you'll still be thirty-two.

Reimagine what your organization and your career can be.

Move forward with the understanding that we shouldn't just do stuff or make stuff because we can, but that we should do it because it helps.

In the end futurism is envisioning what your future could be. But instead of getting caught dreaming, jot those ideas down and work them into an executable plan. Then get out of your own way and realize you deserve that seat at the table in half the time you feel it will take to get there.

Want to run for Congress in four years? Why not the next cycle in two?

Want to become a VP at your local community foundation as your next career step? Why not apply for a CEO role out of town?

Want to wait for your kids to start school before you have time to join a nonprofit board? Join it now. It should be an honor to serve, not a perceived obligation or trade-off.

And for all that is good in this world, don't wait to be asked. Go get it. Be the change you believe in. Don't believe that all good things come to those that wait.

This book is just as much as a playbook for change as it is a call to arms. The emerging leaders featured in this book should inspire you to dream big. We need you to dream big. Our community needs you to dream big.

All you need to do is step through that door and be the person you know you are and can be.

So what will be your north star? What will be your future?

As the author Seth Godin always says, "Go make a ruckus."

And as I always say, "Time to get shit done."

LEADERS OF COLOR

Breaking Down Barriers for Others to Overcome

If I see farther, it is because I stand on the shoulders of giants. —Isaac Newton

A number of years ago, when I participated in racial equity training as part of my role within Philanthropy California, I appreciated the resource libraries on race that were shared with me, finding them to be quite helpful to both my personal and professional life. Most of these resources extended themselves to books and literature on the history of race, as well as strategies and guides to help discuss race and implement more inclusive policies. They also included a list of consultants who could help advance the discussion further—because, as you may already know, diversity isn't just a box you tick.

Lately, I have seen an explosion of these resource libraries, especially with the elevation of race as a key focal point of civic discourse.

Companies are also now seeing the importance and value of lifting up the discussion as part of their corporate citizenry.

This two-speed approach—those who have been doing this work their entire careers, and those just joining the movement—has already seen big changes to the status quo across both business and sports due to an exertion of informed influence.

But is this a motivation from the head or the heart? And is it another case of corporations washing their products and personas to ensure they are still relevant and have their finger on the pulse?

The answer lies in who curated the libraries and what motivated them in the first place. It also lies in what you want to learn and what you are open to learning.

I challenge you to be more specific in your own self-exploration and reflection on the topic of race and white supremacy. Move beyond simple Google searches or professional bodies that email you a list that has been vetted to what they deem appropriate (or digestible) for their members, and follow folks who are unapologetic in their actions.

For all of the angst and anguish through 2020, this is the chance to make a stand, draw a line in the sand and say, "enough." Enough excuses, enough defaulting to "there isn't enough data." This should be the sector's chance to benchmark change across issues such as civic engagement, participation, funding, advocacy, organizing, economic development, research, power, communications, networks, leadership pipelines, partnerships, and policy.

This isn't a race to wokeness. This is about understanding the issues, how to be a real ally, and how to move your work forward for the benefit of your neighbors and your community at large.

It's easy to curate a list of ten influential books. It's harder to identify a Black-owned bookstore and take the time to go there and seek recommendations.

It's easy to join a committee to discuss these issues. It's harder to cede power and ambition and instead elevate new voices into leadership roles.

It's easy to make a donation to an organization. It's harder to volunteer your time to head down to an organization and listen to those with lived experiences.

When I mapped out this part of the book, it highlighted all the things I am disappointed with in philanthropy's approach and attitudes toward racial justice. Therefore, I doubled down on my commitment to lifting up those who are doing amazing work in the field; have challenged my own understandings, assumptions, and beliefs; and have impressed and inspired me in doing so.

These are folks who I have worked with or seen at a conference or who have impacted my work directly. If we are going to create a list to advance our work it must be as authentic as we can make it, knowing that it can change as we change. Empathy is not an endorsement; it's a symbol of white fragility. Actions speak louder than words, and philanthropy needs to take note. We all need to take note.

Here are some people who I recommend you follow through social media, their own organizations, or their policies. Let their work—not Buzzfeed's interpretation of it—be your resource guide.

AMANDA ANDERE

Amanda Andere currently serves as the CEO of Funders Together to End Homelessness, a nonprofit of 185 foundations, corporations, and United Ways working in the United States and Canada that are committed to preventing and ending homelessness through advocacy, collaboration, and innovative grantmaking. She has spent over fifteen years working in the nonprofit and public sector as a leader committed to racial and housing justice through advocacy for systemic change.

Website: funderstogether.org/amanda_andere
Twitter: @AmandaAndere

FRED BLACKWELL

Fred Blackwell works to ensure shared prosperity, innovation, and equity in the Bay Area. As CEO of the San Francisco Foundation, he leads one of the largest community foundations in the country, one focused on racial equity and economic inclusion. His background roots his approaches in an activist mindset. He attended Oakland Community School, which was founded by the Black Panthers, and his mother is the distinguished Angela Glover Blackwell, who founded PolicyLink.

Website: sff.org/team-members/fred-blackwell
Twitter: @fredgblackwell

KAMALA HARRIS

While Kamala Harris needs no introduction (after all, she's now the first female vice president, as well as the first African American and Asian American vice president in US history), her awareness of racial bias in philanthropy was covered in the section about good systems in chapter 14. Her trajectory shows that, regardless of her current position, she may be the one person who will help invigorate and empower the social sector in new ways, accelerating impact and equity in ways that (still) seem improbable in the near future.

Twitter: @KamalaHarris

TRISTA HARRIS

Trista Harris is a world-renowned philanthropic futurist who Mac-Gyvers her way into the most unexpected situations to discover the signals of the future that will help you make the world a better place. A member of the same graduating class at Howard University as Chadwick Boseman, she once negotiated her way into an interview with Sir Richard Branson and was later invited to his home on Necker Island to give a speech on the future of doing good.

Trista has worked in nonprofits since she was thirteen years old. Previously the president of the Minnesota Council on Foundations, which gave away $1.5 billion a year, she is now the president of FutureGood, a consultancy focused on growing a movement of visionaries dedicated to building a better future. She also has a Magic 8 Ball on her desk.

Website: tristaharris.org

Twitter: @TristaHarris

ALAN JENKINS

Alan Jenkins is a professor of practice at Harvard Law School where he teaches courses on race and the law, communication, and social justice. Before joining the Law School faculty, he was president and cofounder of the Opportunity Agenda, a social justice communication lab dedicated to the idea that the United States can and should be a place where everyone enjoys full and equal opportunity. Prior to that, he was director of human rights at the Ford Foundation.

Website: hls.harvard.edu/faculty/directory/11522/Jenkins

Twitter: @Opportunity1

PENIEL JOSEPH

Peniel Joseph holds a joint professorship appointment at the LBJ School of Public Affairs and the History Department in the College of Liberal Arts at the University of Texas at Austin. He is also the founding director of the LBJ School's Center for the Study of Race and Democracy (CSRD). His career focus has been on Black Power Studies, which encompasses interdisciplinary fields such as Africana studies, law and society, women's and ethnic studies, and political science.

In addition to being a frequent commentator on issues of race, democracy, and civil rights, Dr. Joseph's most recent book is *The Sword and the Shield: The Revolutionary Lives of Malcolm X and Martin Luther King Jr.* He also wrote the award-winning books *Waiting 'Til the Midnight Hour: A Narrative History of Black Power in America* and *Dark Days, Bright Nights: From Black Power to Barack Obama.* His book, *Stokely: A Life,* has been called the definitive biography of Stokely Carmichael, the man who popularized the phrase *black power.* Included among Joseph's other book credits is the editing of *The Black Power Movement: Rethinking the Civil Rights-Black Power Era* and *Neighborhood Rebels: Black Power at the Local Level.*

Website: lbj.utexas.edu/joseph-peniel

Twitter: @PenielJoseph

VU LE

Vu Le runs the *Nonprofit AF* blog, which tackles some of the biggest systems issues in philanthropy and the nonprofit sector—and often with a humorous spin that lays bare the preposterous nature of some of our sector's traditional approaches to funding and racial justice.

Website: nonprofitaf.com

Twitter: @nonprofitAF

MICHAEL MCAFEE

Michael is the president and CEO of PolicyLink, a national research and action institute advancing racial and economic equity. He played a leadership role in securing Promise Neighborhoods as a permanent federal program and is driving a new and growing body of work—corporate racial equity—that includes the first comprehensive tool to guide private-sector companies in assessing and actively promoting equity in every aspect of their company's value chain.

Website: policylink.org/aboutUs/staff/michael-mcafee
Twitter: @mikemcafee06

DR. LEONARD N. MOORE

Dr. Moore is the vice president for diversity and community engagement and the George Littlefield Professor of American History at the University of Texas at Austin. He is also the author of a number of books on Black politics. And thanks to his innovative, unique, and engaging teaching style, his classes on the Black Power movement and a signature course titled Race in the Age of Trump have been attended by over one thousand students each semester.

Website: liberalarts.utexas.edu/history/faculty/lm25645
Twitter: @leonardnmoore

LATEEFAH SIMON

Lateefah Simon is a nationally recognized advocate for civil rights and racial justice in Oakland and the Bay Area. She is the president of the Akonadi Foundation and an advocate for civil rights, racial justice, and juvenile justice. In 2003, at age nineteen, she became the youngest woman to receive a MacArthur Fellowship, for her leadership of the Center for Young Women's Development.

Website: akonadi.org/our-team/lateefah-simon-president
Twitter: @lateefahsimon

MICHAEL TUBBS

Michael Tubbs served as the seventy-ninth mayor of Stockton, California. He was elected to this position in 2016, becoming the youngest mayor and first African American mayor in Stockton's history. He has openly embraced the partnership of organized philanthropy, engaging actively with funders and associations, being a vocal proponent for a universal basic income, and overseeing a pilot project in his city that provided a no-strings-attached stipend of $500 over eighteen months.

Website: mtubbs.com

Twitter: @MichaelDTubbs

EDGAR VILLANUEVA

Edgar is a nationally recognized expert on social justice philanthropy and is currently serving as chair of the board of directors of Native Americans in Philanthropy and the vice president of programs and advocacy at the Schott Foundation for Public Education. His recent work as the award-winning author of *Decolonizing Wealth*, a bestselling book offering hopeful and compelling alternatives to the dynamics of colonization in the philanthropic and social finance sectors, is driving mainstream discussion on his ideas and research throughout the field.

Website: decolonizingwealth.com

Twitter: @VillanuevaEdgar

All of the above are the giants of our sector and the ones who inspire me to do better, be better, and bring more folks to the tables I have the privilege to access. There are many, many more, however, and I hope this book catalyzes a new dialogue about how the sector can use new tools and trends to empower additional voices, ideas, and experiences, and one that can help us be our authentic selves as we strive for a better future and better outcomes as a result of our own philanthropy.

BETH KANTER

Finding Balance: An Organizational Responsibility to Help Tech and Talent Thrive

As I write this afterword, I have not left my house much in the last seven months due to being in a higher risk category for the coronavirus (COVID-19). I'm either living at work or working from home, along with my entire family. Looking out the window from my home office in California, I can't see the sky or mountains through the thick haze. The air quality is in the hazardous range due to the wildfires. If that wasn't enough stress, there is also the fight for racial justice, election worries, a financial crisis, and the looming mental health crisis.

Everyone is feeling it. I realized after the first days of the pandemic that I needed to gather every tool from my Happy Healthy Nonprofit toolkit to try to keep calm, focused, and positive. This is a marathon, not a sprint.

I will be honest with you: It isn't always easy, but practicing self-care does help to create calming norms for yourself. For me, it includes getting enough sleep, exercise, time off, mindfulness, keeping optimistic, and—perhaps most importantly—practicing digital wellness, or using technology intentionally in a healthy way.

Technology can be an agent of distraction or calm. Emerging technology tools and apps can monitor our health, show us how to improve our happiness, and even teach us to meditate. But apps can't do the work required to maintain our work-life balance and well-being or reduce our stress levels when we overwork. Humans actually need to change their behaviors within organizations if they are to create a robust culture of resilience.

Workplace culture is the environment that you create for your people whether you work in an office together or as a remote distributed team. It is a mix of your organization's leadership, values, traditions, beliefs, interactions, behaviors, and attitudes that contribute to the emotional and relational conditions of your workplace. While some may view culture as "fluff," it has a significant impact on productivity, achieving results, and collective well-being.

The pandemic prompted the largest global work-from-home experiment. Many nonprofit staff were suddenly prevented from working face-to-face together in their physical offices. Many nonprofits had to abruptly pivot to virtual distributed teams while quickly adapting the delivery of their programs and services amid spikes in demand. They were not simply working from home—they were working from home during a global health crisis.

As nonprofits have been rightly focused on the external impact of the COVID-19 pandemic, a mental health crisis is also emerging. Qualtrics recently published the results of "The Other COVID-19 Crisis: Mental Health," a survey of more than two thousand employees, and found that 67 percent of people report higher levels of stress since the outbreak and 44 percent report their overall mental health has declined. Nonprofit staff well-being and productivity are taking a hit.

Even before COVID-19 hit, workplace burnout was rampant. In 2019, the World Health Organization classified workplace burnout as an illness to call attention to the negative impact of work-related stress. As with everything else, bad situations are accelerating due to the pandemic. Here's why:

- **Uncertainty:** Without a clear end date for the pandemic and a vaccine, there is financial uncertainty for many nonprofits as well as the people they serve, not to mention furloughs and layoffs for staff. It is compounded by postponed events and interrupted program or service delivery, with a higher demand for services already stretched thin. This makes planning difficult.

- **Isolation:** Social distancing and quarantine have prevented us from engaging with our normal day-to-day lives and interacting with friends and family. Working at home, even if you are used to it, can feel lonely. And the more we are confined to interacting with a small number of people, the more likely we are to become socially awkward.

- **Work-Life Balance:** Many nonprofit staff have found it hard to manage the boundaries between work and life due to unrealistic expectations from managers or a lack of downtime activities outside of the home. The workweek and weekend have become blurred, and people are losing track of days. With restricted travel opportunity, vacations have become staycations that do not really recharge our batteries.

- **Technology Overload:** The onslaught of using video conference platforms and other virtual tools for everything in our lives—from work meetings to family holiday celebrations—has caused a new type of techno overload and exhaustion just from staring at people's faces on screens. Another ailment, "doomscrolling," or infinitely scrolling through bad news online and social networks, is also a detriment to our mental health that is leading increased anxiety and depression.

Despite these enormous and unprecedented challenges, nonprofits are learning how to build a robust virtual workplace culture that not only addresses the burnout and mental health issues but also helps them be productive and get work done. And the good news is, the data shows you can improve the well-being of your team and mitigate some of the negative effects. But you must be willing to listen and then lead with radical empathy. Caring is an important first step, but it is just a start. We must take the responsibility of fostering a healthy workplace culture (online and offline) seriously in the nonprofit sector.

Use Rituals to Increase Human Connection

Rituals are small acts done routinely as a group and help create positive connections and relationships. Nonprofit workplace rituals may include meeting check-ins, staff recognition, celebration of work milestones, and other activities. All of these help build social cohesion and relationships. Rituals can be established for your department, team, or entire organization. With the pandemic, it is more important than ever to adapt to the online workspace or establish rituals.

Rituals offer a key productivity benefit: people are more likely to learn from each other, share, and combine their ideas more freely. Stronger relationships at work help us to feel more at ease in sharing our concerns and insights and seek new information and innovative ways of working and can give us more confidence to speak out if there's something that can be done more efficiently and effectively.

Here are a few simple ways to establish or adapt rituals to the online space:

- **Appreciation:** Create rituals of appreciation to recognize staff or a team that has been working hard or reached a successful milestone. Giving shoutouts and applause during a virtual meeting is easy to do. If your organization is using Slack, you can use "Hey Taco" to give props to staff. A number of tools and plug-ins can also help you automate saying thank you for a job well done.

- **Celebrations:** Many nonprofits have celebration rituals, from work anniversaries, successful completion of projects, or other organizational accomplishments. TechSoup has been hosting weekly themed happy hours, while Packard Foundation OE staff hosted a birthday party on Zoom where everyone wore a funny hat. In addition to happy hours, your virtual workplace can host virtual coffee hours and more.

- **Meeting Rituals:** Meetings should always start with a great opener that orients participants to the agenda, introductions, and a check-in ritual. During the quarantine, a round of check-ins allows people to share how they are coping. It doesn't have to be a therapy session. Instead, you can do fun check-in activities that help people de-stress. If you are facilitating a larger staff meeting, you can use the Zoom breakout feature for speed networking activities. And, of course, if you have staff members who hate check-ins, you can also establish a ritual of "I pass."

- **Simulate the Water Cooler:** When all your interactions with your team are through structured work sessions, you can quickly lose the human-to-human connection. Water-cooler chats or informal socializing in the breakroom are among the rituals that your employees may be missing as they work remotely. Make sure your meetings and virtual communication aren't overly buttoned up. Some nonprofits have experimented with remote walking meetings for one-on-one check-ins using Facetime or Zoom, coworking together, virtual water-cooler threads on Slack, or drop-in office hours for quick chats.

Establish Rules of Engagement

If you or any of your team members feel like you're missing something important or being seen as a slacker if you are not able to respond 24/7, one way to lower that anxiety is to establish rules on engagement that spell out your team's work hours, which tools to use, who to contact if something is urgent, the mode of contact, and expectations for response times. A worksheet for this can be found at MindfulTechie.com along with more tools and resources for living a balanced life in a digital world.

It is unclear when or how our work and personal lives will go "back to normal." What is clear, though, is that the pandemic has taught us that paying attention to organizational culture, whether online or off, is more critical than ever for our individual and collective well-being and effectively advancing our missions in uncertain times.

Glossary

A glossary of terms is one of the most underrated items in an industry nonfiction book. It's also an essential part of any book on futurism that is introducing new concepts to a sector that is still focused on making payroll rather than thinking about how to drive impact and efficiency ten years in 2030.

We shouldn't be embarrassed about what we don't know or understand, especially with new buzzwords being created, identified, and introduced to our sector annually. So, if we truly mean that there are no stupid questions when we onboard a new staff member, then let's take the time to hear them, jot them down, and then find ways to add them to our organizational lexicon.

1023-EZ: A streamlined application form for recognition of exemption under section 501(c)(3) of the internal revenue code. Organizations with total assets up to $250,000 and those expecting annual gross receipts up to $50,000 are eligible to use Form 1023-EZ.

5G: The fifth-generation technology standard for cellular networks, projected to fully replace the 4G networks that provide connectivity to most current cellphones and provide stronger network reliability, faster downloads, and more connected devices.

Artificial Intelligence: A wide-ranging branch of computer science concerned with building smart machines capable of performing tasks that typically require human intelligence.

Augmented Reality: The overlay of digital content and information onto the physical world.

Automation: The creation and application of technology by which a process or procedure is performed with minimal human assistance.

Blockchain: A digital record of transactions. The name comes from its structure, in which individual records, called blocks, are linked together in a single list, called a chain.

Call (or Click) to Action (CTA): A marketing term that refers to the next step a person or organization wants its audience or reader to take.

Cause Selling: A relationship-centered, collaborative approach to professional fundraising. The model integrates valuable systems from the for-profit realm, with a more intentional focus on building long-term connections that benefit both the donor and the organization.

Chatbots: Artificial intelligence software that can simulate a conversation (or a chat) with a user in natural language through messaging applications, websites, mobile apps, or through the phone.

Civic Engagement: Actions a person or group take that protect public values or make a change or difference in the community through both political and nonpolitical processes. This also includes developing a combination of knowledge, skills, values, and motivation to make that difference.

Civic Literacy: The knowledge and skills to participate effectively in civic life through knowing how to stay informed, understanding governmental processes, and knowing how to exercise the rights and obligations of citizenship at local, state, national, and global levels.

CivicTech: A technology that enables engagement or participation or enhances the relationship between the people and government by enhancing citizen communications and public decision.

Cloud Computing: The on-demand availability of computer system resources, especially data storage and computing power, without direct active management by the user.

Community Development Block Grants: Federal grants that fund local community development activities with the stated goal of providing affordable housing, anti-poverty programs, and infrastructure development.

Community Development Financial Institutions (CDFIs): Private financial institutions that are solely dedicated to delivering responsible, affordable lending to low-income, low-wealth, and other disadvantaged people and communities.

Credentialing: The process of obtaining professional qualifications such as licensure, education, training, or additional experience.

Cryptocurrency: A digital or virtual currency designed to work as a medium of exchange.

Cryptography: The use of special codes to keep information safe in computer networks.

Data Philanthropy: The sharing of data from various sectors in ways that the public can benefit.

Dependent Variable: The variable being tested and measured in an experiment.

Disaster Analytics: Modeling the risk of natural disaster and understanding the impact of disasters on society.

Donor-Advised Fund (DAF): A giving vehicle established at a public charity. It allows donors to make a charitable contribution, receive an immediate tax deduction, and then recommend grants from the fund over time.

Economic Development Council: An organization whose mission is to promote economic development within a specific geographical area.

Equality: Treating everyone the same and giving everyone access to the same opportunities.

Equity: Refers to proportional representation (by race, class, gender, etc.) in those same opportunities.

Explainable AI: Frameworks that develop interpretable, high-confidence machine learning models.

Fiscal Sponsorship: The practice of nonprofit organizations offering their legal and tax-exempt status to groups—typically projects—engaged in activities related to the sponsoring organization's mission. It typically involves a fee-based contractual arrangement between a project and an established nonprofit.

Futurism: The exploration of predictions and possibilities about the future and how they might enhance, impact, or emerge from the present.

Giving Circle: A form of participatory philanthropy where groups of individuals donate their own money or time to a pooled fund, decide together where to give these away to charity or community projects, and, in doing so, seek to increase their awareness of and engagement in the issues covered by the charity or community project.

GivingTuesday: Refers to the Tuesday after Thanksgiving in the United States. It is a movement to create an international day of charitable giving at the beginning of the holiday season.

Good Systems: Human-AI partnerships that address the needs and values of society, such as trust, transparency, agency, equality, justice, and democracy.

GovTech: Applying emerging technologies to improve the delivery of public services through increasing efficiency and lowering costs.

Graphics and Visualization: Generating graphics with the aid of machine learning.

HX: How a human experiences your product or service.

Impact Investing: Investments made into companies, organizations, and funds that generate financial returns alongside positive social and environmental impact.

Independent Variable: The variable the experimenter changes or controls and is assumed to have a direct effect on the dependent variable.

Internet of Things (IoT): The network of physical objects—"things"—that are embedded with sensors, software, and other technologies for the purpose of connecting and exchanging data with other devices and systems over the internet.

Job Ladder: A formal process within an organization that allows employees to advance their careers to higher levels of salary, responsibility, or authority.

Justice Philanthropy: The practice of making contributions to nonprofit organizations that work for structural change and increase the opportunity of those who are less well off politically, economically, and socially.

Knowledge Broker: An intermediary that aims to develop relationships and bridges with, among, and between producers and users of knowledge by providing linkages, knowledge sources, and, in some cases, knowledge itself to organizations in its network.

Machine Learning: The study of computer algorithms that improve automatically through experience.

Mixed Reality: An extension of augmented reality that not just overlays, but anchors virtual objects to the real world and allows these elements to interact.

National Taxonomy of Exempt Entities (NTEE) Codes: A classification system for nonprofit organizations developed by the National Center for Charitable Statistics. Also used by sector researchers to classify both grants and grant recipients.

Natural Language: A field that gives machines the ability to read, understand, and derive meaning from human language.

New Markets Tax Credits: A financial program that aims to stimulate business and real estate investment in low-income communities via a federal tax credit.

Nonprofit Overhead: The percentage of a nonprofit's spending that goes to administrative expenses instead of going directly to beneficiaries (not to be confused as a bad thing).

Open Data: The idea that some data should be freely available to everyone to use and republish as they wish, without restrictions from copyright, patents, or other mechanisms of control.

Opportunity Zones: A designation and investment program allowing for certain investments in lower-income areas to have tax advantages.

Organized Philanthropy: Nonprofit, nongovernmental entities such as community foundations, endowments, and charitable trusts that invest donated assets to generate income that provides social services and grants.

Participatory Budgeting: A democratic process in which community members directly decide how to spend part of a public budget.

Pay Audits: A process where you identify pay disparities among your workers (and then fix them!).

Power Mapping: A visual tool used by social advocates to identify the best individuals to target to promote social change.

Promise Zones: High-poverty communities where the federal government partners with local leaders to increase economic activity, improve educational opportunities, leverage private investment, reduce crime, enhance public health, and address other priorities identified by the community.

Public-Private Partnership (PPP): A cooperative arrangement between two or more public and private sectors, typically of a long-term nature that tackles a project and/or to provide services to the population. Can also be referred to as a public/private-philanthropic partnership.

Quantum Computing: Computers that perform calculations based on the probability of an object's state before it is measured—beyond the binary of just 1s or 0s—which means they have the potential to process exponentially more data compared to classical computers.

Racial Justice: The work to uproot historically racist systems and replace them with fair, just, and equitable policies and practices.

Recommender Systems: The use of machine learning methods in a manner that seeks to predict user preferences.

Redlining: A discriminatory practice that puts services (financial and otherwise) out of reach for residents of certain areas based on race or ethnicity.

Regional Association of Grantmakers: Membership associations that promote the growth and effectiveness of philanthropy to improve lives in their communities.

Regression Analysis: A set of statistical processes for estimating the relationships between a dependent variable and one or more independent variables.

Reinforcement Learning: The training of machine learning models to make a sequence of decisions. The artificial intelligence gets either rewards or penalties for the actions it performs from its programmer with its goal being to maximize the total reward.

Return on Immersion: A term I originally coined in 2017 at the PRSA International Conference to mean a proposed performance measure used to evaluate the impact, empathy, and investment of a user exposed to virtual, mixed-use, and augmented realities.

Robotics: The study of devices that can move and react to sensory input.

Salary Cloaking: A (debatable) belief that not posting a specific salary will encourage more applicants.

Smart Contracts: A computer program or transaction protocol that is intended to automatically execute, control, or document legally relevant events and actions according to the terms of a contract or an agreement.

Social Emotional Learning (SEL): The process through which children and adults understand and manage emotions, set and achieve positive goals, feel and show empathy for others, establish and maintain positive relationships, and make responsible decisions.

Social Impact Bonds: A contract with the public sector or governing authority, whereby it pays for better social outcomes in certain areas and passes on the part of the savings achieved to investors.

Talent Optimization: A science-based approach to define job requirements, identify ideal internal and external candidates, align teams to accomplish business goals, and effectively manage and inspire employees to achieve superior results.

Trust-Based Philanthropy: An approach to grantee relationships that is seen as an ongoing partnership rather than a one-time transaction.

User Experience (UX): Encompasses all aspects of the end-user's interaction with the company, its services, and its products.

User Interface (UI): Anything a user may interact with to use a digital product or service.

Virtual Reality (VR): A simulated experience that can be similar to or completely different from the real world.

Vision: Training computers to interpret and understand digital images and videos.

White Labeling: A legal protocol that allows one product or service to be sold and rebranded under another company's brand.

Wireless Communication: The transmission of information from one point to other without using a connecting physical medium.

Notes

Acknowledgments

1. 123RF, "The Iceberg Illusion," https://www.123rf.com/pho-
    to_140527345_stock-vector-iceberg-illusion-diagram-vector-illustra-
    tion-what-people-see-and-what-is-success-hidden-part-of-hard.html.

2. Kickstarter, Future Philanthropy, https://www.kickstarter.com/proj-
    ects/futurephilanthropy/future-philanthropy.

Introduction

1. Queensland Floods Commission of Inquiry, *Final Report*, March 16,
    2012, http://www.floodcommission.qld.gov.au/publications/final-re-
    port/.

2. *Queensland Times*, "$4.15 Million Sale Shows 2011 Flood Woes Are
    History," February 9, 2017, https://www.qt.com.au/news/goodna-sale-
    for-415-million-renews-confidence/3141537/.

3. *U.S. News & World Report*, "Austin, Texas, Is the No. 1 Best Place
    to Live, According to U.S. News & World Report," April 9, 2019,
    https://www.usnews.com/info/blogs/press-room/articles/2019-04-09/
    austin-texas-is-the-no-1-best-place-to-live-according-to-us-news.

4. University of Texas at Austin, "UT Austin Selected as Home of Na-
    tional AI Institute Focused on Machine Learning," *UT News*, August
    26, 2020, https://news.utexas.edu/2020/08/26/ut-austin-selected-as-
    home-of-national-ai-institute-focused-on-machine-learning/.

Chapter 2

1. Julia Gillard, "2020 Summit: Golden Gurus," Ministers' Media Centre,
    Department of Education, Skills and Employment, April 23, 2009,
    https://ministers.dese.gov.au/gillard/2020-summit-golden-gurus.

2. Durfee Foundation, "Sabbatical", https://durfee.org/our-programs/sabbatical/.

3. Fieldstone Leadership Network San Diego, "Clare Rose Sabbatical Program," https://fieldstoneleadershipsd.org/clare-rose-sabbatical-program/.

4. Timothy Sandoval, "Keys to Low Staff Turnover: One Nonprofit's Advice," *Chronicle of Philanthropy*, May 1, 2017, https://www.philanthropy.com/article/keys-to-low-staff-turnover-one-nonprofits-advice/.

5. Susannah Birkwood, "Fundraisers' Job Titles Can Affect Likelihood of Donors Talking to Them About Donations, Research Indicates," *Third Sector*, October 25, 2016, https://www.thirdsector.co.uk/fundraisers-job-titles-affect-likelihood-donors-talking-donations-research-indicates/fundraising/article/1413420.

6. Nonprofit Finance Fund, "2018 State of the Nonprofit Sector Survey," https://nff.org/learn/survey.

7. XpertHR, *HR Staffing, Costs and Structures in the Nonprofit Sector: Headline Results of the 2014 Survey*, https://www.nonprofithr.com/wp-content/uploads/2014/08/HR_staffing_costs_structures_NONPROFIT_2014_short_rev.pdf.

8. Tom Popomaronis, "Here's How Many Google Interviews It Takes to Hire a Googler," CNBC, April 17, 2019, https://www.cnbc.com/2019/04/17/heres-how-many-google-job-interviews-it-takes-to-hire-a-googler.html.

9. Aaron Smith and Monica Anderson, "Americans' Attitudes Toward Hiring Algorithms," Pew Research Center, October 4, 2017, https://www.pewresearch.org/internet/2017/10/04/americans-attitudes-toward-hiring-algorithms/.

10. Philanthropy New York, "So, You Want a Job in Philanthropy?" https://philanthropynewyork.org/so-you-want-job-philanthropy.

11. Knight Foundation, "What We Fund," April 8, 2015, https://knightfoundation.org/programs/journalism/ .

12. Trista Harris, "How a Jeffersonian Dinner Can Change the World," August 20, 2016, http://www.tristaharris.org/new-voices-of-philanthropy/Tristaharrisorg/how-a-jeffersonian-dinner-can-change-the-world.

13. Maria Paegler Digital, "21 Ways to Extend the Life of Your Content," https://mariapaeglerdigital.com/21-ways-to-extend-the-life-of-your-content-infographic/.

Chapter 3

1. HR Dive, "Salary History Bans," https://www.hrdive.com/news/salary-history-ban-states-list/516662/.

2. Grace Dean, "Tulsa, Oklahoma, Is Paying Remote Workers $10,000 to Move There for a Year," *Business Insider*, November 25, 2020, https://www.businessinsider.com/tulsa-oklahoma-remote-workers-pay-move-there-for-year-2020-11.

3. Business Wire, "Hawai'i Launches Movers & Shakas Temporary Resident Program," November 30, 2020, https://www.businesswire.com/news/home/20201130005306/en/Hawai%E2%80%98i-Launches-Movers-Shakas-Temporary-Resident-Program.

4. Technology Association of Grantmakers, "TAG Releases Findings of 2020 State of Philanthropy Tech Survey," October 23, 2020, https://www.tagtech.org/news/531543/TAG-Releases-Findings-of-2020-State-of-Philanthropy-Tech-Survey.htm.

5. Jarret O'Brien and Katharine Bierce, "Announcing the Latest Nonprofit Trends Report," Salesforce, February 18, 2020, https://www.salesforce.org/blog/nonprofit-trends-report-second-edition-research/.

6. *Yale Insights*, "Can Technology Transform the Nonprofit Sector?" May 29, 2018, https://insights.som.yale.edu/insights/can-technology-transform-the-nonprofit-sector.

7. Technology Association of Grantmakers, "TAG Launches Digital Infrastructure Guide with NetHope, NTEN, TechSoup," August 12, 2020,

8. https://www.tagtech.org/news/521162/TAG-Launches-Digital-Infra-structure-Funding-Guide-with-NetHope-NTEN-TechSoup.htm.

9. Organisation for Economic Co-operation and Development, "OECD Broadband Statistics Update," July 22, 2020, http://www.oecd.org/digital/broadband-statistics-update.htm?utm_source=newsletter&utm_medium=email&utm_campaign=whatsnewhealth#:~:text=Swit-zerland%20leads%20the%20pack%20with,be%20gradually%20replaced%20by%20fibre.

10. EveryCRSReport.com, "Broadband Infrastructure Programs in the American Recovery and Reinvestment Act," January 4, 2011, https://www.everycrsreport.com/reports/R40436.html#:~:text=American%20Recovery%20and%20Reinvestment%20Act%20of%202009%2C%20P.L.,-111%2D5&text=On%20February%2017%2C%202009%2C%20President,billion%2C%20primarily%20for%20broad-band%20grants.

11. Adia Coalr, "Candid's 2020 Nonprofit Compensation Report Finds an Increase in Female Leadership—and an Increase in the Female Pay Gap," Candid, September 21, 2020, https://candid.org/about/press-room/releases/candid-s-2020-nonprofit-compensation-report-finds-an-increase-in-female-leadership-and-an-increase-in-the-female-pay-gap#:~:text=Candid%20today%20released%20the%202020,orga-nizations%20for%20fiscal%20year%202018.

12. National Partnership for Women and Families, "America's Women and the Wage Gap," September 2020, https://www.nationalpartnership.org/our-work/resources/economic-justice/fair-pay/americas-women-and-the-wage-gap.pdf.

Chapter 4

1. Dina Gerdeman, "Minorities Who 'Whiten' Job Resumes Get More Interviews," *Harvard Business School Working Knowledge*, May 17, 2017, https://hbswk.hbs.edu/item/minorities-who-whiten-job-re-sumes-get-more-interviews.

2. Cue Health, "Cue Health Closes $100 Million Series C Financing to Support Launch of Rapid Molecular Testing Platform," June 10, 2020, https://www.cuehealth.com/about/press/cue-health-closes-$100-mil-

lion-series-c-financing-to-support-launch-of/.

3.   Harder+Company, *Status of Bay Area Nonprofit Space & Facilities*, March 2016, https://harderco.com/sample_work/status-of-bay-area-nonprofit-space-facilities/.

4.   *KnowledgeNudge*, "I Got the Job! . . . So, Um, What's a Knowledge Broker?" October 29, 2015, https://medium.com/knowledgenudge/i-got-the-job-so-um-whats-a-knowledge-broker-45519db96cb0.

5.   National Philanthropic Trust, "Charitable Giving Statistics," https://www.nptrust.org/philanthropic-resources/charitable-giving-statistics/.

Chapter 6

1.   Jonathan Greenblatt, "Celebrating 100 Years of Community Foundations," Obama White House, December 2, 2014, https://obamawhitehouse.archives.gov/blog/2014/12/02/celebrating-100-years-community-foundations.

2.   Michael Moody and Sharna Goldseker, "Generation Impact: How Next Gen Donors Are Revolutionizing Giving," Philanthropy News Digest, November 28, 2017, https://philanthropynewsdigest.org/off-the-shelf/generation-impact-how-next-gen-donors-are-revolutionizing-giving.

3.   Supreme Court of the United States, Brief of Amici Curiae Foundations and Philanthropy-Serving Organizations in Support of Respondents, April 1, 2019, https://www.supremecourt.gov/DocketPDF/18/18-966/95035/20190401200604897_18-966bsacFoundationsAndPhilanthropy-ServingOrganizations.pdf.

4.   Katie Smith Milway, Maria Orozco, and Cristina Botero, "Why Nonprofit Mergers Continue to Lag," *Stanford Social Innovation Review*, Spring 2014, https://ssir.org/articles/entry/why_nonprofit_mergers_continue_to_lag.

5.   Lawson Bader, "It's Time More Nonprofits Consider M&A," *Forbes*, October 28, 2019, https://www.forbes.com/sites/forbesnonprofitcouncil/2019/10/28/its-time-more-nonprofits-consider-ma/?sh=622a535915c0.

6. Northwestern University School of Communication, "Network for Nonprofit and Social Impact, Nonprofit Merger Study Released: Implications for Nonprofit Management," https://nnsi.northwestern.edu/nonprofit-merger-study-released-implications-for-nonprofit-management/.

7. Forefront, "Mission Sustainability Initiative," https://myforefront.org/programs-services/msi/.

8. Venable LLP, "Mergers, Alliances, Affiliations and. Acquisitions for Nonprofit Organizations: Financial and Legal Issues," December 6, 2010, https://www.venable.com/-/media/files/events/2010/12/mergers-alliances-affiliations-and-acquisitions-fo/files/event-handout/fileattachment/nonprofit_combinations_program.pdf.

9. Nordson, "Community Investment," https://www.nordson.com/en/our-company/corporate-responsibility/community-investment.

Chapter 7

1. Christopher Sirk, "Diffusion of Innovations: How Adoption of New Ideas and Technologies Spread," CRM.org, August 21,2020, https://crm.org/articles/diffusion-of-innovations.

2. comScore, "14 Million Americans Scanned QR or Bar Codes on Their Mobile Phones in June 2011," August 12, 2011, https://www.prnewswire.com/news-releases/14-million-americans-scanned-qr-or-bar-codes-on-their-mobile-phones-in-june-2011-127585148.html.

3. Carol Cluppert, "QR Codes Make a Marketing Comeback," Walsworth, August 18, 2020, https://www.walsworth.com/blog/qr-codes-make-a-marketing-comeback.

4. Kit Eaton, "Why Microsoft Is Buying Skype For $8.5 Billion," *Fast Company*, May 10, 2011, https://www.fastcompany.com/1752492/why-microsoft-buying-skype-85-billion.

5. Charity Navigator, "America's Most Charitable Cities," June 13, 2017, https://www.charitynavigator.org/index.cfm?bay=content.view&cpid=5025.

6. Giving USA, "Giving USA 2020: Charitable Giving Showed Solid Growth, Climbing to $449.64 Billion in 2019, One of the Highest Years for Giving on Record," June 16, 2020, https://givingusa.org/giving-usa-2020-charitable-giving-showed-solid-growth-climbing-to-449-64-billion-in-2019-one-of-the-highest-years-for-giving-on-record/.

7. Urban Institute, National Center for Charitable Statistics, "The Nonprofit Sector in Brief," June 18, 2020, https://nccs.urban.org/project/nonprofit-sector-brief.

8. Philanthropy Roundtable, "Who Gives Most to Charity?" https://www.philanthropyroundtable.org/almanac/statistics/who-gives.

9. AmeriCorps, "Volunteering in U.S. Hits Record High; Worth $167 Billion," November 13, 2018, https://www.nationalservice.gov/newsroom/press-releases/2018/volunteering-us-hits-record-high-worth-167-billion.

10. Nancy Jamison and Emily Young, "Is San Diego America's Most Generous City?" *San Diego Union-Tribune*, August 3, 2017, https://www.sandiegouniontribune.com/opinion/commentary/sd-utbg-philanthropy-charity-navigator-20170803-story.html.

11. Rachel Sheppard, "Only 3% of Business Investment Goes to Women, and That's a Problem for Everyone," Crunchbase, April 8, 2020, https://about.crunchbase.com/blog/business-investment-to-women/.

Chapter 8

1. Ky Pham, "HX (Human Experience)—We All Should Keep It in Mind to Create More Value," UX Collective, September 27, 2019, https://uxdesign.cc/hx-human-experience-we-all-should-keep-it-in-mind-to-create-more-value-82d760bc5eae.

2. Andi Kemp, "How Long Does It Take to Write a Grant?" Upward Development, http://upward-development.com/wp-content/uploads/2016/11/ajk-time-it-takes-to-write-grants_2015.pdf.

3. Kristen Bialik, "7 Facts About Americans with Disabilities," Pew Research Center, July 27, 2017, https://www.pewresearch.org/fact-tank/2017/07/27/7-facts-about-americans-with-disabilities/.

4. WebAIM, "The WebAIM Million," https://webaim.org/projects/million/.

Chapter 10

1. F. Duke Haddad, "Are There Too Many Nonprofit Organizations in the US?" NonProfit PRO, October 20, 2017, https://www.nonprofit-pro.com/post/many-nonprofit-organizations-us/.

2. Anna Koob, "Key Facts on U.S. Nonprofits and Foundations," IssueLab, April 22, 2020, https://candid.issuelab.org/resource/key-facts-on-u-s-nonprofits-and-foundations.html.

3. Allegiance Fundraising Group, "This State Has the Most Nonprofits Per Person," March 21, 2016, https://blog.wedid.it/this-state-has-the-most-nonprofits-per-person.

4. Internal Revenue Service (IRS), "IRS Revises Form 1023 for Applying for Tax-Exempt Status," January 31, 2020, https://www.irs.gov/newsroom/irs-revises-form-1023-for-applying-for-tax-exempt-status.

5. Jacob Bogage and Lisa Rein, "Trump Administration Considers Leveraging Emergency Coronavirus Loan to Force Postal Service Changes," *Washington Post*, April 23, 2020, https://www.washingtonpost.com/business/2020/04/23/10-billion-treasury-loan-usps/.

6. Marcia Coyle, "The Postal Clause's Grant of 'Broad Power' to Congress over a System in Crisis," *Constitution Daily*, August 17, 2020, https://constitutioncenter.org/blog/the-postal-clauses-grant-of-broad-power-to-congress-over-a-system-in-crisis.

7. Sarah Anderson, Scott Klinger, and Brian Wakamo "How Congress Manufactured a Postal Crisis—And How to Fix It," Institute for Policy Studies, July 15, 2019, https://ips-dc.org/how-congress-manufactured-a-postal-crisis-and-how-to-fix-it/.

8. Jory Heckman, "House Passes Smaller USPS Reform Bill to Eliminate Pre-Funding Benefits," Federal News Network, February 6, 2020, https://federalnewsnetwork.com/agency-oversight/2020/02/house-passes-smaller-usps-reform-bill-to-eliminate-pre-funding-benefits/.

9. Bureau of the Fiscal Service, "Gifts to the U.S. Government," https://fiscal.treasury.gov/public/gifts-to-government.html.

10. Dave Bier and Kristie De Peña, "Can We Give to the Parts of the Government We Like?" Niskanen Center, May 10, 2016, https://www.niskanencenter.org/can-we-give-to-the-parts-of-the-government-we-like/.

11. Keith Combs, "One Way to Honor Vets? Protect the Postal Service," Inequality.org, November 11, 2019, https://inequality.org/research/usps-veterans.

12. *NonProfit Times*, "Live From DMA: Direct Mail Hiatus Cost ACS $30 Million," August 5, 2015, https://www.thenonprofittimes.com/npt_articles/live-from-dma-direct-mail-hiatus-cost-acs-30-million/.

13. United States Postal Service, "Size and Scope," https://facts.usps.com/size-and-scope.

14. Philanthropy Northwest, *A Foundation Guide to Investing in CDFIs* (Seattle, WA: Philanthropy Northwest, 2017) https://philanthropynw.org/resources/foundation-guide-investing-cdfis.

15. LA n Sync, "Successes," https://lansync.org/successes/.

16. Whitehouse.gov, "Proclamation on National Volunteer Week, 2020," https://www.whitehouse.gov/presidential-actions/proclamation-national-volunteer-week-2020/#:~:text=TRUMP%2C%20President%20of%20the%20United,2020%2C%20as%20National%20Volunteer%20Week.

17. Catherine Kim, "Pete Buttigieg Calls for Expanding National Service," Vox, July 3, 2019, https://www.vox.com/2019/7/3/20680963/pete-buttigieg-expand-national-service.

18. City of South Bend, Indiana, "South Bend Wins Cities of Service National Competition to Revitalize Neighborhoods," July 16, 2018, https://southbendin.gov/2018/07/16/south-bend-wins-cities-of-service-national-competition-to-revitalize-neighborhoods/.

19. Independent Sector, "Independent Sector Releases New Value of Volunteer Time of $25.43 Per Hour," April 11, 2019, https://independentsector.org/news-post/new-value-volunteer-time-2019/.

20. Jessica Semega, Melissa Kollar, Emily A. Shrider, and John Creamer, US Census Bureau, Current Population Reports, P60-270 *Income and Poverty in the United States: 2019* (Washington, DC: US Government Publishing Office, 2020) https://www.census.gov/data/tables/2020/demo/income-poverty/p60-270.html.

21. Derek Thompson, "Why Child Care Is So Ridiculously Expensive," *Atlantic*, November 26, 2019, https://www.theatlantic.com/ideas/archive/2019/11/why-child-care-so-expensive/602599/.

22. Cheryl Dorsey, Jeff Bradach, and Peter Kim, "Racial Equity and Philanthropy: Disparities in Funding for Leaders of Color Leave Impact on the Table," Bridgespan Group, May 4, 2020, https://www.bridgespan.org/insights/library/philanthropy/disparities-nonprofit-funding-for-leaders-of-color.

Chapter 11

1. Jonathan Eggleston and Donald Hays, "Many U.S. Households Do Not Have Biggest Contributors to Wealth: Home Equity and Retirement Accounts," United States Census Bureau, August 27, 2019, https://www.census.gov/library/stories/2019/08/gaps-in-wealth-americans-by-household-type.html.

2. Jacobs Center for Neighborhood Innovation, *Community Development Initial Public Offering: Market Creek Plaza Evaluation Synthesis Report* (San Diego, CA: Jacobs Center for Neighborhood Innovation, 2013) https://www.jacobscenter.org/_pdf/IPO_synthesisreport.pdf.

3. Debbie L. Sklar, "Local Organizations Form Investment Partnership to Fund New Nonprofit Facility," *Times of San Diego*, January 16, 2019, https://timesofsandiego.com/education/2019/01/16/local-organizations-form-investment-partnership-to-fund-new-nonprofit-facility/.

4. Maria Di Mento, "The Philanthropy 50," *Chronicle of Philanthropy*, February 9, 2021, https://www.philanthropy.com/article/the-philan-

thropy-50/#id=browse_2019.

5. Harmony Social and Emotional Learning, "Healthy Relationships Start with Harmony SEL," https://www.harmonysel.org/.

6. City of New York, "Transcript: Mayor de Blasio, First Lady McCray, Chancellor Carranza Announce Major Expansion of Social-Emotional Learning and Restorative Justice Across All City Schools," June 20, 2019, https://www1.nyc.gov/office-of-the-mayor/news/315-19/tran-script-mayor-de-blasio-first-lady-mccray-chancellor-carranza-major-ex-pansion-of.

7. Matthew M. Chingos, "Don't Forget Private, Non-Profit Colleges," Brookings Institution, February 16, 2017, https://www.brookings.edu/research/dont-forget-private-non-profit-colleges/.

8. Benefactor Group, "Stop the Revolving Door in Nonprofit Develop-ment," https://benefactorgroup.com/revolvingdoor/.

9. Steven Sarabia, "Austin FC Sells Out of Season Ticket Memberships," Fox 7 Austin, August 31, 2020, https://www.fox7austin.com/sports/austin-fc-sells-out-of-season-ticket-memberships.

Chapter 12

1. GovTech Fund, "Govtech: The $400 Billion Market Hiding in Plain Sight," January 3, 2016, http://govtechfund.com/2016/01/govtech-the-400-billion-market-hiding-in-plain-sight/.

2. State of Vermont Agency of Commerce and Community Develop-ment, "Remote Worker Grant Program," https://accd.vermont.gov/economic-development/remoteworkergrantprogram.

3. Ana Swanson, "America's Biggest Charity Is No Longer What Most People Think of as a Charity," *Washington Post*, October 27, 2016, https://www.washingtonpost.com/news/wonk/wp/2016/10/27/ameri-cas-biggest-charity-is-no-longer-what-most-people-think-of-as-a-char-ity/.

4. Alex Daniels, "Gifts to Fidelity Charitable Soar to $6.85 Billion," *Chronicle of Philanthropy*, October 10, 2017, https://www.philanthro-

py.com/article/gifts-to-fidelity-charitable-soar-to-6-85-billion/.

5. Fidelity Charitable, "2020 Fidelity Charitable Giving Report," https://www.fidelitycharitable.org/insights/2020-giving-report.html.

6. Fidelity Charitable, "Largest Grantmaker Eliminates Minimum Contribution Amount," September 30, 2020, https://www.fidelitycharitable.org/about-us/news/largest-grantmaker-eliminates-minimum-contribution-amount.html.

7. Charity Navigator, "#GivingTuesday 2020: A Record-Breaking Day," December 7, 2020, https://www.charitynavigator.org/index.cfm?bay=content.view&cpid=8357.

8. Andria Cheng, "Record Black Friday Online Sales Likely Not Enough To Make Up For Lost Store Visits," *Forbes*, November 30, 2020, https://www.forbes.com/sites/andriacheng/2020/11/30/black-friday-online-sales-hit-a-record-but-likely-not-enough-to-make-up-for-lost-store-visits/?sh=78627c564b1a.

9. Shelley E. Kohan, "Cyber Monday Sales Hit $10.8 Billion: Black Friday Weekend by the Numbers," *Forbes*, December 1, 2020, https://www.forbes.com/sites/shelleykohan/2020/12/01/cyber-monday-sales-hit-108-billion-black-friday-weekend-by-the-numbers/?sh=6fdeeec76eb0.

10. WealthEngine, "Making the Most of Year-End Giving Trends," https://www.wealthengine.com/making-the-most-of-year-end-giving/amp/.

11. Will Schmidt, "Infographic: Giving Tuesday 2020 Totals Hit Record High," Classy, December 3, 2020, https://www.classy.org/blog/giving-tuesday-2020-infographic/.

12. Drew Lindsay, "Who's Raising the Most: The 100 Charities That Are America's Favorites," *Chronicle of Philanthropy*, October 30, 2018, https://www.philanthropy.com/article/whos-raising-the-most-the-100-charities-that-are-americas-favorites/.

13. GivingTuesday, "#GivingTuesdayNow Creates Global Wave of Generosity in Response to COVID-19 Crisis," https://www.givingtuesday.

org/blog/2020/05/givingtuesdaynow-creates-global-wave-generosity-response-covid-19-crisis.

Future Focus

1. Prime Minister's Community Business Partnership, "Giving Australia 2016," https://www.communitybusinesspartnership.gov.au/about/research-projects/giving-australia-2016/.

2. Australian Charities and Not-for-Profits Commission, *Australian Charities Report 2018* (Melbourne, VIC: ACNC, 2020) https://www.acnc.gov.au/tools/reports/australian-charities-report-2018.

3. Australian Charities and Not-for-Profits Commission, *Australian Charities Report 2017* (Melbourne, VIC: ACNC, 2019) https://www.acnc.gov.au/tools/reports/australian-charities-report-2017.

4. Australian Charities and Not-for-Profits Commission, *Australian Charities Report 2016* (Melbourne, VIC: ACNC, 2018) https://www.acnc.gov.au/tools/reports/australian-charities-report-2016.

5. Australian Government, "Budget 2018–19," https://archive.budget.gov.au/2018-19/.

6. Just Reinvest and KPMG, *Unlocking the Future: Maranguka Justice Reinvestment Project in Bourke, Preliminary Assessment* (N.p.: KPMG, 2016) https://www.justreinvest.org.au/wp-content/uploads/2016/11/KPMG-Preliminary-Assessment-Maranguka-Justice-Reinvestment-Project.pdf.

7. International Specialised Skills Institute, *The Doveton Model and Implications for Other Sites* (Melbourne, VIC: International Specialised Skills Institute, 2017) https://www.issinstitute.org.au/wp-content/uploads/2017/04/McMahon-Final.pdf.

8. Shaima Hamidaddin, "Saudi Arabia's Answer to 21st Century Philanthropy," *Alliance* magazine, September 4, 2018, https://www.alliance-magazine.org/feature/saudi-arabias-answer-to-21st-century-philanthropy/.

9. UBS, "New Report Reveals that Global Philanthropy Is Booming, Yet

Most Foundations Still Work in Isolation," April 26, 2018, https://www.ubs.com/global/en/media/display-page-ndp/en-20180426-global-philanthropy.html.

10. Scholaro, "Education System in Saudi Arabia," https://www.scholaro.com/pro/Countries/Saudi-Arabia/Education-System; Hollie Nielsen, "Literacy in Saudi Arabia: Striving for Excellence," Federation of American Women's Clubs Overseas (FAWCO), September 22, 2019,

11. https://www.fawco.org/global-issues/education/education-articles/4158-literacy-in-saudi-arabia-striving-for-excellence.

12. Y20—Saudi Arabia, *Y20 Summit 2020 Communiqué*, October 17, 2020, https://reports.youth20saudi.org/Y20_Communique.pdf.

Chapter 14

1. The Opportunity Agenda, "Media Representations and Impact on the Lives of Black Men and Boys," 2011, https://www.opportunityagenda.org/explore/resources-publications/media-representations-impact-black-men/executive-summary.

2. Jeffrey Dastin, "Amazon Scraps Secret AI Recruiting Tool that Showed Bias Against Women," Reuters, October 10, 2018, https://www.reuters.com/article/us-amazon-com-jobs-automation-insight/amazon-scraps-secret-ai-recruiting-tool-that-showed-bias-against-women-idUSKCN-1MK08G.

3. San Diego Foundation, *Our Greater San Diego Vision—Full Report*, (San Diego, CA: San Diego Foundation, 2012) https://issuu.com/the-sandiegofoundation/docs/ogsdv-final-hires.

4. Sunlight Foundation, "Roadmap to More Informed Communities," https://sunlightfoundation.com/our-work/open-cities/projects-resources/.

5. Bruce Katz, "The New Localism: Think Like A System, Act Like an Entrepreneur," The New Localism, March 29, 2018, https://www.thenewlocalism.com/research/the-new-localism-think-like-a-system-act-like-an-entrepreneur/.

6. Jonathan Nafarrete, "How Pencils of Promise Raised $1.9M with the Help of VR," VR Scout, November 2, 2015, https://vrscout.com/news/pencils-of-promise-virtual-reality/.

7. Adi Robertson, "The UN Wants to See How Far VR Empathy Will Go," The Verge, September 19, 2016, https://www.theverge.com/2016/9/19/12933874/unvr-clouds-over-sidra-film-app-launch.

8. Marty Swant, "How Virtual Reality Is Inspiring Donors to Dig Deep for Charitable Causes," Adweek, May 31, 2016, https://www.adweek.com/performance-marketing/how-virtual-reality-inspiring-donors-dig-deep-charitable-causes-171641/.

9. Amnesty International, "'Virtual reality Aleppo' Street Fundraising Campaign Launched," May 8, 2015, https://www.amnesty.org.uk/press-releases/virtual-reality-aleppo-street-fundraising-campaign-launched.

Chapter 15

1. HUD User, Office of Policy Development and Research, "Using Data to Understand and End Homelessness," https://www.huduser.gov/portal/periodicals/em/summer12/highlight2.html.

2. Centre for Public Impact, *Social Impact Bonds: An Overview of the Global Market for Commissioners and Policymakers*, 2017, http://socialspider.com/wp-content/uploads/2017/04/SS_SocialImpactReport_4.0.pdf.

3. Campaign Monitor, "2017 Consumer Email Habits Report: What Do Your Customers Really Want?" July 2017, https://www.campaignmonitor.com/resources/guides/insights-research-report/.

4. Saima Salim, "Do the Consumers Prefer Chatbot to Humans?" Digital Information World, January 8, 2019, https://www.digitalinformationworld.com/2019/01/digital-consumers-want-a-little-less-automation-but-a-little-more-human-interaction.html.

5. Rachel Kraus, "Facebook Is Really Proud of Its 300,000 Business Bots, Despite Claiming it Will Put 'People First,'" Mashable, May 1, 2018, https://mashable.com/2018/05/01/messenger-bots-f8-2018/.

6. MarketsandMarkets Research, "Chatbot Market Worth $9.4 Billion by 2024," https://www.marketsandmarkets.com/PressReleases/smart-advisor.asp.

Chapter 16

1. Adele Peters, "This 'Donation Dollar' Coin Is Designed to Be Given Away," Fast Company, September 2, 2020, https://www.fastcompany.com/90546516/this-donation-dollar-coin-is-designed-to-be-given-away.

2. *Giving Block*, "The Pineapple Fund Donated $55,000,000 in Nonprofit Bitcoin Grants. Here's What Happened," October 1, 2019, https://www.thegivingblock.com/post/pineapple-fund-bitcoin-donated-to-nonprofits-here-s-what-happened.

3. Danny Nelson, "Inside a Crypto 'Ponzi': How the $6.5M Banana. Fund Fraud Unravelled," Nasdaq, August 3, 2020, https://www.nasdaq.com/articles/inside-a-crypto-ponzi%3A-how-the-%246.5m-banana.fund-fraud-unravelled-2020-08-03.

4. IBM, "Coming Soon to Your Business: Quantum Computing," https://www.ibm.com/thought-leadership/institute-business-value/report/quantumstrategy.

5. Hand Foundation, "Helping Hand: 3D Printing Prosthetic Hands," http://www.thehandfoundation.org/newsletter-article.php?Helping-Hand-3D-Printing-Prosthetic-Hands-23.

6. Anastasia Moloney, "Can 3D-Printed Houses Provide Cheap, Safe Homes for the World's Poor?" Reuters, March 15, 2018, https://www.reuters.com/article/us-el-salvador-housing-technology/can-3d-printed-houses-provide-cheap-safe-homes-for-the-worlds-poor-idUSKCN-1GR36H.

7. Will Anderson, "Austin Startup Catches SXSW's Eye with 3D-Printed Tiny Home That Costs Less Than a Car," *Austin Business Journal*, March 14, 2018, https://www.bizjournals.com/austin/news/2018/03/14/austin-startup-icon-sxsw-3d-printed-home.html.

8. Eillie Anzilotti, "The Chan Zuckerberg Initiative Has a $500 Million Plan to Ease the Bay Area Housing Crisis," Fast Company, January 24, 2019, https://www.fastcompany.com/90294576/the-chan-zuckerberg-initiative-has-a-500-million-plan-to-ease-the-bay-area-housing-crisis.

About the Author

Ryan Ginard is a civic connector and fundraiser with more than fifteen years of experience in government, higher education, nonprofits, and organized philanthropy, leveraging more than $2.5 billion in infrastructure funding and directly raising over $15 million for charities. He currently lives in the growing tech hub of Austin, Texas, where he works at the University of Texas at Austin to identify individual donors with an interest in making major gifts to Texas Computer Science in machine learning, artificial intelligence, and robotics.

Ryan's career in organized philanthropy has seen him lead dedicated efforts in civic engagement, public policy, operations, and fundraising at a $1 billion endowed Community Foundation, a regional association of grantmakers, and most recently as chief of staff for a $185 million philanthropic program across early education and charitable giving, impacting more than nine million students and twenty-two thousand schools across twenty countries, including the top ten school districts in the US.

Ryan moved to the United States from Brisbane, Australia, where he spent five years as a policy and media adviser in the federal government on the portfolios of financial services, industry, and innovation.

An active writer and thinker about future directions in philanthropy, Ryan has had his work highlighted in numerous national publications and has been a speaker at internationally renowned conferences such as the Public Relations Society of America's International Conference (PRSA ICON), Social Media Week, and South by Southwest (SXSW), on themes focused on civic technology and immersive storytelling.

LOVE. LEARN. WIN/LOSE. PIVOT.

I have never been much of a traditional learner. I find it hard to get through a book from start to finish. So, the concept of writing one initially blew my mind. Am I ever going to be able to read it myself?!

That is why tech and its ability to absorb knowledge in new ways— ways that work for you—are helping our world evolve in such a rapid way. Technology also doesn't judge you for getting it wrong. It just tells you there is an error so that you can review it, update it, and move on.

Maybe that's why I find myself building platforms, groups, and networks as a way to understand industries and tech—and with great excitement. As you will see in this Future Feature, the major projects I have undertaken in the past decade developed from things that I enjoy (like soccer, civic engagement, and technology) as well as challenges to myself to find ways to make them better and more impactful for a broader audience.

I would love to have seen these projects realized and to have built something that advanced society. But despite the few wins and the long trail of losses, I already have in my own little way. Engagement creates ripple effects that may seem small or inconsequential but actually help folks challenge themselves, explore new ways of thinking, new ways to approach their work. And down the road, perhaps something will have a profound impact on someone's life.

I have never been bored either. My explorations have helped me gain unique skills, provided me with surreal experiences that money can't buy, and have been complementary to my values and life story. The majority of these projects were also done in addition to my day job and raising two young children with my wife. If you believe in what you do, you'll find the time. Trust me.

It was great to reminisce about some of these old projects, and hopefully they will provide a spark for your own future endeavors.

ARE YOUTH BEING SERVED?

This was my first ever project and the hardest to dig up info on due to our website being a simple MySpace page. My two mates and I would discuss politics and current affairs, and we had a really fun couple of years, with one of the highlights being our interview with the deputy prime minister of Australia. It was your quintessential youth radio show, where some weeks you couldn't even get into the studio to record because the previous "show" forgot to leave the keys, some people didn't show up for in-studio interviews because they were hungover (hosts included), and it was up to you to take things to the next level—including all the fundraising that went with it.

For me, this experience highlighted the importance of free speech, lifting up the youth voice, and using satire as a way to educate and inform civic engagement and discourse. (Also, there's no doubt in my mind that *Pod Save America* was inspired by an old MP3 recording they found of our show from back in the day.) We also enjoyed the perks, such as performing at community fetes, being invited to large city events to interview participants, and, my personal favorite, getting free music festival tickets with VIP access.

Our show was featured on Switch 1197AM, Brisbane's youth community radio broadcaster, which provided opportunities to students seeking experience in the media industry. Over the years, Switch has seen a number of its volunteers go on to both commercial television and radio positions all around the country. We weren't one of them. After my travel schedule increased exponentially as I took a role as a political staffer in the federal parliament, I just didn't have the time to commit to pre-show prep, or even recording, for that matter. I tried to prep for my exit from the show by recruiting a producer to help with the administrative aspects, but the show ran out of steam a few months later.

SPRINGFIELD UNITED FOOTBALL CLUB

One New Year's Eve, at some big fancy gala for an investment fund, my friends and I discussed how soccer teams didn't espouse the culture or identity of their communities, nor were they engaged with them beyond sharing the same zip code. This conversation lingered with me the next morning, long after the hangover had subsided. That was when I decided that I was going to form a brand-new soccer club that would be a staple of the community, an inclusive organization that provided more than just a place to play soccer, but a place where people felt they belonged regardless of whether they were a player, volunteer, or supporter.

The journey began in 2008 as City West United playing in a recreational league in the western suburbs of Brisbane. A year later, our team was encouraged to move to the Greater Springfield area to build roots in one of the fastest growing communities in Australia. We hit the ground running, holding stalls at community fetes, donating food to those in need, and even having an annual Peace Cup against a local Afghani refugee team that was played to support UNICEF's One Day, One Goal program. In three short years, the built-from-scratch club became affiliated with FIFA (futsal), the Football Federation of Australia, Football Queensland, and Football Brisbane, seeing a 450 percent growth in membership two years in a row and having teams from under the age of five to senior men's and women's.

Being the founder and founding president of this club is one of the proudest moments in my life. The fact that it has just celebrated its tenth anniversary, moved to a permanent home, and has its own beer goes to show that with hard work and surrounding yourself with those who share your vision, great things can happen.

SOCCER STAR SAN DIEGO

After all of the successes in Australia with Springfield United, I was keen to explore how far my experiences and passion for the administrative side of soccer could go in the US, where soccer was truly the sleeping giant of the sporting landscape (and, truth be told, still is). San Diego was a unique place to explore this, given that it was the largest metro area in the country that didn't have a Major League Soccer franchise and that it constantly delivered the highest TV ratings for the World Cup and similar large international tournaments.

So I looked around trying to latch onto something, and that something was the semi-professional team, the San Diego Flash. The Flash was the perfect match for me. It was challenging the ownership structures of traditional sports teams by selling shares in its club as part of a shared ownership model and also had a number of high-profile partners, including former England international Warren Barton (who was the team's coach) and former US men's national team striker Eric Wynalda. Both were pundits for the Fox Soccer Channel at the time, so the Flash had a captive national audience.

My role was leading a new community relations strategy where I helped build community with local teams and business, onboard new tech to help stream live games including the NPSL Final Four tournament for which we got the host city nod that year, and, most exciting of all, was given free reign to ideate and try out new ways of lifting up the club as one of the most innovative teams in the country. This included a National Day of Action with multiple events to promote soccer using the hashtag #GrowTheGame and saw us convene a local meeting for a potential Street Soccer USA chapter, which uses soccer to help homeless people transition off the streets; a panel at the San Diego Hall of Champions on the future of soccer in this city; and a number of associated games that celebrated the sport.

One idea that caught fire was the creation of a reality TV series of an underdog story inspired by the career of former USA player Jay DeMerit, who showed that it's never too late to follow your dreams of playing pro soccer. The winner of the series would win a training contract with the San Diego Flash Soccer Club. On the word of Coach Barton, in June 2011, Flash player Ryan Guy was signed to New England Revolution of Major League Soccer, so there was a real incentive for local youth to try out.

After a series of trials, the finalists competed in a series of challenges, games, and educational classes (in PR, nutrition, college scholarships, and injury prevention) to show what it takes to be a professional soccer player. We even took the team to watch the LA Galaxy and captured footage of David Beckham playing, which is by far his best cameo that he has never seen.

As with all things reality TV, the recording wasn't without drama. One player was kicked off the show due to smoking weed, and we couldn't produce the final episodes due to our videographer leaving the project and his replacement losing the hard drive of all the footage. (Amateurhour.) However, the winning player ended up making the senior squad and scoring a couple of goals. If you are interested in seeing the pilot, it can still be found on YouTube!

FUTBOL FOCUS

Futbol Focus was the first social network I helped design and build. It was first and foremost a news site but had elements of gamification woven through every aspect of the platform, assigning points for generating new content and fan viewpoints. Those points could then be redeemed for soccer merchandise and to unlock additional features on the site.

This was my first foray into building a business, and I learned very quickly that having a vision and doing the hard work are two things that need to run concurrently rather than hoping one catches up with the other. The site eventually ran out of steam, and I had to go get a real job. The honeymoon of moving to the US and working in soccer had passed.

SOCCER TECH CONFERENCE

Soccer Tech 2012 was an audacious attempt to help connect the sports administrators with soccer tech innovators. Held in downtown Los Angeles and featured as an official partner event of the world-renowned Social Media Week, the daylong conference featured a number of workshops and presentations that discussed the future opportunities and advancement for the sport in the US. It was streamed live via Social Media Week and was one of the major events reported on in the final wrap-up by organizers. Social Media Week sounded out my interest in participating again, but this time in New York City, something that logistically was too much of a stretch at that point in time.

BI-POLITICO

After being reenergized by politics and civic engagement after a year of working on campaigns and at the San Diego Foundation, I performed my first real "pivot" in the tech world by rebadging and enhancing the original Futbol Focus model to build out a platform to help improve civil discourse and amplify people's views and ideas in a bipartisan manner. The gamification part was next level. Folks could register as Democratic, Republican, or Independent; the aim of the game was to share ideas for new policy and find bipartisan support to move forward in the process, where it would eventually go to a vote of the users, and then be formally adopted by the platform as a policy position that we would then take up with the relevant body. Bi-Politico also had a free political PR system for media releases and blogs, classifieds for jobs and services providers, and redeemable points that you could use for campaign support, such as graphic design or something for yourself, such as *TIME* magazine subscriptions or Amazon gift vouchers.

While the name was terrible, the way this platform ended was worse. Once Futbol Focus shut down—and unbeknownst to me—the developer did his own pivot and created a very adult-oriented website. When we reconnected to build Bi-Politico he lazily rebuilt the site on top of the code of his more recent endeavor. So when I clicked through on one of the classified links . . . let's just say it was not the kind of consultant I was expecting. There was no way I could move forward with this, being a values-driven individual. So I severed ties with my developer and moved on. Quickly.

I swear you can't make this stuff up. Sheesh.

YOUNG PROFESSIONALS GIVE

I am fascinated by networks and the science of networking. This was only reaffirmed by a number of peer-reviewed studies that showed being in an open network instead of a closed one is the best predictor of career success. The more closed your network, the more you repeatedly hear the same ideas, which reaffirm what you already believe. The more open, the significantly more successful you were, or whatever that means.

Young Professionals Give (YPG) was a networking group of the first instance, but one where a deeper connection beyond your industry could pay dividends for your career later on. That deeper connection in my eyes would be forged through philanthropy with the aim of creating and generating better community outcomes as a result. Some of those outcomes included more intentional corporate giving, the fostering of more innovation through public-private partnerships, and more socially responsible decision-making. This wasn't anything groundbreaking by any means. But if I could help foster win-win connections between emerging leaders from both the corporate and nonprofit sectors to help advance their respective careers, and if those who benefitted from these expanded networks used their growing influence, experience, and skills to give back to the community and advance the common good, it was worth hosting.

At this time, I became chair of the local chapter of Emerging Practitioners in Philanthropy during a period when generational change had left the group searching for people and a purpose. YPG ended up being that purpose, and we rolled it into EPIP as a new giving circle, helping to increase membership and awareness of both the chapter and a number of impactful nonprofits across the region.

BLUE PICKET FENCE

Having been a campaign director, candidate, and organizer from a country with compulsory voting, the US had me fascinated with movement building and all things civics—literacy, participation, and engagement. Blue Picket Fence (BPF) was my first ever foray into tech and really what stoked my passion for futurism. I keep coming back to this one, and it has had a number of iterations now. If the politics were stripped from it, it could be a great tool for our elections and increasing participation by getting out the vote virtually.

Here was the premise for BPF: What if we could increase voter turnout and outreach through new tech such as geofencing? I conceptualized a new app that would first tackle getting out the vote the four days prior to Election Day in the following ways:

- **Polling Place Hubs:** Supporters coming into a specific radius of a polling booth will be sent a notification that will help direct them to that booth, along with information on who to vote for, depending on your political affiliation.

- **Volunteer Reminders:** Timely reminders that will be viewed and delivered more efficiently than late evening calls and no-show follow-ups during the day.

- **Election Day Tactics:** See how many volunteers are currently walking in each precinct and seamlessly redistribute volunteers to other areas of identified need.

- **Voter Protection:** Send photos and a summary of the alleged incident directly to the boiler room. The photo will be time- and location-stamped, enabling representatives to get to the place of the incident quickly.

Blue Picket Fence has always been a tough sell as an independently created platform given that it would need the requisite marketing and consumer education to get people onto the app and scale the platform up. That can only come from the government or the political parties, and some of the feedback was that this doesn't change votes, which is obviously where the immediate money and interest lies.

UPCENTIV

Upcentiv was my first attempt at philanthropy tech application and a way of tackling the issues I saw with accessibility to the tools and networks that were being wielded by foundations and other charitable titans such as Fidelity and Charles Schwab. This applied mainly to donor-advised funds (DAFs) and the fact that it cost between $5,000 and $25,000 to establish them. In a way, DAFs are the key to democratizing and enhancing philanthropy, though not as they are currently set up or administered. Charitable bank accounts that move money with informed research, curated giving based on donor intent and the causes those donors are most passionate about, and ensuring the data derived from that giving through impact dashboards and visualization are helping drive more and larger gifts to the areas of most need.

The concept for Upcentiv was loosely built around the Acorns app, which allows users to grow an investment portfolio through stocks, bonds, and other securities. The DAF platform, as my cofounder and I envisaged, would help users invest their spare change automatically by rounding up transactions from everyday purchases to the nearest dollar and depositing it directly into a charitable checking account. Users could then make grant recommendations from the balance in their account to a 501(c)(3) nonprofit at any time but receive immediate tax benefits at a higher rate.

My cofounder and I received great initial traction on this and were selected to the Unreasonable Institute's (now Uncharted) San Diego Impact Accelerator with a number of San Diego–Tijuana impact entrepreneurs. It was a great experience and a chance to validate our product and work with a number of local investors. However, shortly after the conclusion of the lab, my cofounder received a job at an iconic restaurant chain and is now their VP of information technology—which, while unfortunate for me, was fantastic for him.

I still haven't seen anything like Upcentiv on the market, and I remain optimistic that something like it will indeed hit the market in the future. There is no doubt it could be a viable and integral way to build a new culture of informed giving for Gen X, millennial, and Gen Z budding philanthropists of the future.

VICTORY URBAN SOCCER

Victory Urban Soccer was an attempt to disrupt the near $1 billion indoor soccer industry with a new type of indoor facility, one that provided more personalization, connectivity, and value to players and transformed venues into unique soccer hubs that players, supporters, friends, and families could come together and enjoy. The focus on combining an enhanced player experience with personalized technology (including an app, in-game video, and packaged highlights) was a key differentiator in the market. My business partner and I also wanted to use gamification to design new kits, logos, and other items that forged stronger links with players beyond merely providing a pitch and league to participate in.

This one was so close to kicking off (excuse the pun) that we had in place a master lease agreement for a new sixteen-thousand-square-foot venue in National City, California. Again, changes in circumstances halted momentum and, with it, our funding. This approach was well ahead of its time, and there still isn't anything like it on the market. One day, folks, one day.

MVMT BUILDER AND GOTEAM.FUND

MVMT Builder (an abbreviated play on the word movement) was an interesting one. It was the platform I invested the most time in, teaching myself how to code as a way to build up and build out on white-label tech, and one where I had really strong partners. Yet it was one that I really wasn't overly enthused about because it wasn't new, it was just a niche.

The concept here was a US-focused crowdfunding platform that would help build the essential resources needed to ensure grassroots campaigns are successful by radically simplifying political action. The site helped individuals and groups to raise small batched funds, recruit volunteers, and seek buy-in on policy ideas and community issues. We supported their work by providing advice on messaging, strategy, and whatever it took to increase the campaign's chances of success.

Ultimately, MVMT Builder meandered in the noise. The real opportunity was when we rebadged it as the GOTeam.Fund (Grassroots Organizing Team Fund) and looked at the Australian market, noting that fundraising was still centrally controlled and not optimized in any shape or form. We saw it as a way to supplant the traditional fundraisers and bring more people under the tent.

GOTeam.Fund focused on finding new contributions that support the election of Labor candidates and governments. This platform was an ideal opportunity for candidates, potential candidates, Australian Labor Party (ALP) members, ALP supporters, trade union members, and Labor-affiliated not-for-profit organizations and affinity groups, such as LEAN and Country Labor, to raise the money they need for their campaigns or projects. This was all about making the process of fundraising more personal and creative so that a new group of donors and volunteers could be leveraged through personal networks. The mechanisms to empower individual members to expand the reach of Labor campaigns hadn't been available before then.

Sadly, the Federal Party couldn't lend its support to the platform as it didn't want to push people onto a non-party fundraising tool, and the state branches all had their own established processes for candidates to fundraise. While they were happy for us to go it alone, they also advised candidates against it; our consensus was that it was best that we not continue if any of our team harbored any ambition to run in the future. You can do the math on that one.

OUR ENDORSEMENT

The more I delved into the possibilities of civic tech as a way to embolden and equip residents in the United States with the tools to support campaigns, self-organize, and lift up their communities, the more I was committed to ensuring everyone has a voice in building a future we can all thrive in. And one truly undervalued way of sharing one's voice at the local level was through endorsements, or publicly declaring one's personal or group's support of a candidate for elected office.

However, it was evident that endorsements had essentially become a vanity metric for candidates to either legitimize their candidacy (or electability), be distinguishable to their base, or be the impetus for another press release or weekend canvass. (I love the latter, by the way!) They had essentially become lines of text or wordsmithed quotes from major influencers. At the same time, I saw endorsements as a real opportunity to provide context to a candidacy, a more authentic viewpoint of why a candidate is deserving of someone's vote, and ultimately a way of improving political discourse across the whole spectrum.

Our Endorsement was a video platform that highlighted the positive attributes and outcomes of a candidate's experiences as well as what potentially made them an effective representative of the community of which they were seeking office. This allowed folks to record and upload their own endorsement videos to candidates' pages to show a different side of those on the ballot and through the eyes and shared experiences of your family, friends, neighbors, and broader community. For example, Candidate A helped with your immigration papers. That's great! Share that. Or maybe Candidate X pulled over on the side of the road when you had broken down and gave you a lift somewhere. Awesome! Share that too.

The idea was also to use the qualitative data from Our Endorsement to identify the qualities that residents would like to see in their precinct's elected officials. This would help political parties identify and recruit future candidates that reflect these values instead of the high name ID or "tapped" candidates who sometimes were not a real fit.

We tried this tech with a number of candidates up and down the ballot, with the tech working seamlessly and some authentic endorsements proving our hypothesis. The mistake I made here was rolling this all up within the Silicon City Hall project to beef that up, when all it did was make it more of a bonus application rather than a game-changing platform. Focusing on this simple yet powerful tool could have helped the large swath of independent voters see through the clutter and see who the real candidates were as people—especially since decency had been sorely lacking from leadership at the time.

POLITICS IN THE PUB

Given the fun I had with Are Youth Being Served?, it was only a matter of time before the rapidly growing podcasting scene would bring up happy memories and convince me to try my hand at this new medium. I saw podcasts through a different light from those that did the usual interview in a studio or create a criminal melodrama out of an old cold case. My hunch was that they would become a more dynamic recording of a conference panel, using the audience in ways that both enhanced key insights but also challenged the panelists in real time. Again, emerging leaders were the voices I wanted to lift up, since their viewpoints and approaches could inspire listeners to lean in to new ways of thinking.

My new cohost and I agreed that the most authentic conversations about current affairs have taken place in the pub with a pint in hand. Being in San Diego we also had the perfect backdrop: the litany of small, intimate tap houses that fueled our local economy. And so *Politics in the Pub (Live!)* was born.

The show sought to cultivate an honest conversation with San Diegans about the most pressing issues of the day, and my God, was it fun. We ended up having around twenty-five to fifty folks showing up to each event and even had a few regulars who helped thread some of the ongoing humor that was a key ingredient to the show. Our two-hour shows followed one main subject area to allow a deeper dive into the issues, tackling housing policy, unionism, and civic technology, to name but a few.

We also had two special editions of the show. One featured candidates who were running in the 2018 California primaries to discuss their races and share what running for office is really like. The other, which was in partnership with the San Diego Diplomacy Council and State Department, gave us the opportunity to interview a delegation of young political leaders from India who helped provide an international perspective on the 2018 midterm election result, including what the results could mean for future relations between the two nations. This was my favorite episode as we dabbled in a bit of citizen diplomacy and heard firsthand how the world's largest voting event (Indian national elections) works from those who participate, work, and are elected as a result of it.

After the midterm elections, my cohost and I took a break to see what improvements could be made. Alas, we both got new jobs that were all-consuming, but *Politics in the Pub* was a terrific creative experience nonetheless.

SAN DIEGO NONPROFIT ALLIANCE

After the collapse of the San Diego Nonprofit Association, which had been floundering for years due to internal divisions (the nonprofit side versus the healthcare groups) and a failed rebranding/relaunch that focused more on programming and networking than representation, I spoke to a number of key folks in the sector. They agreed that representation matters, especially when changes to federal budgets, the tax code, and the possible repeal of the Johnson Amendment had either occurred or was being actively discussed in Congress. We even had discussions about the possibility of San Diego Grantmakers expanding its support to nonprofits, very much like Forefront in Illinois. But I knew deep down that this was more about an opportunity for expansion rather than supporting the sector, something that on reflection was probably true given the hat that I was wearing at the time.

The conversations continued. After I moved on from San Diego Grantmakers, where my conflicts of interest thus ended, some of my sector peers and I envisioned a structure for a potential San Diego Nonprofit Alliance that could serve as a collective voice for the 11,500-plus nonprofits and focused more on advocacy, resource building, and educating and empowering members on a lot of the themes contained in this book. We were ready to start building out a founding board when my impending move to Texas came into full view—and with it, much of the momentum I was trying to generate amongst my peers.

PROGRESSIVE INFRASTRUCTURE AND TECHNOLOGY PAC

Civic engagement, civil discourse, and trust in government are at all-time lows, and our communities suffer as a result (voter participation prior to the record turnout of the 2020 presidential elections was also concerning). And with increased levels of societal isolation and constantly growing inequities in what is the most technologically connected age in history, it's no wonder people feel the system is rigged. I felt I could bring something different to the table.

The best way at that moment was to form a super PAC to help support these principles in a way my team, donors, and I felt we could make a measurable difference and impact. If we could find a way to leverage, fund, or subsidize the latest and greatest campaign technologies, apps, and platforms available, then our efforts could help win important races up and down the ballot for those candidates we supported. We also wanted to find a solution to something that irked us in politics and movement building: Each election sees the recruitment of hundreds of thousands of engaged people, only for that dynamic scaffolding created to drive citizens to the polls to be quickly disassembled after all the ballots have been counted.

Campaigns are inherently wasteful when it comes to nurturing activism beyond elections. What if we finally shifted the *moment* of an election to building a real social *movement*?

The PAC's name is often misrepresented. While it was indeed "progressive" the PAC actually focused on progress through the lens of integrated voter engagement, or Progress+IVE. It seeks to synergize voter mobilization over multiple election cycles with ongoing organizing work and is something we should strive for. We can have both short-term wins and build long-term movements by leveraging the passion and purpose of those involved in individual campaigns to build a more permanent infrastructure of grassroots power for real systemic change.

The PAC was super small, and we ended up having more conversations than we did expenditures. What was evident from these conversations was that our impact was better focused on local and state races. But that's not to say we didn't foster great dialogue on how to move from moments to movements. A real highlight was hosting an exclusive screening of *Knock Down the House*, which highlighted the campaigns of a number of first-time female candidates, including Alexandria Ocasio-Cortez. We also had a panel of first-time female candidates running for San Diego City Council, which highlighted the importance of cause and effect in political action.

SILICON CITY HALL

Silicon City Hall was a direct result of the aforementioned substantive conversations I had with campaigns, activists, and civic technologists.

There was a genuine need and urgency from the field that we needed to build a more sustainable campaign tech ecosystem that would ensure progressive candidates and social change organizations were equipped with the best digital tools to build power and win regardless of capacity constraints.

What my cofounder and I ultimately wanted to create was a mechanism that would support both the supply and demand sides of the political technology industry. By offering an online marketplace where we could deliver curated packages at largely discounted prices, we felt we could level the playing field. However, we found that the barriers to civic tech adoption are too expensive, too cyclical (it's hard to keep users engaged and tech staff employed through the boom and bust of campaign cycles), and not accessible due to centralization and being geared toward decision makers.

In the end we tried to do too much, which left large cracks and question marks around the process. We tried to be everything to everyone, which went against our better judgement. We wanted to build tech where it didn't exist, causing perceived conflicts of interest. We also wanted to assign digital specialists to each race to cultivate larger adoption and identify data trends, which raised concerns of scalability and cost. In addition, we wanted to raise participation when people said it's solely about targeting those winning votes.

Silicon City Hall made it through a number of rounds of a prominent civic tech investment fund. This was exciting, since it definitely proved there was a need for our concept and that it was indeed feasible. And while their selection committee applauded the concept as well as the fact that we wanted to build a new tech culture that would tackle issues of racial bias in coding and allow people of color an opportunity to build wealth through ownerships of the platforms they cocreate, they couldn't move us forward. They felt that we were the wrong team and that we didn't have the tech talent on board to make this successful. Some of the additional feedback was pretty blunt, but I actually agreed with it and that was ultimately that. My cofounder also went back to college to pursue her master's around that time, and my family's move to Austin was rapidly gathering pace.

So while I keep learning, growing, and identifying the potential applications and implications of technological advances for the benefit of philanthropy through a social change lens, I admit that I might not be the leader in this process. Perhaps my role is to inform those much smarter than I am of what is possible and let them work it out. I truly enjoy being part of the ecosystem; in a way, this book captures the lessons I have learned to potentially inspire the ideas that can catalyze the change I believe in.

Projects sometimes end, but the fight continues. Leveraging tech for good is a fight worth being in, and the social benefits should never be overlooked in pursuit of the financial and commercial benefits. If you believe technology can truly play that generational role in building a reinvigorated civil society where people can both build power and influence the majority, then you should consider joining this fight.